the
nordic
kitchen

Claus Meyer

the nordic kitchen

One year of family cooking

Photography by Anders Schønnemann

MITCHELL BEAZLEY

6
Introduction

12
Spring

62
Summer

122
Fall

182
Winter

250
Index

256
Acknowledgments

Introduction

I come from a part of the world where ascetic doctors and puritanical priests have led a 300-year-long crusade against sensuality and the pleasure-giving qualities of food. For centuries the idea of preparing wonderful meals for loved ones was considered a sin, in line with theft, wild dancing, incest, and masturbation. The philosophy peddled by these fine people was that, if you want to live a long and healthy life and avoid going to hell, just eat something bland and get it over with quickly.

It was in this spirit that I was brought up in a middle-class family in the Sixties—the darkest period in Danish food history. My mother represented the first generation of Danish women to work outside the home. It was an era of canned meatballs, powdered potatoes, sauce coloring, and the stock cube. My parents raised me on a diet of chopped fatty meat of the cheapest-possible quality and frozen vegetables preboiled years before in Kazakhstan.

Most of the meat was coated in toasted bread crumbs, three or four times, before it was deep-fried in margarine packed with transfatty acids—we used the excess margarine for dipping. At the age of 15, I weighed 207 pounds and was one of the fattest kids in the region. Eating during my childhood was never a matter of reaching out for the beauty of life. It was a matter of economic efficiency; food should cost very little, and be prepared and eaten in less than 30 minutes.

What subsequently changed my life was one transcendent year spent in France after high school. I started out working as an au pair with a dentist in Paris but fell ill. I was sent to recuperate with a French baker and *traiteur*, Guy Sverzut, and his wife Elizabeth, in Agen, Gascony. I recovered surprisingly quickly and decided to spend most of my remaining time in France with Elizabeth and Guy, who treated me like the son they never had. Guy quickly realized that I was

obsessed with food and cooking, and he invited me to work at his side. His bakery, Au Petit Marquis, was a time capsule representing the golden age of French culinary craftsmanship. He was a man who always bought the best produce and never challenged a price. He regularly offered free bread and cakes to friends, family, neighbors, and loyal clients. In Denmark, our evening meal would take my mother no more than 30 minutes to assemble from semiprepared food and the three of us a maximum of 10 minutes to eat. In Agen, every single day we would spend lots of time cooking and would frequently enjoy hours having dinner with friends and family. Coming from divorced parents, I simply felt I had found paradise on earth, and if I had fallen in love with food itself in Paris, in Agen I lost my heart to French food culture. I had also found my calling (or a calling had found me): I wanted to change the food culture of my country.

During the next 15 years, while I was studying and, later, launching my first food companies, I believed that changing the food culture of my country was pretty much a matter of introducing the virtues of French cooking into Denmark, and, through cookbooks, TV shows, and my food school, I did my best to do so. Then, in the late 1990s, I happened to be a contributor to a book about Spanish food and was charged with covering Andalucia and the Basque Country. In San Sebastian I met Pedro Subijana and Juan Marie Arzak, and I was blown away by the food—it was like nothing I had ever eaten before. But it was not just the food, it was also the underlying culture—the tapas bars, the more than 300 food societies (*Cofradias*) established with the sole purpose of honoring and celebrating iconic Basque produce, not to mention the public food clubs (*Las Sociedades Populares*), where men sharing the same profession meet once a week to cook together. During my encounter with San Sebastian, I understood that in 1978

the leading Spanish chefs had met to write a manifesto pronouncing that Spanish cuisine would one day be counted among the greatest in the world, and they went on to launch a process of revitalization deeply rooted in Spanish food history. As we all know, just 25 years later everyone in the sphere of gastronomy was talking about Spanish food, and El Bulli and Arzak were both ranked among the top five restaurants in the world.

In 1998 I watched two Danish movies that made a strong impression on me along with a large number of others in Denmark and internationally. *The Celebration* and *The Idiots* were the concrete result of an avant-garde filmmaking movement launched in 1995 by the Danish directors Lars von Trier and Thomas Vinterberg. With their *Dogme 95 Manifesto* they sought to define a modern cinematic expression that excluded the use of elaborate special effects or technology and emphasized the traditional values of filmmaking and storytelling, in the hope that the industry would give power back to the artist as opposed to the studio. It's fair to say that von Trier and Vinterberg, who were soon joined by other Danish filmmakers, inspired filmmakers around the globe, and today they are regarded as some of the most accomplished and influential directors in world cinema.

Influenced by these experiences, and provoked by the onslaught of the global junk- and fast-food industry, particularly in countries lacking a strong food culture, I decided in 2003 to open a restaurant that would work solely with Nordic produce and basically restore the link between cooking and nature in our region. I hired René Redzepi, just 25 years old, as head chef and offered him a partnership in the restaurant that we named noma. Had I known the full potential of this young man I may have had even higher ambitions on behalf of the restaurant itself, but initially the idea was not just to build one

of the best restaurants in the world but to spearhead a process of change in the way we cooked in our restaurants as well as in our homes. With noma we wanted to create a restaurant that explored the potential of Nordic produce that would stand out internationally, and we wanted to identify a common regional culinary identity and engage as many stakeholders as possible in the process of change.

We asked ourselves this: If our food culture should not only bring joy and pleasure, but also one day be counted among the most admired and respected on the planet, which values should we lean on down the road? An answer to that question was given when, in 2004, prior to the New Nordic Cuisine Symposium that we arranged, we collaborated with a number of leading chefs from the region to work out a culinary manifesto, a sort of belief system if you will, that became a guiding light to most of us, and to a large number of other important stakeholders on the food scene, during the following decade, and beyond.

My dream year of family food

This book is the result of my desire to understand and communicate what the values embedded in the Nordic Cuisine Manifesto could mean for home cooking. It's also a kind of a testimony to the food we have been eating in my family for the past four to six years. And then it reflects my life-long interest of our culinary heritage. Which dishes from Danish food history deserve to be defended in their original state, which ones should be left behind us, and which just need a sensitive update in order to remain relevant for the next generation?

How does this food and the recipes in this book, differ from, for example, classical French food? Well, apart from featuring different produce from a different territory, as a general rule, the sauces are less concentrated and contain less fat. Sometimes they are even made from other ingredients than stock, and the result is

that the food is lighter and more succulent. Vegetables are also treated differently and play a more distinct role in the New Nordic Cuisine. The same goes for fresh herbs, grains, and legumes.

Frying, baking, braising, sautéeing, poaching, and grilling are cooking techniques widely used throughout this book, just as they would be in an average French cookbook. Having said this, a number of dishes feature fish, shellfish, meat, or vegetables that are simply pickled, cured, or marinated. From the beginning of this journey, the idea of celebrating the ingredient, nature, rather than honoring a complex process or the chef's magical wisdom, has been one of the core culinary aims of The New Nordic Cuisine. Food served raw, I believe, is an expression of that.

Eating with the seasons

I am sure that today most readers of this book value the concept of seasonality and place, something that is also the structural principle of this book. Our priorities have changed in very few years.

In the Nordic region—and generally speaking in the northern hemisphere—we have four distinct seasons and we have a large number of wild and cultivated foods that are unique to each.

With an immense garden, full of wonderful vegetables, berries, fruits, grains, nuts, and herbs that are just waiting to be harvested and eaten, it's crazy not to use them. I believe we should eat what is in season, here, now. With few exceptions the crops you buy frozen aren't produced with the highest levels of deliciousness in mind, and there is no reason to use frozen products when the fresh equivalents are in season. Of course, it's nice to have a stash of blackcurrants, green beans, and peas in the freezer, thus prolonging the summer. But frozen produce can never replace the freshly harvested, ultimately juicy, and aromatic version of the same product.

That's just the way it is. Cooking with frozen greens from a random source, which have been preboiled has a tendency to make the entire cooking process less soulful, when the purpose should be the opposite.

I could have easily compiled a book of recipes with a guarantee that it wouldn't take you more than a maximum of 30 minutes to cook each dish. I did, honestly, give it some thought, but I came to the conclusion that other cookbook authors are better qualified for such a dogmatic exercise. After careful consideration I selected these EXACT recipes because I think the level of deliciousness they represent justifies the little bit of extra work in the kitchen they may involve. I also have a book of recipes that I am proud to hand down to my children.

Sustainable *and* delicious

In 2003, Harvard University published the result of a large study led by Professor David Cutler, that showed it was difficult to make a clear link between the level of macro nutrients or the content of vitamins and minerals in a diet and personal health. We shouldn't rule out that it may be healthy to eat according to our blood type or sperm quality, or live off raw food or cut out meat. It is just that there is just not much evidence to support these dietary approaches. Some people appear to attain excellent health by consuming a very high-protein diet, while others achieve similar results by eating food that is disproportionately high in fat or by eating predominantly carbohydrates. The Harvard study showed that, as far as food is concerned, the single most important factor to indicate whether you will live a long and healthy life is how often you cook your food yourself. From this perspective, I could theoretically dismiss everything we know about food and health. But of course, the study didn't show that what you eat doesn't matter to your health. In a world where Type 2 diabetes is rising in almost epidemic proportions, where 1.4 billion people are suffering from obesity, and where one in three children is likely to die 10 years younger than their parents, when every other Dane between the ages of 30 and 60 is slightly or heavily overweight—other nations being worse off—I think we have a duty to do our best to create a new food culture, where day by day we eat better and eat fewer processed foods.*

Your personal health is one thing, but the health of the planet is quite another. We have long thought that the two have nothing to do with each other. It's a view that is harder and harder to maintain. What we eat has a profound influence on our surroundings. The way most of us in the Western world eat is not sustainable. Livestock production, for example, accounts for 18 percent of global emissions—a higher emission than the entire transport sector. Other consequences of our food production are less well known: soil erosion; deforestation; overuse of freshwater resources; loss of biodiversity; and the use of pesticides and fertilizers that contaminate soil, water, and air. Furthermore, we are using enormous amounts of fossil fuel to transport massive quantities of food over long distances.

We can easily take greater account of the planet's health without compromising our quality of life. It's actually more doubtful whether we can sustain that quality of life without changing our eating habits if we think it's important that future generations should also have the opportunity to live a good life on this planet.

If you live in the northern hemisphere in a temperate climate zone, by cooking the recipes from this book, a larger proportion of your energy will come from the plant kingdom and less from animal products than is standard. I believe we should all eat fresh, local produce and more whole grains, eat food from the wild, a variety of vegetables and fruits, and avoid endangered fish species. Choose organic when you can, and try to reduce food waste by cooking no more food than you need and using any leftovers in your next meal. By following these basic principles you will feel closer to nature, and you will find that you enjoy more food that reflects the seasons and connects you to your surrounding landscape.

Bon Appétit
Claus Meyer, 2016

Foraging code of conduct

It's always lovely to take a walk in the woods, and, once you become familiar with how and when things can be eaten, you will rarely come back empty-handed. It's a very special treat to eat a dish made from ingredients you've collected in the wild. Do keep in mind that there are some rules to respect, however.

On public land, you must pick plants, berries, mushrooms and nuts for personal consumption only. Do not dig up plants or cut off branches. Use secateurs or a sharp knife to avoid damaging the plant unnecessarily. Think of the people who will come along after you and take no more than you need.

On private land, you can only pick what you can reach from public roads and paths. If in doubt, ask the owner! As a rule, they will be happy that you are interested, and you get the opportunity to talk about the area you're planning to visit.

And of course before eating any wild ingredient, be absolutely certain that you have identified it correctly and that it is safe to eat.

*Footnote

The recipes in this book are extracted from Claus Meyer's Almanak. The recipe compilation represented by Almanak follow the nutritional principles of the OPUS research center project the New Nordic Diet under the leadership of Professor Arne Astrup, MD, PhD, DM.Sc. Department of Nutrition, Exercise, and Sports, University of Copenhagen, Denmark:

- **Total fat is not a particular concern but is kept in the range 25 to 40 percent of calories**
- **A minimum of 50 percent of all fat is unsaturated**
- **On average, more than 15 percent of total calories comes from proteins**

- **Carbohydrates predominantly originate from wholegrain products, root vegetables, fruits, and berries**
- **The fiber content exceeds an average of 3g per megajoule /25 to 35g per day**
- **The total calorie intake is the responsibility of each individual**

It's all about flavor

Our daily bread

I believe you should eat good bread with your meals. It doesn't necessarily have to be freshly baked—bread can be reheated and good bread is great toasted. Let it be the rule rather than the exception that your bread has a high content of whole grains. The dough should be properly risen, with as little yeast as possible, and baked at high temperatures. Good bread makes meals better, aids digestion, and strengthens your health. It's also extremely fun to make, and a discipline where everyone—with a little guidance—can become a better baker the more bread they bake.

Season well

Although I have carefully tested the recipes, I have to say that you always need to taste the food during the cooking process. Quite simply, taste the food and add a little of what you think is missing—salt or pepper, sourness or sweetness. You might have to check the seaoning several times until you are satisfied. If you follow the recipes as they are, you will, of course, end up with a good result, but season the food carefully to get both a satisfying experience in the kitchen and more flavor in the end result. The art of seasoning is about the balance between the four basic tastes: sour, sweet, salty, and bitter. It's very easy to correct and will make for a better end result.

I have taught about 10,000 people in cooking classes over the past 10 years, and in general people don't use enough salt. 39 out of 40 agree that the taste is better with the addition of more salt, because salt enhances the flavor of the food. Once you have added the salt, you must ask yourself whether the balance between on the one hand the sweet and rich attributes of the dish and on the other the bitter and sour elements are at the level you would like them to be. The sweetness keeps the sour and bitterness in check and makes the flavor smoother, in, for example, gravies, soups, dressings, and dips.

I often find that acidity is missing. For instance, cooked vegetables can taste very plain if there is no sour element. If a dish is sweeter or richer than you would prefer, you can balance that out with some good vinegar or lemon juice. If you are missing bitterness in the dish, the easiest way to adjust it is to add a little beer and tasting it along the way, or by adding minced raw shallots, chives, parsley, citrus peel, or bitter lettuce leaves. In my own kitchen, I always keep "gastrique" on hand. Gastrique is an acidic, bittersweet, caramelized vinegar syrup that you make by caramelizing sugar in a pan and then adding some good vinegar (not balsamic) and letting the caramel dissolve in it. The gastrique adds bitterness to your gravies and dressings and enhances the overall flavors. It is also good to adjust the "heat" of your dishes, seasoning them with freshly ground pepper, horseradish, ginger juice, chile, or mustard. Select an ingredient that is already a part of the dish but that could also act to balance out the heat. The hot feeling in the mouth is the result of a chemical reaction in the trigeminal nerve. It doesn't actually have anything to do with taste—it just feels like it.

When making gravy, soup, or a stew, you need to consider if the aromas are intense enough, otherwise you will have to reduce the liquid—this is always the best way to enhance all the flavors at once. If you don't have time for that, you can add aromatic ingredients. These could be herbs, chile paste, tomato paste, mustard, spiced salt, elderberries, soy, or chopped olives. This was all taken into consideration in these recipes, so I am confident that the end result will be good food. I would recommend that you look back and remind yourself of these tips from time to time until you are completely familiar with the techniques. You will find that following the seasoning processes takes the taste of your food to another level.

Using this book

I don't expect you to cook the food in this book recipe by recipe. I do, however, hope that you will use it as a source of inspiration. If your farmers' market happens to have beautiful beets one day, or if you can get hold of a load of elderflowers, then do look them up in the index and check if there are any recipes you would liketo make.

The exact moment when ramsons are in season or apples are ripe in fall may vary from year to year, so keep an eye on nature and make friends with your local fresh produce retailer or fish dealer, so they can advise you on what is in season.

I am not an overly didactic person, so that is why, for example, I will never say "turn on the oven," but rather "bake in a preheated oven at 400°F for 40 minutes."

All the recipes in this book are designed for 4 people unless I have indicated otherwise. Bread, cake, and drink recipes are often given in slightly larger quantities. The same is sometimes the case with larger roasts.

Always read a recipe thoroughly. If, in addition to the main recipe, a separate side dish is included, it will be listed after the main recipe. But be aware that it may sometimes be best if you make the side dish first. The combinations reflect the way we eat the dishes in Denmark, but feel free to combine them whichever way works best for you.

At the start of each chapter are two lists of ingredients that define that season. One lists cultivated produce, in alphabetical order. The other lists foraged ingredients chronologically, according to the order in which they can be found in the wild. Some ingredients straddle the seasons, and therefore appear at the end of one season's list and the top of the next.

Spring

Seasonal ingredients

Cultivated produce

asparagus
beetroot
brill
carrots
celeriac
chervil
chicory
chives
cicely
cod roe
dandelion leaves
eggs
flounder
garfish
green strawberries

grey mullet
horseradish
Jerusalem artichokes
kohlrabi
lamb
leeks
lovage
lumpfish roe
morels
mussels
Norwegian lobster
onions
oysters
parsley
parsnip

pointed cabbage
prawns
radish
rhubarb
sparlings
spinach
squid
turnip

In the wild

dandelion leaves
ramsons
ground elder
rowan sprigs
nettles
sorrel
garlic mustard
beech leaves
St George's mushrooms
bird cherries
venison

woodruff
fjord shrimps
horse mushrooms
sea arrowgrass
broadleaved pepperweed
winkles
sea plantain
bolete mushrooms
elderflower
rosehips

Soups and appetizers

Nettle soup
with potato pillows and smoked curd cheese

Potato pillows
2¼ lb large baking potatoes
coarse sea salt
1⅔ cups all-purpose flour, plus extra for dusting
1 organic egg, lightly beaten
sea salt flakes and freshly ground pepper

Soup
2 large baking potatoes, about ¾ lb
4 cups water or vegetable stock
1 shallot
½ garlic clove
1 tablespoon cold-pressed canola oil
3½ oz blanched nettles (*see* right)
sea salt flakes and freshly ground pepper

To serve
¼ cup Smoked Curd Cheese (*see* right) or full-fat quark
⅓ cup grated hard cheese, such as Høost or Cheddar

Start with the potato pillows. Put the potatoes in an ovenproof dish lined with coarse salt and bake in the oven at 350°F for 45 to 50 minutes or until soft.

Cut the potatoes in half and use a spoon to scrape the flesh out into a bowl. Mix in the flour and egg using a potato masher or a whisk, then season with salt and pepper. The texture of the mixture should be soft, but definitely not sticky.

On a floured work surface, roll the potato mixture out into a thin sausage shape about the same diameter as your thumb. Cut into bite-sized pieces and then stamp lightly with a fork to give them a cute little pattern. Place the potato pillows on a large baking pan and let chill in the refrigerator until the soup is ready.

To prepare the soup, peel and thinly slice the potatoes, then add them to a pan with the water or stock and cook for about 15 minutes or until soft.

Peel the shallot and garlic and slice thinly. Heat the canola oil in a large pan and lightly sauté the shallot and garlic without browning. Add the blanched nettles and cook for a further 30 seconds.

Pour the potatoes and their cooking liquid into the pan with the shallot, garlic, and nettles and simmer the soup for 2 minutes before it goes in the blender. Swiftly blend until smooth—it's important not to blend it for too long or the soup will become sticky in texture. I normally can't be bothered to pass the soup through a sieve back into the pan, especially as I don't mind a lump of potato or a little nettle here and there, but if you wish, feel free to do so. Season the soup to taste with salt and pepper.

Cook the potato pillows in a pan of lightly salted water for 2 to 3 minutes, a few at a time so they don't stick to one another. Serve the soup in bowls with some potato pillows, a spoonful of smoked curd cheese, and a sprinkle of freshly grated hard cheese on top.

Blanching nettles

Use the small young shoots or only the tops of older plants. Bring a pan of salted water to a boil, add the nettles, and cook for about 30 seconds. Remove the nettles and immediately submerge in cold water to stop the cooking process so that the nettles keep their flavor and color. Wring out all the cold water before cooking the nettles any further.

NETTLES
Look for the first nettle shoots to sprout in spring.

Smoked curd cheese
MAKES 1 LARGE CHEESE

Pour 3 quarts whole milk and 1 cup buttermilk into a pan and season with salt (about a tablespoon). Heat to 79°F.

Add 10 drops of rennet to the milk mixture whisking continuously. Pour the milk mixture into a bowl, cover with plastic wrap, and let stand in the kitchen for 24 hours.

Pour the cheese curds into a sieve lined with a thin cloth (I would recommend using a piece of clean cheesecloth), set over a large bowl. Let the curds drain in the refrigerator for 8 hours.

Flip the cheese over and return it to the refrigerator to drain for another 8 hours.

Now the cheese is ready to be smoked. I normally use a barbecue charcoal chimney starter for this purpose. Put some straw into the barbecue starter and pack it down tightly. If you like, you can put some nettles on top of the straw to add flavor. I use a small wooden pallet as a rack on which to sit the cheese for smoking, placing it on top of the starter, but a metal colander would work well, or even a barbecue grill. Now light the barbecue starter—from the bottom. I use a weed burner because it is much easier to control the heat and ignition process, but a flame lighter for lighting a barbecue can also be used.

Start smoking the cheese when the smoke is thick and warm—beware of the straw catching fire—and it should be smoked for approximately 3 minutes, depending on the heat of the smoke. Let the cheese sit for 1 hour before serving to allow the smoke flavor to mature, if you have the time.

TIP The cheat's shortcut would be simply to take a full-fat fromage blanc or fromage frais and season it with smoked salt!

Potato soup
with ramsons and parsley

3 large potatoes
4 cups water
1 shallot
½ garlic clove
1 tablespoon cold-pressed canola oil
10 to 15 ramson leaves
1 handful of flat-leaf parsley
sea salt flakes and freshly ground pepper

Peel and thinly slice the potatoes, then add them to a large pan with the 4 cups of water and cook for about 15 minutes until soft.

Peel the shallot and garlic and slice thinly. Heat the canola oil in a separate large pan and lightly sauté the shallot and garlic without browning. Add the ramson and parsley and sauté for a further 30 seconds.

Pour the potatoes and their cooking water into the pan with the shallot and herbs and let the soup simmer for 2 minutes. Then blend the soup swiftly until smooth—it's important that you don't blend it for too long, otherwise the consistency will become sticky, almost like glue. Season to taste with salt and pepper.

Simmer the soup for a little longer, then serve by itself with some good bread or garnish with a spoonful of ramson pesto, a dollop of Homemade Mayonnaise (see page 68), or crème fraîche. This recipe is a lighter version of the traditional soup, so a touch of cream will enrich it.

TIP You could fill out the soup by adding some lumpfish caviar, shellfish, or fish.

Mussel soup
with spinach, ramsons, and barley

2¼ lb mussels
2 to 3 shallots
1 carrot
1 small parsnip
1 to 2 leeks, trimmed and rinsed
¼ red or green chile
1 tablespoon canola oil
1 to 2 glasses white wine
½ cup heavy whipping cream
1¾ oz fresh spinach
8 to 10 ramson leaves
sea salt flakes and freshly ground pepper
finely grated zest and juice from
    1 organic lemon, or to taste
½ cup pearl barley, cooked

Clean the mussels by scrubbing them thoroughly under cold water and removing the beards. Discard any mussels that don't close after lightly tapping them on the work surface, or those with damaged shells.

Peel the shallots, carrot, and parsnip, and slice them very thinly, along with the leeks. Seed and thinly slice the chile. Sauté in the canola oil in a pan for about 2 minutes so that they start to soften and become sweet. Add the mussels and the wine, cover the pan with a lid, and steam for 4 to 5 minutes or until the mussels have opened. Discard any that haven't opened—they are not safe to eat. Lift the mussels out, remove from their shells, and set aside.

Add the cream to the pan and simmer for a few minutes. Rinse the spinach and ramson leaves, then add to the soup.

Pour the soup into a blender and blend to a smooth consistency. Pass the soup through a sieve back into the pan and reheat until it is just about to boil. Add salt, pepper, and lemon zest and juice to taste. Return the shelled mussels to the soup and add the cooked pearl barley. Heat the soup for a minute before serving it with a hearty slice of good bread.

Chervil soup
with poached eggs

1 shallot
2 carrots
3 cups chicken stock
2 handfuls of chervil
3 tablespoons heavy whipping cream
sea salt flakes and freshly ground pepper
4 to 6 Poached Eggs (see below), to serve

Peel the shallot and carrots, and slice thinly. Add to a pan with the stock. Bring to a boil, then simmer for 10 minutes over low heat.

Coarsely pluck the chervil leaves from the stems and place in a blender with the cream. Pour the vegetables and stock into the blender as well and blend until smooth.

Pour the soup back into the pan and reheat. Add salt and pepper to taste. Serve the soup in bowls with a poached egg (see below) in the center of each, and perhaps with some Crispy Croûtons on top (see page 128).

Poached eggs

4 to 6 very fresh organic eggs
sea salt flakes and freshly ground pepper

Fill a pan with water, add some salt, and bring to a boil. Crack the eggs individually into cups, making sure that no pieces of shell find their way into the cups. If the eggs are really fresh, the whites should look bouncy and sit tightly around the yolks. Season the eggs with salt and pepper.

Use a spoon to swirl the boiling water around in the pan, then carefully drop an egg into the middle of the swirl and let it poach for 2 to 3 minutes. When the egg is poached, immediately lift it out into a bowl of cold water to stop the cooking process. Repeat with the rest of the eggs.

Soup of green asparagus
with shrimp and smoked curd cheese

1 handful of green asparagus
2 shallots
1 tablespoon standard canola oil
2 cups water or chicken stock
3 tablespoons full-fat crème fraîche
sea salt flakes and freshly ground pepper
2 tablespoons apple cider vinegar, or to
    taste, divided
3½ oz small cooked, peeled shrimp
    (*see* page 45)
1 tablespoon Smoked Curd Cheese
    (*see* page 16)
1 tablespoon cold-pressed canola oil

Break off and discard the woody stem ends of the asparagus, then rinse the spears in cold water. Slice the lower two-thirds of the stems finely, reserving the tips for garnishing later.

Peel the shallots and chop them very finely, then sauté lightly in a pan with the sliced asparagus in the standard canola oil.

In another pan, bring the water or stock to a boil, then add to the shallots and asparagus and cook for 2 minutes. It's important to keep the cooking process swift so that the asparagus retains its green color and fresh taste.

Pour the soup into a blender, add the crème fraîche, and blend together. Pass the soup through a sieve back into the pan to get rid of any stringy bits of asparagus that haven't blended. Season to taste with salt, pepper, and some of the vinegar.

Cut the asparagus tips in half lengthwise and mix with the shrimp, smoked curd cheese, cold-pressed canola oil, salt, pepper, and the remaining vinegar to taste.

Reheat the soup and serve with a spoonful of the asparagus and shrimp mixture in each bowl.

White asparagus
with smoked curd cheese cream

20 white asparagus
sea salt flakes
7 oz small cooked, peeled shrimp
    (*see* page 45)
freshly ground pepper
a pinch of sugar

To serve
Smoked Curd Cheese Cream (*see* right)
chopped fresh herbs, such as chervil,
    chives, and parsley

Peel the asparagus and break off the woody stem ends (see the panel on preparing asparagus, below).

Bring a large pan of water to a boil, add a little salt, and cook the asparagus for 2 to 3 minutes, depending on their thickness and to taste: 2 to 3 minutes will give you crisp asparagus, as I like them, but if you prefer them tender, give them 3 to 4 minutes, or up to 5 to 6 minutes if you like your asparagus completely meltingly tender, tending toward the overcooked. Lift the asparagus out of the water and let them drain on a clean cloth napkin or dish towel on a platter. Or, if you wish to serve the asparagus warm, wrap them in the cloth, place on the platter, and pour a little of the warm asparagus cooking water over them.

Season the shrimp with salt and pepper and just a pinch of sugar (the sugar highlights the fine shrimp flavor, but be careful not to overdo it). Arrange the asparagus on a platter, adorn with little dollops of the Smoked Curd Cheese Cream (*see* below), and scatter the shrimp on top. Finish with a sprinkle of chopped herbs to taste, and serve immediately.

This is one of the most sophisticated spring appetizers I can think of, and when asparagus and shrimp are in season, I do not hesitate to bring the two ingredients together at every given opportunity. It is simply a very happy marriage.

Smoked curd cheese cream

2½ oz Smoked Curd Cheese
    (*see* page 16)
1 cup lowfat milk
3 tablespoons heavy whipping cream
1 grating of nutmeg
finely grated zest of ½ organic lemon
sea salt flakes and freshly ground pepper

Mix the smoked curd cheese with the milk and cream in a bowl to a soft cream. Add a hint of nutmeg, the lemon zest, and salt and pepper to taste.

How to prepare asparagus

There are different methods for preparing white and green asparagus. White asparagus should be peeled before cooking, and the easiest way to do this is to lay spears on a cutting board and use a speed peeler to peel from under the tip down the spear. Once peeled all over, bend the spear at the base and it will naturally snap where the woody part of the stem begins—if you try to trim the end with a knife, you risk not cutting away enough of the woody part and you'll be chewing on unpleasant fibers.

Green asparagus does not require peeling—just snap off the base of the spear to break off the woody part.

Both types of asparagus require only a short cooking time in order to retain their fresh and crisp texture—white asparagus will require a little longer cooking than the green.

Asparagus
and chervil mousseline

8 white asparagus
8 green asparagus
sea salt flakes
1 teaspoon superfine sugar
Chervil Mousseline (*see* below), to serve

Prepare the asparagus. Peel the white ones and break off the woody stem ends (see the panel on preparing asparagus on page 19). Rinse the green asparagus in cold water.

Bring a pan of water to a boil with salt and the sugar added, but don't cook the asparagus before the mousseline sauce is ready (*see* below) and your guests are seated.

Asparagus varies slightly in girth, and the white usually needs to be cooked a little longer than the green. Boil the white asparagus for 2 to 3 minutes and then the green for 1 to 2 minutes.

Transfer the freshly cooked asparagus spears to a bowl of cold water to keep their color and freshness, then remove them again immediately to prevent them from losing too much heat. Let them dry briefly on a clean dish towel, then serve the asparagus warm with the Chervil Mousseline (*see* right) and great bread.

· ·

TIP If your guests are not ready to eat asparagus the moment you pull them out of the boiling water, place them on a platter, cover with a napkin or clean dish towel, tuck the cloth around them, and pour a little of the hot cooking water over them. This way they will keep warm until the party is seated.

· ·

Chervil mousseline

3 organic egg yolks
2 tablespoons apple cider vinegar, plus extra for seasoning
2 tablespoons water
sea salt flakes
1 stick butter
1 handful of chervil (save some to garnish), chopped
freshly ground pepper
3 tablespoons heavy whipping cream

Whisk the egg yolks, vinegar, measured water, and a little salt together in a bain-marie (a heatproof bowl set over a pan of barely simmering water) to a creamy consistency and until the whisk leaves a trail when you lift it from the foam.

Melt the butter gently in a saucepan. Some people take the time to remove the whey, which sinks to the bottom, to clarify the butter, but I never do. Mix the butter into the eggs by pouring it in a thin stream and whisking until all of it is incorporated and the sauce is rich and smooth. Season with plenty of chopped chervil, salt, pepper, and a little more vinegar.

Whip the cream lightly and fold into the mousseline just before serving—this makes it light, airy, and creamy. Serve the chervil mousseline, scattered with chervil, with the warm asparagus as a wonderful start to a May dinner.

Toast with mussels
and sweet cicely

8 thin slices of white bread
1 tablespoon olive oil
1 tablespoon Homemade Mayonnaise (*see* page 68)
3 tablespoons Greek yogurt (2% fat)
1 teaspoon prepared mustard
finely grated zest and juice of ½ organic lemon
a pinch of curry powder
7 oz steamed and shelled mussels (*see* tip)
sea salt and freshly ground pepper
½ handful of sweet cicely, chopped

Drizzle the bread slices with the olive oil toast on a ridged grill pan for about 1 to 2 minutes on each side. The toasted slices should be very crisp and golden.

Combine the mayonnaise, yogurt, mustard, lemon zest and juice, and curry powder in a bowl to make a dressing. Mix the mussels in the dressing and season with salt, pepper, and the chopped sweet cicely.

Serve the mussel salad on the warm toast as a small appetizer, maybe with a little salad.

· ·

TIP You can use canned mussels here, but fresh mussels will elevate the taste to a whole new level, and by spending the few minutes it takes to steam them (*see* page 18), you will also have one of the best stocks around—perfect for the nettle soup on page 16.

· ·

Asparagus and chervil mousseline »

Ramsons

In early April, the forest floors teem with the first 1- to 2-inch wide, bright green leaves of ramsons (Allium ursinum), also known as Nordic garlic. They grow to about 6 to 8 inches in height and, later in the season, sprout white starlike flowers in small sphere-shaped clusters atop triangular stems. Ramsons may be confused with lily of the valley, which is highly toxic, but if you smell the plants, you should be left in no doubt, since ramsons have a very strong garlicky scent and taste. Good places to look for it are in moist, humus-rich, leafy deciduous forests and woodland populated with ash and hazel, or along damp riverbanks. Place the leaves in a sealed bag with a few drops of water and they will keep fresh for up to a week in the refrigerator.

Using ramsons

Cut as many leaves as you need, rinse them, and use them chopped in a potato salad, soup, or stew, or on a slice of rye bread. Mix the shredded leaves with a little oil and some salt to make a paste to use as a dip for fish, chicken, or smoked meats, for example. You can store the ramson paste in small containers in the freezer, which will preserve both its flavor and color, but it will also keep well in the refrigerator. The white flowers are perfect as a garnish, and have a delicious crunchy texture and a distinct leek flavor. The green buds that appear in June can be scattered over dishes or pickled as capers.

Ramson pesto

You will need about 20 ramson leaves, 1 handful of parsley, 1 ounce fresh crustless bread, ½ cup skinned hazelnuts (see page 156), 1 cup cold-pressed canola oil, sea salt flakes and freshly ground pepper, and a little jaggery or honey.

Rinse the herbs and let to drain thoroughly before you tear them into smaller bouquets (you can include some of the stems, too). Add to a blender with the bread, hazelnuts, and oil and blend to a coarse paste. Season to taste with salt, pepper, and the sugar or honey. The pesto is really good with baked root vegetables or potatoes and a piece of fried fish, meat, or poultry.

Pickled ramson buds

You will need 7 ounces ramson buds, ½ cup coarse sea salt, 1 cup apple cider vinegar, ½ cup water, ½ cup sugar, 5 whole black peppercorns, and 2 bay leaves.

Check that the ramson buds are fresh, then rinse them thoroughly, place them in a bowl, and sprinkle with the salt. Let stand in the kitchen for 12 hours. Wash the buds and put them into sterilized preserving jars. Combine the vinegar, measured water, sugar, and spices in a saucepan and bring to a boil. Remove from the heat and let cool, then pour the brine over the ramson buds, seal the jars tightly, and let stand in the refrigerator to pickle for 7 days before you start using them. They will keep fresh for up to 6 months in the refrigerator.

Ramson salt

You will need 10 ramson leaves and 2 tablespoons coarse sea salt—that's all.

Put the ramson leaves and salt in a food processor and blend to a beautiful green salt. Store the salt in a glass jar or other airtight container and use it to sprinkle onto soft-boiled eggs, scrambled eggs, or bread, or to season a steak or a piece of fish.

Meat

Roast leg of lamb
with crust of herbs

1 whole leg of lamb on the bone,
  about 4½ lb
sea salt flakes and freshly ground pepper
3 garlic cloves
1 tablespoon English mustard
2 to 3 tablespoons fresh bread crumbs
7 oz chopped fresh herbs, such as
  parsley, rosemary, and thyme
2 tablespoons softened butter

Rub the leg of lamb thoroughly with salt and
pepper. Peel and chop 1 garlic clove and
mix it with the mustard, then glaze the lamb
with the mixture.

Place the lamb in a roasting pan and
cook in a preheated oven at 425°F for
about 10 minutes to glaze, then lower the
temperature to 350°F and roast for a further
30 minutes.

Peel the rest of the garlic cloves, then crush
them into a small bowl and mix them with
the bread crumbs, chopped herbs, and
softened butter until you have a smooth
paste. Take the roast out of the oven and
spread the butter mixture on top of the
leg, then return to the oven for a further
30 minutes. You may wish to use a meat
thermometer to check the temperature of
the meat by inserting it into the thickest
part, but without sticking it all the way into
the bone. When it reaches 140°F, the meat
should be pink and juicy.

Take the lamb out of the oven and let rest
for 15 minutes. Cut the meat into thin slices,
carefully, so that the delicate herby crust
doesn't fall off. Serve with cooked grains
and a nice green salad.

Pan-fried lamb kidneys
with beets and kohlrabi in gastrique

2 tablespoons sugar
5 fennel seeds
5 whole black peppercorns
½ cup cherry vinegar
3 early-season beets or 1 large one
1 kohlrabi
2 tablespoons cold-pressed canola oil
sea salt flakes and freshly ground pepper
2 lambs' kidneys (order from your butcher)
4 bay leaves
1 tablespoon standard canola oil
1 tablespoon chopped rowan sprigs
  (see right)

Start by making the gastrique. Caramelize
the sugar by heating in a pan until it is lightly
golden in color (make sure it doesn't get too
dark or burn), then add the fennel seeds,
peppercorns, and vinegar and let simmer
until you have a syrup consistency.

Take the pan off the heat and let the
gastrique cool. Peel the beets and kohlrabi
and slice very thinly, either with a sharp
knife or using a mandoline. Mix the cold-
pressed canola oil into the gastrique, then
add the vegetables and let them soak for
approximately 15 minutes before seasoning
with salt and pepper.

While the vegetables are soaking, remove
the cores and fat from the kidneys. Rinse
the kidneys under cold running water for
about 15 minutes until they have no aroma.
Dry the kidneys with paper towels, then fry
them with the bay leaves in a skillet in the
standard canola oil for about 2 to 3 minutes
on each side. Season with salt and pepper.

Prepare a plate with the kidneys, some
of the beets and kohlrabi, and a little of
the gastrique. Finish off by scattering the
kidneys with the chopped rowan sprigs and
serve with some good bread.

Rowan sprigs

The European rowan (*Sorbus
aucuparia*) is typically found in forests
and woodland, often growing in slightly
poor soils, and also thrives at high
altitudes, hence its other name
of mountain ash. It is also commonly
seen by the side of country roads or
in the parks of our cities. The tree
can grow to a height of 50 feet, but
frequently takes the form of a shrub
10 to 20 feet tall. The bark of the tree
is smooth and shiny and gray in color.
The distinctive compound leaves of
the rowan are made up of six to eight
serrated leaflets. The white flowers
have a sweet scent and grow in clusters.
Around August to September, the
edible berries, which are ¼ to ⅓ inch
in diameter, will start to mature and
turn orangey red in color, although they
taste very bitter if not dried or frozen.
However, the young tender sprigs that
sprout in April are a great delicacy for
your salad bowl, their flavor resembling
that of bitter almonds. Pick the sprigs
while they are still small and use them
fresh—whole or chopped up. But don't
worry; you won't damage the tree—it
will simply grow more new shoots.

Grilled lamb chops
with mashed vegetables and green salsa

**8 bone-in lamb chops, about
  2¾ to 3½ oz each**
1 tablespoon olive oil
sea salt flakes and freshly ground pepper

Inspect the lamb chops thoroughly and use a knife to remove any bone fragments from the meat. Oil the chops with the olive oil and season well with salt and pepper.

Cook the chops in a very hot skillet or on a ridged grill pan for about 2 minutes on each side or until their surface is beautifully golden but they are still pink and juicy at the bone.

Serve with Mashed Vegetables (*see* below) and Green Salsa (*see* right). A nice salad on the side would also be a good accompaniment, for example, my White Cabbage Salad (*see* page 210) with orange and chile.

Mashed vegetables

**2¼ lb mixed root vegetables, such as
  celery root, carrots, and parsnips**
⅔ stick butter
sea salt flakes and freshly ground pepper
**finely grated zest and juice of
  ½ organic lemon**

Peel and coarsely dice the vegetables. Cook in a pan of boiling water for about 20 minutes until very soft. Drain and let stand for 1 minute so the steam can rise.

Start mashing the vegetables coarsely using a whisk. Cut the butter into little cubes and add one cube at a time as you continue mashing. Season to taste with salt, pepper, and the lemon zest and juice. Give the vegetables another stir and season with some more salt and pepper if needed.

Green salsa

1 handful of flat-leaf parsley
1 handful of basil
**6 slices of yesterday's white bread,
  coarsely diced**
1 garlic clove, peeled
½ cup good-quality olive oil
3 tablespoons white wine vinegar
sea salt flakes and freshly ground pepper

Pick all the leaves from the herb stems, rinse them, and put in a food processor with the diced bread, garlic clove, olive oil, vinegar, salt, and pepper. Blend to a thick salsa.

Serve in a bowl to accompany the lamb chops, or with soup, potatoes, as a dip for bread, or really with anything that could use a bit of a green kick.

Oven-roasted shoulder of lamb
with potatoes and ramsons

**1 boneless shoulder of lamb,
  about 3¼ to 4½ lb**
1 to 2 garlic cloves
3¼ lb potatoes
4 to 5 red onions
10 ramson leaves or 2 garlic cloves
2 handfuls of flat-leaf parsley
1 rosemary sprig
standard canola oil, for oiling
sea salt flakes and freshly ground pepper
**2 cups water or light stock (chicken, veal
  or vegetable)**

Using a sharp knife, score a criss-cross pattern into the meat. Peel the garlic and rub the meat with half a clove (save the piece of garlic). Peel the potatoes and cut into not-so-thin slices. Peel and slice the red onions. Chop the ramson leaves (or extra garlic cloves), parsley, rosemary, and the rest of the garlic finely and mix with the onions.

In a roasting pan oiled with canola oil, lay out the potato slices in rows slightly overlapping one another. Then cover with a layer of the onion and herb mixture, then a layer of overlapping potatoes and so on, seasoning each layer with salt and pepper as you go. Pour the 2 cups of water or stock over the potatoes.

Season the lamb with salt and pepper and set it onto the potatoes with the criss-cross pattern facing down. Roast in a preheated oven at 400°F for 15 minutes, then reduce the heat to 325°F and cook for a further 1½ hours. You can use a meat thermometer to check the temperature at the center of the roast, which should be about 150°F. Take the meat out of the oven and let rest, covered, for 5 to 8 minutes.

Meanwhile, finish the potatoes under a hot broiler until the surface is crispy.

Slice the lamb and serve it on top of the potatoes or in a warmed serving dish with the potatoes on the side. With the potatoes already soaking in the delicious herb broth, there is really no need for a sauce, so this is definitely one of those all-in-one dishes. The only additional item that might accompany the dish to the table would be apple chutney or some onion and horseradish marmalade.

Lamb meatballs
with potato compote, cream cheese, and lovage

10 coriander seeds
10 cumin seeds
1 onion, peeled
½ apple, peeled
1 lb 2 oz ground lamb, 6 to 8% fat
2 thyme sprigs, chopped
6 to 8 mint leaves, chopped
sea salt flakes and freshly ground pepper
1 tablespoon prepared mustard
canola oil, for frying

Toast the coriander and cumin seeds in a dry skillet until they pop, then grind them using a mortar and pestle.

Peel and grate the onion and apple finely, then mix with the ground lamb and spices, herbs, salt, pepper, and mustard. Let the meat mixture rest in the refrigerator for 20 minutes or so before starting to cook it.

Heat up a little canola oil in a skillet and then start forming the meat mixture into meatballs. Fry the balls for about 2 to 3 minutes on each side or until they are still slightly pink and juicy in the middle.

Serve the lamb meatballs with the Potato Compote, Cream Cheese, and Lovage (see below), some good bread, and maybe a green salad, if you like. Another nice accompaniment would be Baked Turnips with Sorrel and Honey (see page 50).

Potato compote, cream cheese, and lovage

2¼ lb new potatoes
sea salt flakes
1 tablespoon cold butter
3 tablespoons cream cheese
freshly ground pepper
½ handful of lovage, chopped

Wash the potatoes thoroughly, scrubbing them using a sponge or a brush, but don't remove all the skin. Add the potatoes to a pan of salted water to just cover and bring to a boil, then simmer, covered, for 8 minutes. Turn off the heat completely and let the potatoes sit in the hot water for a further 8 minutes.

Drain the potatoes but save some of the cooking water for the compote. Mash the potatoes and mix in the cold butter, cream cheese, salt, pepper, and chopped lovage. Thin to the desired consistency with the reserved potato-cooking water, but add it little by little to avoid making the compote watery. Serve the potato compote with the lamb meatballs.

Veal stew
with young vegetables, shrimp, and dill

1 lb 5 oz veal blade or shoulder
4 cups water
sea salt flakes
3 bay leaves
1 lb 2 oz new potatoes
5 turnips
½ young celery root, about 10½ oz
8 scallions
1 fennel bulb
1 tablespoon butter
3 tablespoons all-purpose flour
2 organic egg yolks
½ cup heavy whipping cream
freshly ground pepper
3½ oz small cooked, peeled shrimp
  (see page 45)
1 handful of dill, chopped

Cut the veal into 1¼-inch pieces, add to a Dutch oven, and pour in the 4 cups of water until it just covers the meat. Bring to a boil and then add some salt as well as the bay leaves. Skim off any foam or impurities that rise to the surface. Cover the pan with a lid, reduce the heat, and let cook for about 1½ hours until the meat is nice and tender.

Meanwhile, prepare all the vegetables. Since the vegetables should be very young and fresh, it really isn't necessary to peel them, so just scrub the potatoes, turnips, and celery root thoroughly in the sink. Cut the vegetables into slightly smaller dice than the meat. (The meat shrinks a little during the cooking process, so both meat and vegetables will end up bite-sized when the stew is done.) Cut off the tips of the scallions, leaving about 2 inches of the green top, then wash them thoroughly. Dice the fennel coarsely and rinse it in cold water.

Once the meat is done, remove it from the stew and start blanching the vegetables in the broth, vegetable by vegetable, as they each require a different cooking time: 6 to 7 minutes for the potatoes; 3 to 4 minutes

for the turnips; 2 to 3 minutes for the fennel; and 1 minute for the celery root and scallions. When all the vegetables are cooked and set aside, strain the broth into a bowl through a sieve to remove any remaining impurities.

Melt the butter in the Dutch oven and add the flour while stirring vigorously with a whisk. Slowly add the broth back into the pan, little by little, still stirring vigorously, then simmer for about 5 minutes. Combine the egg yolks and the cream and stir into the sauce so that you have a nice creamy consistency. Return the meat and vegetables to the pan and heat it all up again. (You can let the stew simmer for a while if you like; the flour will prevent the egg yolks from coagulating.) Season to taste with salt and pepper. Scatter the shrimp and the chopped dill on top and serve straight from the Dutch oven or in a large bowl with some good bread or cooked grains on the side.

· ·

Tip You can serve the stew without shrimp, but if using shrimp, it is important to use fresh shrimp rather than frozen ones or those in brine, otherwise you will end up with an unpleasantly rubbery consistency and you will lose most of their flavor when they are heated through.

· ·

Boiled smoked saddle of pork
with spinach in lemon cream sauce

1 onion
1 carrot
2 bay leaves
10 whole black peppercorns
1¾ lb smoked saddle of pork
   (smoked, cured pork loin)

Peel the onion and carrot, add to a large pan of water with the bay leaves and peppercorns, and bring to a boil. Add the piece of smoked pork and make sure that the water just covers it. Let the water return to a boil, then lower the heat, cover the pan with a lid, and cook for about 45 minutes.

Turn the heat off and let the pork sit in the cooking water for 15 to 20 minutes. Take the meat out, remove any string or netting and cut into thin slices. Serve immediately with the Spinach in Lemon Cream Sauce (*see* below) and boiled potatoes.

Spinach in lemon cream sauce

3 lb 5 oz fresh spinach leaves
2 teaspoons butter
½ cup heavy whipping cream
freshly grated nutmeg, to taste
finely grated zest and juice of
   1 organic lemon
sea salt flakes and freshly ground pepper

Rinse the spinach very thoroughly, several times if necessary to make sure all the dirt is washed away. Put in a sieve to drain.

Melt the butter in a pan, add the spinach, and sauté for 1 to 2 minutes until it starts to soften. Add the cream and cook for about 30 seconds, then season to taste with nutmeg, the lemon zest and juice, salt, and pepper. Serve immediately.

Parsley-stuffed pork tenderloin
with warm radishes and butterhead lettuce with cream vinaigrette

1 trimmed pork tenderloin
½ handful of flat-leaf parsley,
sea salt flakes and freshly ground pepper
2 teaspoons butter
½ cup water or light stock (chicken or veal)

Cut away the large sinews from the tenderloin, then dry the meat with paper towels. Slice the tenderloin halfway through lengthwise, then place in a double layer of plastic food bags and pound it using a meat tenderizer.

Rinse the parsley, let it dry, and then chop it coarsely. Season the tenderloin on both sides with salt and pepper and then stuff it with the parsley. Roll it up into a tight roll with the parsley inside and tie some butcher's twine around the roll to secure it.

Heat the butter in a pan until it turns golden in color before adding the tenderloin. Fry on all sides, then add the water or stock, cover the pan with a lid, and cook over low heat for 7 to 8 minutes. Turn the meat over and cook for a further 7 to 8 minutes so that it cooks for no more than 15 minutes in total.

Take the tenderloin out of the pan, wrap it in foil, and let rest for about 10 minutes. Cooking the meat for a relatively short time and then letting it rest for so long afterward gives it a perfect, slightly pink and juicy center. Cut into slices and serve with some of the gravy from the pan, along with Warm Radishes and Butterhead Lettuce with Cream Vinaigrette (*see* right).

Warm radishes

20 radishes
2 tablespoons apple cider vinegar
3 tablespoons cold-pressed canola oil
1 teaspoon acacia honey
sea salt flakes and freshly ground pepper

Cut off the base of each radish and remove the largest leaves while leaving the smaller ones in place. Cut the radishes in half and add to a pan with the vinegar, canola oil, honey, salt, and pepper. Heat up and cook for 1 to 2 minutes until the radishes are cooked through but still al dente. Serve while they are warm.

Butterhead lettuce with cream vinaigrette

1 to 2 tablespoons apple cider vinegar
3 tablespoons heavy whipping cream
1 to 2 tablespoons superfine sugar
sea salt flakes and freshly ground pepper
1 butterhead lettuce

Mix the vinegar into the cream in a bowl and let stand until it thickens. Add the sugar and stir well. Season to taste with salt and pepper.

Rinse the lettuce well and dry in a salad spinner or using a clean dish towel. Tear the leaves into smaller pieces and toss them with the cream dressing. Serve immediately so that the lettuce doesn't get soggy.

Pork roast
with herbs, fennel, and new potatoes

SERVES 6
1 scallion
4 rosemary sprigs
5 sage sprigs
5 chervil sprigs
1 organic lemon
1 boneless pork loin, skin on
sea salt flakes and freshly ground pepper
2¾ lb new potatoes
2 tablespoons cold-pressed canola oil
3½ oz fresh spinach
1 fennel bulb

Peel the scallion and slice it thinly. Rinse the herbs and pluck the leaves from the stems, but keep the stems for the roast to sit on in the oven. Finely grate the zest of the lemon.

Cut the pork almost in half, leaving a small portion uncut on one side so that you can open out the meat, and fill it with the herb leaves, lemon zest, salt, and pepper. Close it again and tie it tightly together with butcher's twine to seal all the goodness inside the meat.

Rinse the potatoes thoroughly and cut in half. Put them into an ovenproof dish together with the zested lemon, cut into quarters. Drizzle with the canola oil, season with the herb stems, salt, and pepper, and mix well. Put the pork on top of the potatoes and roast in a preheated oven at 350°F for 1 to 1¼ hours until the crackling is nice and crisp and the potatoes are golden and crisp on the outside but soft in the middle. If you like, use a meat thermometer to check the temperature at the center of the roast, which should be about 150°F.

Take the roast out of the oven and let it rest for 5 to 10 minutes. Meanwhile, rinse the spinach several times in cold water and let drain in a sieve. Rinse the fennel and then slice thinly. Mix the fennel and spinach with the potatoes—enough to warm them a little, but not so much that they get soggy.

Carve the roast and serve with the fried potatoes and all the lovely greens. You don't really need any other accompaniments, because you have everything in one dish. With this recipe, once you have put the meat in the oven, the work is done and dinner is on its way!

Mock chicken

Originally, pork tenderloin wasn't a piece of meat that you would cook by itself. The lean muscle was usually ground together with a fattier part of the pig and used as ground pork or to stuff sausages. In the second half of the 19th century, when fresh meat became more abundant, we started frying tenderloin either sliced up or whole, stuffed with, for example, apples and prunes, or parsley, as in this recipe. The first time parsley-stuffed tenderloin appeared was in the recipes of Frøken Jensen, and was called "mock chicken." Until well into the 20th century, chicken was considered an expensive food item, and was reserved for Sundays, typically stuffed with parsley and butter.

DANDELION LEAVES
These little leaf rosettes are perfect in a salad.

Roasted duck breast
and baked rhubarb with horseradish

2 duck breasts
3 lemon thyme sprigs
1 tablespoon apple cider vinegar
sea salt flakes and freshly ground pepper

Prepare the duck breasts by cutting away the sinews and removing any remaining bits of feather. Using a sharp knife, lightly score a criss-cross pattern into the skin.

Sauté the breasts in a hot pan, first on the skin side for a couple of minutes so that the fat renders and the skin gets crisp, then on the other side for about a minute. Don't forget to save the duck fat afterward—it is great for sautéing potatoes!

Put the breasts into an ovenproof dish and marinate in the lemon thyme, vinegar, salt, and pepper—simply shower the ingredients over the duck and massage them into the flesh, then let them soak into the duck for about 15 minutes.

Cook in a preheated oven at 325°F for 8 to 10 minutes.

Remove the duck breasts from the oven and let rest for 2 to 3 minutes, then cut them into slices. Serve with Baked Rhubarb with Horseradish (see below) and a large dish of boiled new potatoes.

Baked rhubarb with horseradish

5 to 6 rhubarb stalks
3 tablespoons jaggery
sea salt flakes and freshly ground pepper
2 tablespoons elderflower vinegar
2 teaspoons freshly grated horseradish
1 tablespoon cold-pressed canola oil
½ handful of chervil

Cut off the tops and bottoms of the rhubarb stalks, but be careful not to remove the white "foot" of the stalk, which is where the rhubarb flavor is most concentrated and best. Rinse the stalks in cold water, cut into 3-inch pieces and put into an ovenproof dish.

Sprinkle the sugar, salt, pepper, and vinegar over the rhubarb and bake in a preheated oven at 315°F for 8 to 10 minutes. The stalks should be soft, yet al dente, but don't worry if you accidentally bake them for too long—it happens, believe me—because then you will simply have a compote instead, which really isn't a bad thing.

Take the dish out of the oven and carefully mix in the grated horseradish and canola oil. (If the rhubarb has turned into a compote, mix in the horseradish first and then drizzle the oil on top.) Pick the chervil leaves from the sprigs and use to garnish the rhubarb. Serve while warm with the roasted duck breast or a classic roast chicken.

Honey-glazed chicken with black pepper
and fennel-asparagus crudités

SERVES 6
1 large organic chicken, about
    3¼ to 4½ lb
3 rosemary sprigs
3 thyme sprigs
½ organic lemon
1 tablespoon honey
2 tablespoons elderflower vinegar
1 tablespoon olive oil
15 whole black peppercorns,
    lightly crushed
sea salt flakes

Check the chicken for any feather stumps and pluck them out. Remove any blood or intestine residues from the cavity and wipe with paper towels. Stuff the chicken with the whole rosemary and thyme sprigs, then cut the lemon into large cubes and add to the cavity.

Mix the honey, vinegar, oil, and crushed peppercorns together in a bowl to make a marinade, then lubricate the skin of the chicken all over with the marinade.

Season the chicken all over with salt.

Place the chicken in an ovenproof dish and roast in a preheated oven at 350°F for 1 hour.

Take the chicken out and let it rest for 10 to 15 minutes before you carve it into pieces. Serve the chicken with boiled new potatoes and the Fennel-asparagus Crudités (see below).

Fennel-asparagus crudités

2 fennel bulbs
10 green asparagus
2 tablespoons cold-pressed canola oil
2 tablespoons apple cider vinegar
sea salt flakes and freshly ground pepper

Cut the fennel bulbs in half, rinse them thoroughly in cold water, and drain. Break off the woody stems of the asparagus and discard (or save them to make soup), then rinse the spears in cold water, too.

Slice the fennel and asparagus thinly lengthwise—use a mandoline if you have one or otherwise a sharp knife—then put them in a bowl.

Add the oil, vinegar, salt, and pepper to the raw vegetables and toss to coat, then let stand for 2 minutes before serving.

Fish

Steamed mussels
with lovage, chervil, and beer

4½ lb mussels
3 shallots
2 garlic cloves
white part of 1 leek, rinsed
2 teaspoons butter
1 cup apple cider or tart apple juice
1¼ cups lager or pale ale, plus extra to
    season if you like
2 cups heavy whipping cream
½ handful of lovage
½ handful of parsley
½ handful of chervil
sea salt flakes and freshly ground pepper

Prepare the mussels as described on page 18.

Peel and chop the shallots, garlic, and leek finely, and put them in a large pan with the butter. Lightly sauté, and before they start to brown, add the mussels and stir well. Pour the apple cider, or apple juice, and lager into the pan, cover with a lid, and steam the mussels for 4 to 5 minutes until they have opened up. Discard any that haven't opened—they are not safe to eat.

Strain the mussel broth into a saucepan, add the cream, and bring it to a boil, then simmer for about 5 minutes. Meanwhile, set the mussels aside in their cooking pan with the lid on.

Add the fresh herbs (reserving some to garnish) to the broth, then pour it into a blender. Blend to a smooth green sauce. Season with salt, pepper, and a little extra fresh lager if you wish. Pour the sauce over the mussels, scattering them generously with the herbs. Serve with some good wholemeal bread for soaking up the sauce.

. . . .

TIP If you don't eat all of the dish, take the mussels out of their shells and return them to the sauce. Store in the refrigerator, then heat up the next day with small cooked potato cubes or boiled grains to make a nice stew.

. . . .

Pan-fried smelt
with cream-stewed cucumber and dill oil

1 handful of dill
3 tablespoons olive oil
12 to 16 smelt (*see* tip)
sea salt flakes and freshly ground pepper
1 tablespoon standard canola oil
1 cucumber
½ cup heavy whipping cream
2 tablespoons apple cider vinegar

Start by making the dill oil. Take half the dill and pluck the feathery leaves from the stems into a blender. Add the olive oil and blend to a green oil. Save the oil for later.

Now check the smelt—they should smell fresh and a little like cucumber (*see* tip). Clean the smelt and remove the bones, but leave the tail in place to hold together the 2 small fillets. (Alternatively, ask your fish dealer to do the work for you.) Season with salt and pepper, then fry the smelt in the canola oil in a hot skillet for about 30 seconds on each side until they are very crisp on the outside but juicy in the middle.

Peel the cucumber, cut it in half lengthwise, and scrape the seeds out with a teaspoon. Cut the cucumber into chunky pieces.

Heat the cream in a saucepan and let simmer for a while. Season with the vinegar, salt, and pepper to taste. Add the cucumber pieces and cook for a few minutes until the cream clings to the cucumber. Finely chop the remaining dill and scatter it into the pan. Give it a little stir and serve the cucumber with the fried smelt and a drizzle of the dill oil. Serve as an appetizer or add some potatoes or cooked grains and serve for dinner.

. . . .

TIP The smelt (also known as sparling or European smelt) is a small, fjord or freshwater fish that can be caught from February to May. Characteristically it smells like fresh cucumber, so much so that some fishermen call it "the cucumber fish." If you can't find any, just use herring instead and cook for 2 to 3 minutes longer in the pan.

. . . .

ST. GEORGE'S MUSHROOMS
In parks and gardens, these precious little mushrooms will start sprouting in spring.

Pan-fried garfish
with rhubarb chutney

2 large garfish, scales removed
1 tablespoon mustard
sea salt flakes and freshly ground pepper
rye flour, for dusting
2 teaspoons butter, plus extra
    for greasing
1 tablespoon standard canola oil
flat-leaf parsley leaves, to garnish

Remove the bones from the garfish to
create 4 fillets (or ask your fish dealer to do
this). Spread the flesh side of the fillets with
the mustard, salt, and pepper, then cut each
fillet into 4 pieces and fold them together
skin-side out. Dust the pieces with rye flour.

Fry the garfish fillets in the butter and
canola oil in a hot skillet for 2 to 3 minutes
on each side. The skin should be beautifully
golden and crisp. Season if necessary with
a little extra salt and pepper.

Serve the garfish with Rhubarb Chutney
(see below), a little of the frying butter
and oil mixture, and boiled new potatoes.
Scatter with flat-leaf parsley leaves just
before serving.

Rhubarb chutney

8 to 10 rhubarb stalks, trimmed and cut
    into ½-inch pieces
1 large red onion, chopped
1 whole red chile
1 teaspoon curry powder
1 teaspoon coriander seeds
3 tablespoons jaggery
3 tablespoons apple cider vinegar
1 handful of golden raisins

Cook the rhubarb pieces in a saucepan
over low heat along with the rest of the
ingredients, simmering until the rhubarb
has offered up all of its flavor, which should
take about 15 to 20 minutes. Remove and
discard the chile from the chutney, then
pour the chutney into sterilized preserving
jars and let cool. Enjoy immediately or store
in the refrigerator for 2 to 3 weeks.

Skate wings
with pointed cabbage in broth with herbs

2¼ lb skate wing, 1 lb 5 oz pure fillet
sea salt flakes and freshly ground pepper
2 cups fish stock
½ fennel bulb
½ pointed cabbage
8 scallions
2 handfuls of chopped fresh herbs, such
    as chervil, parsley, and tarragon
a little apple cider vinegar

Remove the skin and bones of the skate
wing, or ask your fish dealer to do this—it
can be a little difficult. Scrape the fillet free
of any slime.

Divide the fillet into 4 pieces, season with salt
and pepper, and roll them from the thick end
to the thin end so that each roll seals itself.

Bring the stock to a boil in a pan and poach
the skate wing fillets over low heat for 6 to
7 minutes—they should only just tremble
in the hot liquid. Remove the skate from
the stock, place on a plate, and cover with a
clean dish towel.

Rinse the vegetables in cold water. Slice
the fennel thinly, then cut the cabbage
and scallions into larger chunks. Add the
vegetables to the stock and cook for a few
minutes until tender, but still with plenty of
crunch. Add the chopped fresh herbs and
season with salt, pepper, and vinegar to taste.

Place each skate wing fillet in a wide soup
dish and pour the stock and vegetables
over. Serve immediately with good bread.

Potato salad
with green asparagus, dill, and crispy fried shrimp

1 lb 2 oz new potatoes
sea salt flakes
8 green asparagus
6 radishes
2 tablespoons apple cider vinegar
2 tablespoons cold-pressed canola oil
1 teaspoon honey
freshly ground pepper
1 handful of dill
7 oz raw small shrimp
2 tablespoons standard canola oil

Wash and scrub the potatoes, put them
in a pan with water to just cover, and add
salt. Bring to a boil then lower the heat
and simmer the potatoes, covered, for
8 minutes. Turn off the heat and let the
potatoes sit in the hot water for a further
8 minutes. This way, they will be tender
but not overcooked (I always cook new
potatoes this way).

Drain the potatoes and let cool slightly,
then dice them coarsely and place in a bowl.
Prepare the asparagus by breaking off the
woody stem ends, and prepare the radishes
by cutting off the tops and roots, then
rinse both vegetables in cold water. Slice
the asparagus and radishes thinly and add
them to the potatoes.

Mix the vinegar, cold-pressed canola oil,
honey, salt, and pepper together in a bowl
to make a dressing. Pour the dressing onto
the potatoes, stir well, and add the dill,
freshly chopped.

Now it is time for the shrimp. Snip the
heads off the shrimp. Heat up a skillet with
the standard canola oil, add the shrimp,
and fry them over very high heat for 1 to
2 minutes until the shells are completely
golden and crisp, then season with salt.

Serve the crisp, hot shrimp with the potato
salad and some great bread on the side for
a quick and easy main dish. I know that there
are people who will refuse to eat the shrimp
in all their glory (that is, in all their shell!),
but the intense frying makes the shells
crispy and quite delicious. Sometimes
I even fry the shrimp whole and eat them
with their heads intact, but that is where
my family draws the line.

Pan-fried garfish »

Boiled red king crab
with tomato mayonnaise

2 raw red king crab legs
½ handful of dill
10 whole black peppercorns
1 tablespoon coarse sea salt
2 tablespoons apple cider vinegar, divided
sea salt and freshly ground pepper
2 tablespoons cold-pressed canola oil

Cut the crab legs into sections at the joints and put them in a saucepan with the stems from the dill, the peppercorns, coarse salt, and 1 tablespoon of the vinegar. Cover the crab with water and bring the water to a boil, then skim off any foam or impurities that rise to the surface, and lower the heat.

Cook the crab legs for 5 minutes, then turn off the heat completely and let them sit in the hot broth for about 10 to 15 minutes.

Remove the meat from the crab legs by cutting the shells open with a pair of kitchen scissors. The meat can then be lifted out in whole pieces or prised out with the end of a teaspoon. Put the crabmeat in a bowl and season with salt, pepper, the remaining tablespoon of vinegar, and the canola oil.

Serve the crabmeat with Tomato Mayonnaise (see below), a green salad, and toasted bread. Depending on how hungry you are and the composition of the rest of the meal, the dish may be served either as an appetizer or a main course.

Tomato mayonnaise

2 pasteurized egg yolks (available from online suppliers)
sea salt flakes
1 tablespoon prepared Dijon mustard
2 to 3 tablespoons apple cider vinegar
⅔ cup cold-pressed canola oil
2 tablespoons tomato paste
freshly ground black pepper

Using an electric hand beater or balloon whisk, whisk the egg yolks, salt, mustard, and vinegar together in a bowl until thick and white. Whisk in the oil in a thin stream— it is important to do this slowly to stop the mayo from splitting. If it begins to curdle, rescue it by adding a few drops of cold water while whisking vigorously. Add the tomato paste and possibly a little extra salt and pepper to taste, then serve.

Lumpfish roe
with potato rösti and buttermilk dressing

10½ oz fresh lumpfish roe (see page 188)
sea salt flakes and freshly ground pepper

Rösti
4 to 5 baking potatoes
1 small garlic clove, chopped
2 to 4 thyme sprigs, leaves chopped
2 tablespoons standard canola oil

Dressing
1 cup buttermilk
2 tablespoons apple cider vinegar
1 tablespoon superfine sugar
1 pack growing garden cress, chopped

Remove any membranes from the roe and taste it—you might need to add salt or it may have already been salted. Store it in the refrigerator until serving.

To make the rösti, peel the potatoes and grate them on the coarse side of the grater. Press all the liquid out of the potatoes and put them in a bowl. Season well with salt, pepper, and the chopped garlic and thyme.

Heat a small skillet, about 6 to 7 inches in diameter, and make sure it is nonstick so that the rösti comes off easily. Oil the pan with the canola oil. Press the grated potato into a firm pancake and fry in the skillet over medium heat for about 5 minutes on one side until it becomes golden and crisp. Place a plate or lid securely over the pan, flip the whole thing over, and slide the rösti back into the pan. Then cook for 5 minutes on the other side.

Transfer the rösti to a cookie sheet and roast in a preheated oven at 400°F for about 10 to 15 minutes until it is completely cooked through. Take it out of the oven and cut it into 4 neat pieces.

For the dressing, mix the buttermilk, vinegar, sugar, salt, and pepper together in a bowl, add the chopped garden cress, and whisk until well combined.

Serve the warm potato rösti on individual plates with a dollop of the roe on top. Drizzle with some of the dressing before enjoying the crispy goodness.

Langoustines with tarragon and garlic

2¼lb langoustines (12 to 16)
1 very fresh whole garlic bulb
1 handful of tarragon
sea salt flakes
3 tablespoons olive oil
½ organic lemon
freshly ground pepper

Check that the langoustines are fresh—they should smell of the sea. Place them in a large ovenproof dish. Chop the whole fresh garlic bulb and the tarragon coarsely, and scatter both over the langoustines. Season with salt and drizzle with the olive oil. Squeeze most of the juice from the lemon half over the langoustines, then cut it into chunks and add to the langoustines so that the rind provides extra citrus flavor.

Place the dish in the preheated oven at 500°F and bake the langoustines for 8 to 10 minutes. Of course, you can also cook them outside on the barbecue if you like, and they will cook in no time. Remove the langoustines from the oven and serve immediately, with good bread to dip in the juices in the bottom of the dish.

Light dishes

Warm brioches
with smoked salmon and ramson spread

MAKES 20 BRIOCHES

Pre-dough
1¼ cups cold water
¾ oz (2 tablespoons) fresh compresssed yeast (baker's yeast)
2 cups wheat flour

Brioche dough
½ cup whole milk
1 lb 10 oz (6 cups) all-purpose flour, plus extra for dusting
2 teaspoons sea salt flakes
12 organic eggs
2⅔ stick softened butter
½ cup superfine sugar
1 beaten organic egg, for glazing

Filling
10 ramson leaves
1 cup Greek yogurt, 2% fat
1 teaspoon acacia honey
finely grated zest of ½ organic lemon
sea salt flakes and freshly ground pepper
1 red onion
1 Little Gem lettuce
7 oz smoked salmon

Day 1
Pour the 1¼ cups cold water into a bowl and stir in the yeast. Add the flour and knead the dough well. Cover with plastic wrap and keep in the refrigerator for 12 hours.

Day 2
Take the pre-dough out of the refrigerator a few hours before using to let it return to room temperature. Meanwhile, mix the milk, flour, salt, and eggs for the brioche dough together in a large bowl and knead until smooth. Knead in the softened butter, and continue kneading until the dough is smooth again, then knead in the sugar until completely combined. Add the pre-dough and knead until smooth and supple. If kneading by hand, you should expect to spend 8 to 10 minutes; if using an electric

stand mixer fitted with a dough hook, kneading should take 6 to 8 minutes.

Let the dough rise in the bowl, covered with a damp dish towel, in the kitchen for 2 hours.

Knead the dough by hand on a floured work surface, then cover it and let it rest on the work surface for 30 minutes. Split the dough into 2 pieces, roll each into a sausage shape, and divide each sausage into 10 pieces. Roll the pieces into buns, place them on 2 baking pans covered with parchment paper, and let rise for a few hours until doubled in size.

Glaze the brioches with the beaten egg and bake in a preheated oven at 425°F for about 10 to 12 minutes until golden and fluffy. Remove from the oven and let cool on a wire rack.

While the brioches are cooling, make the filling. Rinse the ramson leaves, then chop coarsely and blend them with the yogurt, honey, lemon zest, salt, and pepper in a blender or food processor, or using a hand-held stick blender, to a smooth green cream. Season with additional salt and pepper if necessary.

Peel the red onion and cut it into very thin slices. Separate the leaves from the lettuce, rinse them, then dry the leaves well. Cut the warm brioches in half, spread the cut sides with the ramson cream, and add the slices of smoked salmon, lettuce, and red onion. Eat the brioches as part of a brunch or as lunch sandwiches—or pack a picnic basket and enjoy them in the spring countryside.

TIP Instead of the ramsons, you can use chives with a little garlic, to create a taste combination similar to ramsons.

Pan-fried chicken livers
with nettles and pickled onions

7 oz fresh chicken livers
2 red onions
2 tablespoons acacia honey
3 tablespoons apple cider vinegar
sea salt flakes and freshly ground pepper
1 tablespoon olive oil
2 handfuls of nettle shoots
½ frisée (curly endive)
1 tablespoon cold-pressed canola oil

Check that the chicken livers are fresh— they must have a beautiful dark red color, smell of flesh and blood, and have a smooth, shiny surface. Remove any sinews or membranes, and place the livers in the refrigerator until it is time to fry them.

Peel the red onions, cut them into thin wedges, and put them in a bowl. Add the honey, vinegar, salt, and pepper, and let marinate for 20 to 30 minutes, stirring a few times at regular intervals.

Heat a skillet with the olive oil and fry the chicken livers for 1 to 2 minutes on each side over high heat so that they have a nice fried surface but remain pale pink in the middle.

Rinse the nettle shoots, chop them coarsely, and add them to the pan with the chicken livers to fry for the last 10 seconds of cooking time, softening them a little but keeping their structure and beautiful green color intact. Season with salt and pepper.

Rinse and tear the frisée, then dry it using a salad spinner or a clean dish towel. Remove the livers from the pan and serve immediately with the pickled onions, lettuce, and some good bread, drizzling the cold-pressed canola oil over the plate. Serve either as an appetizer or a light lunch.

Fried porridge

1¼ cups chicken stock or water
1 cup beer
1 teaspoon sea salt flakes
⅔ cup wholegrain rye flour
⅓ cup wholegrain barley flour
⅓ cup freshly grated hard cheese, such
    as Høost or Cheddar
2 teaspoons butter
1 tablespoon standard canola oil,
    plus extra for greasing

To serve
1¼ lb good-quality fresh sausages
    straight from your butcher's
1 handful of ground elder, garlic mustard,
    or other fresh herb of your choice
Onion Compote (*see* below)

Bring the stock or water, beer, and salt
to a boil in a pan, add the flours, and stir
vigorously. Reduce the heat and simmer for
20 to 25 minutes, stirring frequently, until
the mixture no longer tastes of flour. Add
the grated cheese and butter and stir until
you have a smooth mixture.

Pour into an oiled baking pan. Cover with
plastic wrap and let chill in the refrigerator
to set until firm.

Cut the cold porridge into thin slices and fry
them in the canola oil in a skillet.

If your sausages aren't precooked, it might
be a good idea to fry them before the
porridge; if they are, just quickly fry them in
the same pan after frying the porridge.

Serve the crispy porridge slices warm with
the fried sausages, scattered with the fresh
herbs, and with a dollop of Onion Compote.

Onion Compote

5½ oz red onions
3 tablespoons apple cider vinegar
¼ cup sugar
3 tablespoons water
1 tablespoon mustard
sea salt flakes and freshly ground pepper

Peel the onions and chop them finely.
Add to a pan with the vinegar, sugar, and
measured water, bring to a boil, and then
simmer for about 20 minutes or until you
have a compote consistency. Remove from
the heat and add the mustard, salt, and
pepper until seasoned to perfection.

Raw salmon
with lime, horseradish, and garlic mustard

7 oz very fresh skinless salmon fillet
2 tablespoons water
finely grated zest and juice
    of 1 organic lime
2 tablespoons freshly grated
    horseradish
1 tablespoon cold-pressed canola oil
1 tablespoon jaggery
1 tablespoon sea salt flakes
freshly ground pepper
10 garlic mustard leaves, finely chopped
    or chives, snipped

Check that the salmon is really fresh and
appetizing—it is supposed to smell of the
sea, not the harbor! Slice the salmon thinly
and divide among 4 plates.

Whisk together the water, lime zest and
juice, horseradish, canola oil, sugar, and salt
and pepper to taste in a bowl until smooth.
Pour evenly over the salmon and let stand
for 5 minutes.

Scatter the salmon with the chopped garlic
mustard leaves (or finely snipped chives)
and serve immediately before the acid
"overcooks" the fish. The acid from the
lime doesn't only give flavor but acts as
a cooking agent, changing the structure
and color of the fish. The method could be
referred to as "cold cooking" and is used
in the South American dish ceviche. I like
to stop the process at the stage where the
salmon still remains slightly raw.

Serve the salmon with some good bread,
preferably toasted.

TIP Garlic mustard is a garlic-flavored
herb found in deciduous forests, woodland,
parks, and hedgerows. The leaves are
heart-shaped with barbed edges, somewhat
like nettles, and the herb is often found
growing next to nettles. Later in spring the
plant bears white flowers, which, as with
the leaves, make an excellent condiment
and garnish for anything from a salad to a
sandwich. If you can't find garlic mustard,
you can replace it with finely snipped chives.

GARLIC MUSTARD
The first tender shoots of garlic mustard
are particularly good scattered on an
egg sandwich.

Raw salmon »

Shrimp
with crispy potatoes and smoked curd cheese

7 oz small potatoes
4 cups grapeseed oil, for frying
2¼ lb small cooked, peeled shrimp
**   (see above)**
2¾ oz Smoked Curd Cheese
**   (see page 16)**
a little dill, for scattering
sea salt flakes and freshly ground pepper
1 tablespoon cold-pressed canola oil

Wash the potatoes thoroughly (peeling isn't necessary) and cut into very thin slices using a mandoline or a potato peeler. Soak the potato slices in a bowl of water for 10 minutes, then drain.

Gently heat the oil for frying in a pan to about 315°F—it should sizzle when you dip the wooden end of a match in the oil. Meanwhile, let the potato slices dry on paper towels. Fry the potato slices in the hot oil until lightly golden and crisp—approximately 1 to 2 minutes. Be careful that the oil doesn't become too hot and overbrown the potatoes. Serve the crisp potatoes with the peeled shrimp and smoked curd cheese, scattered with a little dill, salt, and pepper, and drizzled with the canola oil. Serve as a small appetizer or a snack with a glass of bubbly on the terrace.

Open rye bread sandwich
with new potatoes, smoked curd cheese dressing, radishes, ramsons, and cress

4 slices of rye bread
14 oz boiled new potatoes (see method
**   on page 36)**
4 tablespoons Smoked Curd Cheese
**   Dressing (see right), divided**
4 ramson leaves, rinsed
4 radishes, rinsed
½ pack or tray of growing garden cress
sea salt flakes and freshly ground pepper

Place the bread slices on a platter. Slice the potatoes, lay them out on the bread slices and add a tablespoonful of Smoked Curd Cheese Dressing to the top of each slice.

Cut the ramson leaves into very thin strips, cut the cress, and slice the radishes into thin slices, too. Scatter each sandwich with the ramsons and cress, and then the radishes. Season with salt and pepper to serve.

Smoked curd cheese dressing

3 tablespoons Smoked Curd Cheese
**   (see page 16)**
½ cup lowfat milk
1 teaspoon acacia honey
sea salt flakes and freshly ground pepper

Put the smoked curd cheese in a bowl, add the milk, and beat to a smooth cream. Add the honey and salt and pepper to taste.

Omelet
with peppered mackerel, potatoes, and scallions

1 smoked peppered mackerel fillet
1 scallion
14 oz boiled new potatoes (see method
**   on page 36)**
2 teaspoons butter
sea salt flakes and freshly ground pepper
6 organic eggs
1 cup lowfat milk
½ handful of chives

Remove any skin and bones from the mackerel fillet. Chop the scallion finely and cut the boiled potatoes into large cubes.

Sauté the scallion and potatoes in the butter in an ovenproof skillet, and season with salt and pepper. Mix in the mackerel.

Beat the eggs and milk in a bowl and season with a little salt and pepper. Pour the egg mixture into the skillet and place it in a preheated oven at 350°F. Bake the omelet for 8 to 10 minutes until the egg mixture is firm and slightly golden on top. If the omelet lacks a little color, turn on the broiler for the final few minutes.

Finely snip the chives and scatter them on the omelet. Serve with rye bread, mustard, and a green salad or green asparagus with a vinaigrette of Parsley, Anchovies, and Apple Cider Vinegar (see page 50).

Crispy onion rings

2 cups all-purpose flour
1 small organic egg
1 cup beer
⅔ cup warm water
1½ tablespoons standard canola oil
fine salt
a little superfine sugar
3 onions
sea salt flakes
2 organic egg whites
1 to 2 quarts grapeseed oil, for frying

First make the batter. Mix together the flour, egg, beer, measured warm water, canola oil, some fine salt, and a little sugar in a bowl with a whisk and let rest in the refrigerator for about an hour. (The egg whites are not added until immediately before use.)

Peel the onions and cut into rings. Put the onion rings into a bowl, sprinkle with sea salt flakes, and let stand for 10 minutes to soften and release some of their liquid.

Heat the oil in a pan to 315 to 350°F—it should sizzle when you dip the wooden end of a match in the oil. Whisk the egg whites until stiff and then fold them gently into the batter (the trick is to mix the first spoonful of whites in vigorously, then fold the rest of them in gently). Dip the onion rings in the batter, then fry them in the hot oil until golden and crisp. Lift them out with a slotted spoon, place them on some paper towels, and give them a sprinkle of salt.

Serve the crispy onion rings while they are still warm, with a portion of Sweet and Sour Dip with Dill and Horseradish (see right) or Green Salsa (see page 26) for dipping. The onion rings are a great snack to accompany a glass of cold beer and can also be served on top of a piece of boiled or braised meat.

Spinach tart
with cottage cheese

Pastry
¾ cup Öland or organic wholegrain
    wheat flour, plus extra for dusting
½ cup oat flour
½ cup rye flour
1 teaspoon baking powder
⅓ cup standard canola oil, plus extra
    for greasing
2 tablespoons water
1 teaspoon salt
1 cup lowfat plain yogurt

Filling
1½ cups cottage cheese
1 cup lowfat milk
3 organic eggs
3 gratings of nutmeg
sea salt flakes and freshly ground pepper
2 teaspoons butter
1 lb 2 oz fresh spinach leaves, washed
    and drained
1 shallot
⅓ cup grated hard cheese

To finish
1 shallot
1 handful of fresh herbs, such as sweet
    woodruff, chervil, and sweet cicely
a few drops of apple cider vinegar
a few drops of cold-pressed canola oil

First make the pastry. Mix all the ingredients together in a bowl to make a dough. Seal the dough in plastic wrap and let rest in the refrigerator for 30 minutes.

Meanwhile, prepare the filling. Mix the cottage cheese, milk, eggs, nutmeg, salt, and pepper together in a bowl to a smooth paste.

Melt the butter in a saucepan and briefly sauté the spinach, just until it starts to collapse and release its liquid. Season with salt and pepper. Transfer the spinach to a sieve and strain off the liquid.

Roll the pastry dough out into a thin layer on a floured work surface, then transfer it to a tart pan 1¼-inches deep with a diameter of 9½ to 10½ inches, and greased with canola oil. Press the dough firmly into the dish and trim the excess dough from around the edge.

Put the drained spinach into the pastry crust and cover with the cottage cheese paste. Peel and slice the shallot into very thin rings, then spread over the top of the paste. Lastly, scatter the grated cheese evenly over the tart.

Bake the tart on the bottom rack of a preheated oven at 325 to 350°F for 30 to 35 minutes until the filling has set. The tart should be light golden on the top and the pastry crust baked through.

Just before serving, peel and cut the other shallot into thin rings, then toss with the freshly torn herbs in the vinegar and canola oil, just to give them a bit of shine. Arrange the shallot and herb mixture on top of the tart and serve warm. If you want more greenery, serve with a small salad on the side. You can also choose to make the tart a day ahead and serve it cold for lunch or as an accompaniment to a main course.

Sweet and sour dip
with dill and horseradish

¼ cup sugar
2 teaspoons dill seeds
3 slices of peeled fresh horseradish,
    1⁄16 inch thick
1 garlic clove, peeled
1 cup apple cider vinegar
sea salt flakes

Caramelize the sugar by heating in a pan until it is lightly golden in color (make sure it doesn't get too dark or burn), then add the dill seeds, horseradish, the whole garlic clove, and finally the vinegar. Bring to a boil and then lower the heat and cook until reduced by half. Season the dip with a few grains of salt and let cool before serving.

Spinach tart »

Vegetable accompaniments

Boiled leeks
with vinaigrette of parsley, anchovies, and apple cider vinegar

6 winter leeks
sea salt flakes
4 anchovy fillets, chopped
2 tablespoons capers or elderberry capers
1 tablespoon prepared mustard
½ handful of parsley, torn
3 tablespoons apple cider vinegar
1 teaspoon honey
2 tablespoons cold-pressed canola oil
freshly ground pepper

Cut off the roots and tops of the leeks. Rinse thoroughly in cold water. Drain, then cut them into chunks 1½ to 2 inches in length.

Bring a pan of lightly salted water to a boil and add the leeks. When the water returns to a boil continue boiling the leeks until they are tender—about 5 to 7 minutes, depending on thickness.

Make a rustic vinaigrette by mixing together the chopped anchovies, capers or elderberry capers, mustard, parsley, vinegar, honey, and canola oil in a bowl until well combined.

Lift the tender leeks from their cooking water and add them directly to the vinaigrette so that they absorb the flavors. Give them a stir and season to taste with salt and pepper.

Serve the leeks immediately while still warm, either as a small vegetable dish on its own or as a side for fish or meat.

··

TIP For a little luxury, I sometimes replace the anchovies with 3 to 4 coarsely chopped Limfjord oysters.

··

Baked turnips
with sorrel and honey

1 lb 2 oz turnips
2 tablespoons apple cider vinegar
2 tablespoons cold-pressed canola oil
1 tablespoon honey
sea salt flakes and freshly ground pepper
1 oz sorrel (you can use any type of sorrel or even lemon balm)

Wash the turnips well in cold water and cut the tops and bottoms off, as if they were large radishes. Slice the turnips very thinly using a mandoline or a sharp knife.

Mix the turnips with vinegar, canola oil, honey, salt, and pepper, then place them in an ovenproof dish and bake in a preheated oven at 325°F for 6 to 7 minutes until they are just becoming tender and start absorbing the marinade but still remain crisp. Stir and let them cool slightly.

Coarsely chop the sorrel and toss it into the turnips at the last minute, otherwise it will lose its color and freshness due to the acid in the vinegar. Serve with fish or meat.

Potato salad
with ground elder and shallots

2¼ lb large potatoes
sea salt flakes
3 tablespoons apple cider vinegar, plus extra if needed
1 tablespoon acacia honey
2 tablespoons cold-pressed canola oil
freshly ground pepper
3 shallots
2 handfuls of ground elder or flat-leaf parsley or chervil

Peel the potatoes, cut them into ¾-inch cubes, and rinse them under cold water. Bring a pan of salted water to a boil, add the potatoes, and cook for 6 to 7 minutes or until they are cooked but al dente. Drain and put the potatoes in a bowl.

For the marinade, whisk together the vinegar, honey, canola oil, salt, and pepper in a bowl. Add to the potatoes while they are still warm to allow them to absorb the marinade.

Peel the shallots and cut them into thin rings. Rinse the ground elder and pick off all the leaves, or chop it coarsely. Add the shallots and elder to the potatoes and mix well. If needed, season with extra salt, pepper, and vinegar. The salad is delicious warm as well as cold, but remember that the elder will lose its beautiful dark green color if in contact with heat or acid for too long.

SORREL
This plant hibernates during winter, but you'll find it in abundance growing wild in spring.

Baking and sweet things

Swedish syrup bread
MAKES 2 LOAVES

⅔ cup Swedish dark syrup
1¼ cups chopped pitted prunes
½ cup whole blanched almonds,
   coarsely chopped
1 cup rye flour
3 lb 5 oz Dark Rye Bread dough
   (*see* page 55)
butter, for greasing

Mix the syrup, prunes, almonds, and rye flour into the Dark Rye Bread Dough and stir to create a compact, slightly sticky texture.

Divide the dough equally into 2 loaf pans, each 9 x 5 x 3 inches in size, buttered well. Let the dough to rise in the warmth of the kitchen for 1 hour. Bake in a preheated oven at 315°F for 1¼ hours to 1 hour 25 minutes, or until a skewer inserted comes out clean. Turn the loaves out of the pans, place directly on the rack in the oven, and bake for a further 10 minutes.

Remove the loaves from the oven and transfer to a wire rack to cool slightly. Eat the bread warm with cold butter and a little Danish blue cheese—this is a serious grown-ups' treat! The bread is also great for toasting and, if being enjoyed in this way, it will keep for several days after baking.

Barley bread
MAKES 2 LOAVES

2 cups cold water
.1 oz (about the size of a small pea) fresh
   compressed yeast (baker's yeast)
½ cup Sourdough Starter (*see* right)
2 cups barley flour
2½ cups all-purpose flour
2 teaspoons sea salt flakes
2½ tablespoons honey
cold-pressed canola oil, for greasing

Day 1
Pour the measured cold water into a bowl. Stir in the yeast and Sourdough Starter.

Mix in the barley flour, all-purpose flour, salt, and honey, and knead until the dough almost stops sticking to the sides of the bowl. Barley dough is very soft and requires a long kneading time to become smooth and elastic, so knead the dough for about 20 minutes to obtain the right texture. If you do not have an electric stand mixer with a dough hook, you can use a hand mixer fitted with a dough hook or simply work the dough with a wooden spoon and plenty of elbow grease. Pour the dough into a plastic bowl oiled with cold-pressed canola oil, cover it with plastic wrap, and place in the refrigerator for 24 hours.

Day 2
Divide the dough equally into 2 wooden molds (metal molds can also be used) that can hold 6 cups dough each, oiled with canola oil. Let the dough rise until it reaches the top edges of the molds, which will take about 2 to 3 hours at room temperature. Bake in a preheated oven at 350°F for 45 minutes until golden and baked through. Remove from the oven and invert the hot bread out of the molds and onto a wire rack to cool.

Sourdough starter

If you bake regularly, you should always have a sourdough starter in your kitchen. It is by no means complicated, and will make your bread more individual, complex, and healthy. This starter, among experts also called a *biga*, is almost as thin as water, but it adds a wonderful flavor to the bread.

3¾ cups cold water
1¼ cups organic wheat flour
⅔ cup organic wholemeal flour
¾ cup organic rye flour

Place all the ingredients in a bowl and whisk together well. Pour the dough into a pan, or a glass or ceramic bowl. Partially cover the container so that the dough can still breathe, and let stand at room temperature. Whisk the sourdough once a day.

After about 10 days the starter should smell like a good, strong dark beer—and have foam like one. If that is the case, it is ready for use.

Subsequently stir the starter regularly (once a day is preferable, but every second day will be sufficient). Always make sure that you stir to the very bottom, because the sourdough starter will form a sediment that will simply rot if not mixed regularly with the liquid.

Each time you use the sourdough it needs a "refreshment," and the rule is: refresh with the same amount of flour and water that you have removed for baking. Store the starter at room temperature, in a kitchen cupboard, for example, and nourish it with fresh flour and water at least once a week.

TIP If you don't have a sourdough starter, you can replace the starter in a sourdough recipe with a corresponding amount of crème fraîche, buttermilk, sour milk (*see* page 16) or other fermented milk product and a slightly larger amount of yeast. It will obviously reduce the quality of the final outcome, but the method can be used if you are short of time.

Barley bread »

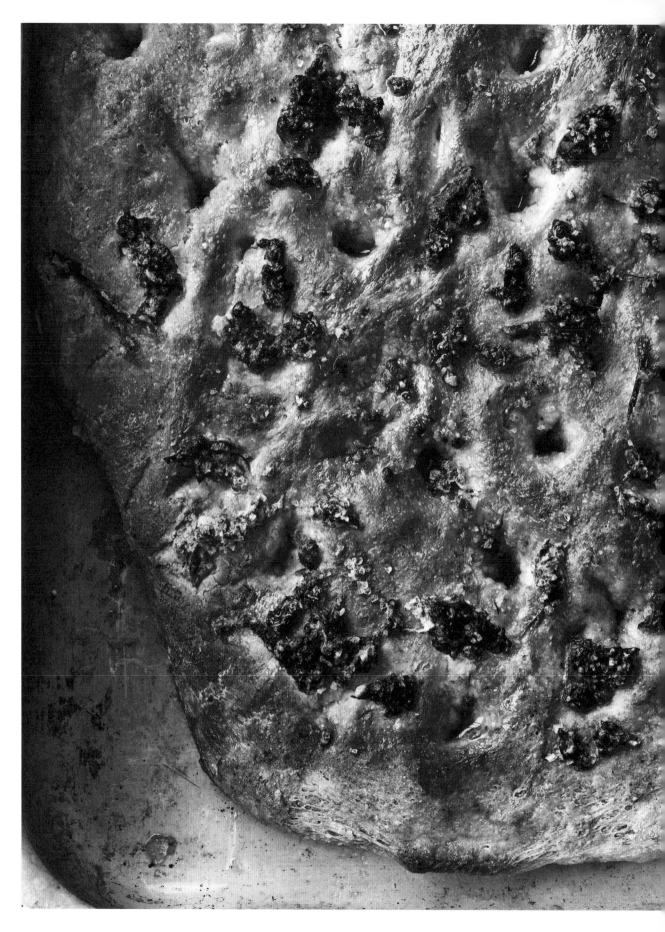

Dark rye bread

MAKES 3 LOAVES

Day 1
**1¾ quarts cold water, divided
1 lb 2 oz cracked rye kernels
1⅔ cups sunflower seeds
1½ cups flaxseeds
½ oz (1½ tablespoons) fresh
   compresssed yeast (baker's yeast)
1¾ lb rye flour**

Day 2
**3 tablespoons sea salt flakes
1½ teaspoons dark malt flour (optional)
sunflower oil, for greasing**

Day 1
Mix 4 cups of the measured cold water with the rye kernels, sunflower seeds, and flaxseeds in a bowl. Cover with a cloth or lid, and let stand at room temperature for 24 hours.

Pour the remaining 2½ cups measured cold water into another bowl and dissolve the yeast in it. Mix the rye flour into the liquid and cover the dough with a cloth or lid. Let stand at room temperature for 24 hours. The two mixtures should not be combined until the next day, otherwise the dough will be too sour, and too much acetic acid will make it difficult to bake the bread through.

Day 2
Mix the 2 mixtures together and add the salt and roasted malt flour, if using (it makes the bread dark), and knead it all together for about 10 minutes.

Divide the dough into 3 loaf pans, each measuring 9 x 5 x 3 inches, and greased well with sunflower oil. Let the dough rise in the warmth of the kitchen for about 2 to 3 hours or until it reaches the top edges of the pans. Bake in a preheated oven at 350°F for about 1 hour 20 minutes. Remove the pans from the oven, invert the loaves onto a wire rack, and let them cool. The bread will keep for 8 to 10 days stored in a bag. Do not store in the refrigerator, as it will quickly dry out.

This is one of the best-selling breads in Meyers Deli and one of the tastiest rye breads I know. Unlike most other rye bread, it is made entirely with rye flour, without any wheat flour added. This creates a really deep rye flavor and a great moistness.

TIP You can save several ounces of the dough for making the next batch of rye bread. The unbaked dough will keep in the refrigerator for up to 3 weeks. Add the dough to the day 1 mixture on day 2, reducing the quantity of fresh yeast in the day 1 mixture to ¼ oz (1 tablespoon).

Rye bread

Rye was the most common grain for bread until the end of the 1800s, when white bread began to be cheaper and slowly took over. In the first millennium of rye-bread consumption, loaves were small, since Iron Age and Viking ovens lacked enough heat or capacity to bake larger loaves. However, using the stone-building techniques of the 12 to 13th centuries, big masonry *cupola* furnaces were built to accommodate many large oval "breads," as they were called then. They were possibly based on sourdough, with added barley flour or similar and, when available, seasoning like aniseed, caraway, coriander, or dill seeds. These seasonings are not as commonly used with rye bread today, but they complement the rye flavor perfectly.

Focaccia
with ramson pesto

**2¾ cups lukewarm water
½ cup standard canola oil
¾ oz (2 tablespoons) fresh compresssed
   yeast (baker's yeast)
2¼ lb protein-rich wheat flour, such as
   Italian "00" flour or Öland or organic
   wholegrain flour, or a mixture (*see* tip)**

**1 tablespoon sea salt flakes
2 tablespoons high-quality cold-pressed
   canola oil
3 to 4 tablespoons ramson pesto
   (*see* page 22)**

Mix the measured lukewarm water and the standard canola oil in a bowl and stir in the yeast. Add the flour and salt and knead the dough well. If kneading the dough by hand, do so for 10 to 12 minutes. If kneading in an electric stand mixer fitted with a dough hook, begin at low speed for the first 3 minutes, then turn to full speed for 6 minutes. Let the dough rise in the bowl covered with a clean dish towel at room temperature for about 3 hours.

Oil a large roasting pan with standard canola oil. Transfer the dough to the pan and gently spread it out by hand until it covers the entire pan. Pour the cold-pressed canola oil onto the dough and spread it around with your fingers. Drizzle the dough with the ramson pesto, and gently press it with your fingers to create small indentations all over the surface, pressing the salt and oil into them. Let the dough rise at room temperature for about an hour.

Bake the bread in a preheated oven at 425°F for about 25 minutes until it is crisp and golden. Remove from the oven and let cool in the pan. When cool, remove it from the pan and serve as an entire loaf of bread, not in slices but by breaking off servings.

TIP You will produce a healthier and tastier bread with the same fine texture as an original focaccia if you bake it using a slightly coarser stone-ground flour, or a mixture of slightly coarser all-purpose flour and wholegrain flour. Just make sure that the flour has more than 12% protein and a good gluten structure.

All about rhubarb

The appearance of rhubarb marks the departure of the cold winter months, during which we have had to resort to almonds and other nuts, citrus fruits, chocolate, and old apples and pears for making desserts. The first rhubarb shoots out of the ground as frozen blue "fists" in April. If you are very eager, you can put a bell jar over the plant. These young stalks are harbingers of spring and are a taste of heaven in the first fresh fruit desserts of the year, or as an accompaniment to roast chicken or a pork chop.

Wild rhubarb

Wild rhubarb is very rare in Denmark, but you will quite often be able to find stray rhubarb in urban areas and in places where garden waste has been disposed of. With smooth leaves measuring 27 to 30 inches in width and strong green or red stalks, it is easily recognized. The edible stalks have a characteristic sour taste due to their oxalic acid. The inflorescence can grow up to 5 feet in length, with a hollow stem and a tuft of white flowers. Varieties of *Rheum rhaponticum*, also known by the misleading name of false rhubarb, are red through the stalk and are the most delicious varieties.

When you harvest rhubarb, pull the stalk up with a firm grip at the bottom, close to the root, otherwise it breaks easily. This would be particularly unfortunate because the lower whitish pieces are the most delicious part of the plant. Never follow rhubarb recipes blindly, as the content of natural sugar in rhubarb varies from variety to variety, from time of year to time of year, and almost from plant to plant. You should always taste as you go, and remember that cooked fruit often becomes slightly more acidic in flavor when it has cooled.

Rhubarb soup

Start the rhubarb season by bringing 4 cups water and 2 cups sugar to a boil in a pan. While the syrup is approaching boiling point, cut about 1 lb 2 oz rhubarb stalks into small pieces (you should have about 4 cups). Add the pieces to a large bowl, pour the boiling syrup over them, and cover the bowl with plastic wrap. After an hour, the rhubarb pieces should be crisp and tender, unless they were cut too thickly. In that case, boil the mixture briefly. Keep the cooled mixture in the refrigerator for later in the day or the day after, when you can serve it as a cold dessert soup with whipped cream, vanilla ice cream, or vanilla cream. While you are enjoying the soup, consider whether you fancy adding any rhubarb-friendly flavorings to the syrup the next time you make it, such as vanilla, mint, rosemary, cinnamon, thyme, or lemon or orange rind.

Rhubarb in baking

Cooked rhubarb pieces can also be used as a filling for pies or trifles, or served with ice cream and cakes. Cook the rhubarb with a little water and sugar until completely tender, like a compote, and when it has cooled completely, fold in a portion of whipped cream. Refrigerate until the next day, when the oxalic acid will have firmed up the whipped cream.

Rhubarb syrup

The juice that forms while boiling rhubarb can be used to make a syrup. Boil 1 cup of the liquid to a thick syrup. Boil ½ to 1 cup white wine vinegar (or other mild vinegar) until reduced to one-fifth of its original volume. Then mix the rhubarb syrup and vinegar reduction together to taste, carefully adjusting the proportions, adding a little cooked rhubarb if you wish. Serve, for example, with fried flounder, fried chicken, or roast lamb. Rhubarb is also highly suitable for chutney (*see* page 36), and it can used in place of plums, tomatoes, apples, or any of your other favorite chutney ingredients.

Rhubarb cordial

I recommend this delicious rhubarb cordial. You will need 2¼ lb rhubarb stalks, 1½ cups jaggery, ½ cup apple cider vinegar, and 2 quarts water. Cut off the tops and bottoms of the rhubarb stalks, rinse the stalks in cold water, and cut into small pieces. Put into a saucepan along with the sugar, vinegar, and water and bring to a boil. Let simmer for 5 minutes, then remove the pan from the heat and let steep for 20 to 25 minutes. Pour it into bottles, seal, and store in the refrigerator for up to 2 to 3 weeks. Leaving the pulp in gives you a thicker consistency, but if you want a thinner cordial, you can strain out the pulp.

Rhubarb compote
with ymer and honey

1 lb 2 oz rhubarb stalks
½ vanilla bean
¾ cup jaggery
finely grated zest and juice
**   of ½ organic lemon**

To serve
ymer (available from Danish food
**   suppliers) or plain full-fat**
**   Greek yogurt**
honey

Cut off the tops and bottoms of the rhubarb stalks, but be careful not to remove the white "foot" of the stalk, which is where the rhubarb flavor is most concentrated and best. Rinse the stalks in cold water, cut into pieces ¾ to 1¼ inches in length, and place in an ovenproof dish. Split the vanilla bean lengthwise and scrape out the seeds into the rhubarb, then add the bean along with the sugar and lemon zest and juice. Toss the mixture together.

Bake in a preheated oven at 300°F for 15 to 20 minutes. Keep an eye on the dish during the cooking time so that you can retrieve it the moment the rhubarb is tender but not mushy.

Let the baked rhubarb cool and serve with a portion of ymer or Greek yogurt and a few drops of honey on top. You can also add some Toasted Oat Flakes (*see* page 121), nuts, or rye bread crumbs if you want to add a crunchy element. Serve the compote as a luxury breakfast or as a small, fresh dessert.

You can make a batch of the compote to store. Once cooled, decant into sterilized preserving jars or an airtight container, seal, and keep in the refrigerator for up to 20 to 30 days.

Rhubarb cake
SERVES 8

Cake layers
4 organic eggs
⅔ cup sugar
1¼ cups all-purpose flour
1 teaspoon baking powder
butter, for greasing

Rhubarb compote
10½ oz rhubarb stalks
¾ cup jaggery
1 handful of lemon balm
½ vanilla bean

To assemble
⅓ cup blanched almonds
1¾ oz white chocolate, plus extra
**   shavings to decorate**
2 cups heavy whipping cream
1 rhubarb stalk
a little sugar, for sprinkling

First make the cake layers. Beat the eggs and sugar together in a bowl until pale and foamy. Mix the flour and baking powder together and sift into the batter, then fold in gently with a spatula.

Grease an 8½-inch springform cake pan with butter and pour in the cake batter. Bake the cake in the middle of a preheated oven at 400°F for about 30 minutes. Remove the cake from the oven and let cool in the pan on a wire rack. When the cake is completely cool, carefully release it from the pan and cut it horizontally into 3 equal layers with a sharp knife.

Now cook the compote. Cut off the tops and bottoms of the rhubarb stalks, but be careful not to remove the white "foot" of the stalk, which is where the rhubarb flavor is most concentrated and best. Rinse the stalks in cold water, then cut into pieces ½ to ¾ inch in size and put in an ovenproof dish with the lemon balm. Split the vanilla bean lengthwise, scrape out the seeds, and mix with a little of the sugar, making them easier to distribute in the dish. Mix the

vanilla sugar into the rest of the sugar, then sprinkle over the rhubarb. Stir well and add the bean to the dish.

Bake in a preheated oven at 300°F for 15 to 20 minutes until the rhubarb is tender but still has a firm bite. Remove the dish from the oven and set the compote aside to cool completely.

Chop the almonds and white chocolate coarsely. Whip the cream, set half aside for decoration, and gently fold the almonds and chocolate into the other half. Add the rhubarb compote and fold in.

Assemble the cake with the flavored whipped cream between each layer, and finish by decorating it with the pure whipped cream (for the best effect, use a pastry bag). Another decorative trick is to create rhubarb shavings by running a vegetable peeler lengthwise along a rhubarb stalk. Toss the shavings with a little sugar before scattering them on the cake and finish with shavings of white chocolate.

Rhubarb cake »

Rhubarb sorbet
with crispy crumbles

SERVES 10 TO 12

1 lb 2 oz rhubarb stalks
½ vanilla bean
4 cups water
1 cup jaggery
10 whole black peppercorns
2 to 3 tablespoons apple cider vinegar
1 organic egg white and 3 tablespoons
confectioners' sugar (optional)

Cut off the tops and bottoms of the rhubarb stalks, but be careful not to remove the white "foot," which is where the rhubarb flavor is most concentrated and best. Rinse the stalks in cold water, cut into chunks, and add to a saucepan. Split the vanilla bean lengthwise and scrape out the seeds into the rhubarb, then add the bean along with the measured water, sugar, and peppercorns (it may sound strange, but the pepper gives a wonderful kick to all that sweetness).

Bring to a boil and cook for 3 to 4 minutes. Remove the pan from the heat and season to taste with the apple cider vinegar. Let the rhubarb mixture infuse for 20 minutes. Remove the vanilla bean and peppercorns and blend in a blender or use a hand-held stick blender. Now strain the blended syrup through a coarse sieve, allowing a little of the rhubarb pulp to pass through.

Place the syrup in the refrigerator to cool completely, then churn it in an ice-cream maker until frozen. Transfer the frozen sorbet to a plastic container with a lid, cover, and place in the freezer, where it will keep its creamy texture for 3 to 4 days.

If you don't have an ice-cream maker, pour the rhubarb syrup directly into a plastic container and freeze it. When the syrup is completely frozen, place the block of rhubarb ice on a cutting board and chop it up coarsely. Whizz the cubes of rhubarb ice in a food processor until smooth and creamy, then pour back into the container and return to the freezer. Stir the mixture 2 to 3 times at 30-minute intervals, and then the sorbet is ready to be served.

Another great way to obtain a creamy sorbet without the use of an ice-cream maker is to create a meringue by whisking the egg white with the sugar until stiff, then mixing it into the sorbet after you have whizzed up the frozen syrup in the food processor. Sorbet with meringue still requires a little freezer time before serving.

Regardless of how you have created your rhubarb sorbet, serve it with Crispy Crumbles (see below) on top.

TIP If the sorbet has been in the freezer for longer than 3 to 4 days and large ice crystals have formed and the texture is hard, you can resuscitate your dessert by melting it and then churning it in the ice-cream maker again. However, this isn't an option if you have mixed meringue into the sorbet, as the mixture won't stand up to the treatment.

Crispy crumbles

2 tablespoons spelt grains
2 tablespoons wheat grains
2 tablespoons rye grains
2 tablespoons sunflower seeds
1 tablespoon flaxseeds
1 tablespoon honey
1 teaspoon sea salt flakes

Day 1
Cover the grains and seeds with cold water. Let stand at room temperature for 12 hours.

Day 2
Drain the contents through a sieve. Pour the grains into a dry skillet and toast them gently over low heat for about 8 to 10 minutes until golden and crisp. Add the honey and salt and mix well to evenly caramelize the grains. Cool the grains on a plate, and then they are ready for crunching.

TIP These crispy crumbles are great as a topping for yogurt, so make a little extra for your Saturday breakfast.

Licorice parfait
with white chocolate, green strawberries, and sweet cicely

¼ cup superfine sugar
2 tablespoons water
¼ cup pasteurized egg yolks
3 tablespoons lowfat milk
1 oz licorice root powder
8 oz good-quality white chocolate, such
as Valrhona Ivoire (35% cocoa solids),
finely chopped
1 cup heavy whipping cream
10 to 15 green strawberries
½ handful of sweet cicely

Bring the sugar and measured water to a boil in a pan until the temperature reaches about 250°F and it has a syrupy consistency.

Place the egg yolks in a bowl and add the hot syrup by pouring it in a thin stream while whisking vigorously. Continue whisking until the yolks have become creamy and white.

Bring the milk and licorice root powder to a boil in a saucepan and then pour it evenly over the finely chopped white chocolate in a bowl to melt it. Stir the hot milk and chocolate until it comes together into a homogeneous cream.

Whip the cream lightly until it has the consistency of sour cream. Gently combine the egg mixture and chocolate mixture, then fold in the lightly whipped cream. Pour the mixture into 4 to 6 small ramekins and store in the freezer until the next day.

Take the parfait out of the freezer 10 minutes before serving. Invert the parfaits out of the ramekins directly into wide flat soup bowls and top with the fresh green strawberries, cut into small cubes and tossed with the cicely, freshly chopped. The fresh green strawberries and the light anise flavor of the sweet cicely is an exceptionally good match for the subtle taste of licorice in the parfait.

• •

TIP You can also freeze the parfait in a loaf shape, and slice it before serving. Remember to take the parfait out of the freezer about 15 to 20 minutes before serving.

• •

Buttermilk ice cream
with lemon and vanilla

SERVES 8 TO 10

1 cup jaggery
¼ cup glucose syrup (*see* tip)
2 cups whole milk
½ vanilla pod
4 cups buttermilk
finely grated zest of 1 organic lemon

Bring the sugar, glucose, and milk to a boil in a saucepan to dissolve the sugar and glucose. Split the vanilla bean lengthwise, scrape out the seeds, and add both the seeds and bean to the milk mixture.

Pour the buttermilk into a bowl and whisk in the boiling sweetened milk. Add the lemon zest and mix thoroughly. Let the mixture cool, then pour into an ice-cream maker. Churn the mixture until frozen, airy, and creamy (this should take about 15 to 20 minutes). Transfer the ice cream to a plastic container with a lid, seal tightly, and freeze for a couple of hours.

The ice cream will keep its creamy consistency for 2 to 3 days in the freezer, then the texture will turn hard and crystalize. As with sorbets, you can defrost the hardened buttermilk ice cream and churn it again in the ice-cream maker, but this trick will work only once.

Enjoy the ice cream on its own or serve it with warm rhubarb pie. This ice-cream flavor is usually a big hit with Danish children because it tastes exactly like the dessert koldskål, made from buttermilk with lemon and vanilla, and I can recommend serving the ice cream with a buttery cookie.

• •

TIP Glucose syrup or liquid glucose contributes to the delicious and creamy texture of this dessert. You will find glucose in grocery stores or from online suppliers specializing in products for baking and for making confectionery. If you are unable to get hold of glucose, replace it with an equal quantity of acacia honey, but bear in mind that your ice cream will have a distinct honey flavor.

• •

LEAVES FROM YOUR FRUIT TREES
Decorate your food with tender leaves picked from currant or gooseberry bushes.

Summer

Seasonal ingredients

Cultivated produce

apples
asparagus
blackberries
blackcurrants
blueberries
cabbage
carrots
cauliflower
chanterelles
cherries
corn
crabs
crayfish
cucumber
dill
eggplant

fennel
flounder
gooseberries
green beans
green elderberries
grey mullet
herring
horseradish
lovage
mackerel
Norwegian lobster
onions
parsley
peas
pointed cabbage
potatoes

raspberries
redcurrants
rose petals
rhubarb
salsify
shrimp
spearmint
spinach
squash
strawberries
summer leeks
tomatoes
venison
wood pigeon

In the wild

rosehips
shore crabs
wild strawberries
marsh samphire
forest raspberries
blueberries
mirabelles
wild berries
wild cherries
bog bilberries
wild apples

woodruff
leaves from berry bushes
   (use them for tea and in salads)
wild thyme
lingonberries
chanterelles
elderberries
sea buckthorn
crowberries
shaggy inkcaps
partridge

Soups and appetizers

Cold cucumber soup
with mint and salt and sugar-cured mullet

2 cucumbers, peeled and cut into chunks
sea salt flakes
1 scallion
½ handful of mint, leaves picked, plus extra to serve
4 cup lowfat plain yogurt
1 cup water
freshly ground pepper

Sprinkle the cucumbers with 1 teaspoon salt flakes and let stand in the kitchen for 10 to 15 minutes.

Chop the scallion and put it in a blender or food processor along with the cucumber, mint, yogurt, and 1 cup water. Blend until evenly combined and smooth. Season to taste with salt and pepper.

Refrigerate the soup for 30 to 60 minutes until well chilled and all the flavors have developed.

Serve the soup ice cold with the Salt and Sugar-cured Mullet (see below), cut into thin slices, some mint leaves, and good bread.

Salt and sugar-cured mullet

3½ oz very fresh skinless grey mullet fillet
1 teaspoon sugar
1 teaspoon coarse sea salt
freshly ground pepper

Check that the mullet is really fresh and smells of the sea, not of the harbor. Check the fish for bones and scrape off any stray scales with a knife. Place in a dish and sprinkle evenly with the sugar and salt. Cover the dish with plastic wrap and place in the refrigerator for 12 hours—or give it 24 hours if you like. Cut the fillet into very thin slices and season with freshly ground pepper.

White asparagus soup
with pearl barley and smoked curd cheese

1 handful of white asparagus
2 shallots
standard canola oil
2 cups chicken stock or water
3 tablespoons full-fat crème fraîche
sea salt flakes and freshly ground pepper
apple cider vinegar, to taste
⅔ cup cooked grains, such as pearl barley, pearled spelt, or pearled rye
1 tablespoon Smoked Curd Cheese (see page 16)

Place the asparagus on a cutting board and, using a fine peeler, peel the spears from just below the tip downward. You may need to go over them with the peeler a second time to make sure you remove every last bit of skin. Break off the woody stem ends of the spears, just where they naturally give way. Throw the peelings and stem ends away, or save them for use in other soups or broths (they are too bitter to use in a pure asparagus soup like this). Cut off the bottom two-thirds of the asparagus and save the last third, the tips, for the garnish.

Peel and chop the shallots very finely, then lightly sauté them with the asparagus slices in a little canola oil in a saucepan. Add the chicken stock or water and simmer for 2 minutes only—if you cook the asparagus for too long, they will lose their beautiful fresh asparagus flavor and be overcooked, tasting like canned ones.

Pour the soup into a blender and blend it with the crème fraîche. You can pass the soup through a sieve back into the pan if you like, to remove the stringiest asparagus bits. Season with salt, pepper, and apple cider vinegar to taste just before serving.

Cut the asparagus tips lengthwise finely. Mix them with the cooked grains, smoked curd cheese, a little canola oil, and some salt, pepper, and apple cider vinegar to taste.

Use this small "asparagus salad" as a garnish—serve the soup in bowls with a spoonful of the "salad" on top.

Tip It is also nice to give the soup some extra substance in the form of chicken meatballs (see page 186).

Cold pea soup
with mint and skyr

sea salt flakes
1⅔ cups freshly podded peas
3 mint sprigs, leaves picked
finely grated zest of 1 organic lemon
1 teaspoon acacia honey
freshly ground pepper
1 cup skyr or Greek yogurt

Bring a pan of salted water to a boil and blanch the peas for 1 to 2 minutes. Remove the peas and immediately immerse them in cold water, reserving the cooking water. This way they will be tender but stay fresh and beautifully green.

Drain the peas and add to a blender with the mint, saving some peas and a few mint leaves to scatter onto the soup. Add the lemon zest, honey, salt, pepper, and finally 1¼ cups of the reserved cooking water, then blend all the ingredients for about a minute to make a smooth green soup.

Pour the soup into a bowl and place it in the refrigerator to cool. Serve the cold soup topped with the reserved peas and mint and a spoonful of skyr or yogurt, along with some good bread.

Tip This soup makes a refreshing small summer appetizer, and can also be served with a piece of fried fish, a little seafood, or some smoked fish added to the serving bowl. If serving the soup as a main course, double the quantity and preferably include one of the aforementioned additions.

Crab claws
with fennel mayonnaise

2¼ lb raw crab claws
sea salt flakes
1 lemon
10 whole black peppercorns, plus
    pepper mill for serving
½ handful of dill

Put the crab claws in a saucepan, cover with water, and add 1 tablespoon sea salt flakes, 2 slices of the lemon, the peppercorns, and dill. Bring to a boil and skim off the foam. Reduce the heat and let the claws cook for 5 to 7 minutes. Turn off the heat and let the claws sit in the hot broth for about 20 minutes or until cooked.

When the claws have cooled slightly, gently crush them with a hammer, just enough for the meat to be accessible with a fork. Serve the claws whole so that your guests can enjoy digging out the good crabmeat, and place sea salt, a pepper mill, the rest of the lemon cut into wedges, and a bowl of Fennel Mayonnaise (see below) on the table. And don't forget the toast. I usually season the mayonnaise with pastis, the French anise apéritif, so I also serve this with the claws instead of white wine, diluted with water and with lots of ice cubes, of course.

Fennel mayonnaise

Homemade mayonnaise
2 pasteurized egg yolks
sea salt flakes
1 tablespoon Dijon mustard
1 to 2 tablespoons apple cider vinegar
⅔ cup cold-pressed canola oil

To finish
1 fennel bulb
½ handful of chervil or sweet
    cicely, chopped
2 tablespoons pastis, or to taste

First make the mayonnaise. Using an electric hand mixer or a balloon whisk, whisk the egg yolks, salt, mustard, and vinegar together in a bowl until thick and white. Whisk in the oil in a thin stream—it is important to do this slowly to stop the mayo from splitting. If it begins to curdle, you can try to save it by adding a few drops of cold water while whisking vigorously.

Cut the fennel in half and rinse it thoroughly in cold water. Drain and then slice it very finely before mixing it into the mayo along with the chopped chervil or sweet cicely.

Finish off the fennel mayonnaise by adding the pastis to taste.

Tip This mayonnaise also makes an uncannily good base for a seafood salad. Mixing the remaining crabmeat and some cooked shrimp or lobster tails and piling it generously on top of toasted rye bread as a late night snack makes me close to being a happy man. Dipping some leftover boiled potatoes into the fennel mayonnaise isn't a bad idea either.

Boiled crayfish
with dill mayonnaise

2 to 3 quarts water
1 tablespoon sea salt flakes
1 teaspoon sugar
5 dill sprigs
2 to 3 slices of lemon, plus lemon wedges
    to serve
2¼ lb live crayfish

Bring the water to a boil in a saucepan along with the salt, sugar, dill, and lemon slices. Throw in the crayfish and boil for 6 minutes.

Remove the pan from the heat and let the crayfish cool in their broth. The cooling-down process must be fairly quick, so either stand the pan in a bowl of water with ice cubes or place it directly in the refrigerator to chill for about 20 to 25 minutes.

Lift the cold crayfish out of the broth and serve them with the Dill Mayonnaise (see below), toast, and lemon wedges as an appetizer or a summer lunch. The tails are good, but the most delicious part, in my opinion, is biting into the head and sucking out all the luscious juices.

TIP On the rare occasion when any crayfish is left over, I always make a salad with the meat, cold new potatoes, and dill mayonnaise. I save the heads from which the juices have not been sucked out as well as the shells for making shellfish bouillon. I am amazed time after time at just how much flavor they add.

Dill mayonnaise

1 quantity Homemade Mayonnaise
    (see left)
1 handful of dill, chopped
sea salt flakes and freshly ground
    pepper, if necessary

Season the prepared mayo with the chopped dill and a little extra salt and pepper, if you think it needs it, then serve.

Shore crabs

When the sea warms up in late summer, shore crabs venture into the shallow waters. The pentagonal shell, or carapace, of a shore crab is about 4 to 4½ inches wide, and vary in color from shades of brown to green. During the day, shore crabs hide under rocks or seaweed, but they are easy to lure out and catch from a jetty or dock.

How to catch crabs

Put a plastic clothespin on the end of a piece of string and attach a lightly crushed mussel to the clothespin—you can also use a small piece of fish or meat. Lower the bait to the sea floor, and soon the crabs will come out and begin to bite. Now, ever so gently, start hoisting up the clothespin with the crab holding onto it and dump it into a bucket. Even more fun is catching crabs at night. Shine a flashlight into the water and simply snatch the crabs out of the water using your hands—grasp them where the shell is at its widest and drop them into your bucket. You can wear a pair of gardening gloves for protection. In the summer in Smålandshavet or Nordsjælland, my family and I often amuse ourselves by swimming around in shallow water equipped with goggles, the top half of an empty, large-size plastic soda bottle in one hand and a glove on the other hand. We then fill the bottle with crabs as we catch them—with one hand gripped around the bottle neck, an adult can maneuver it around in the water without the crabs escaping. Note: In some US states you need a license to fish for crabs, so check local regulations first.

Soup and stew of shore crabs

Shore crabs make a very tasty soup or stew. Quickly kill the crabs by plunging them in boiling water, or by cutting them lengthwise with a sharp knife, as follows:

Place a crab on a cutting board with the top (back) shell facing down and underside facing upward. Using your best kitchen knife, pin the blade against the breast shell, then press down and cut through its head. Continue in the same way with the rest of the crabs, every now and then scraping the prepared crabs and juices from the cutting board into a bowl.

Now you are ready to make your shore crab soup or stew. For the latter, fry your crabs with onion and garlic in butter or oil. Add apple cider or a mixture of apple juice and apple cider vinegar to the pan, then reduce over high heat until it is almost gone. Next, add chopped tomatoes and lots of parsley or dill—preferably fresh dill rather than dill seeds. Heat up, add 1½ tablespoons of butter, and season to taste with salt and pepper. Serve with boiled new potatoes, pearl barley, rice, or pasta. It is mandatory to bite into the crab shells so that all the lovely juices flow into your mouth.

Meat

Roast chicken
and braised peas with baby onions, bacon, and lettuce heart

SERVES 4 TO 6

1 large organic chicken, about 3¼ lb
1 handful of flat-leaf parsley
1 lemon
1½ tablespoons butter
sea salt flakes and freshly ground pepper

Check the chicken for any feather stumps and pluck them out. Remove any blood or intestine residues from the cavity and wipe with paper towels.

Pick the leaves off of the parsley sprigs and rinse them, and cut the lemon into quarters. Stuff the chicken with the parsley and lemon, along with the butter, salt, and pepper. Tie the chicken up with butcher's twine so that the thighs are hugging the breast—that way the chicken will be juicier. Place the chicken on a roasting rack set into a roasting pan to catch the juices. Roast in a preheated oven at 325°F for 1 hour, then turn off the oven and leave the chicken in the oven for a further 10 minutes.

Take the chicken out of the oven and let rest for 10 minutes before carving it. Serve the chicken with Braised Peas with Baby Onions, Bacon, and Lettuce Heart (see below), boiled new potatoes, and some good bread.

Braised peas with baby onions, bacon, and lettuce heart

2¼ lb peas in the pod (yielding about
 1⅔ to 2 cups peas when podded)
1 tablespoon cold butter
5½ oz baby onions
1 oz bacon, cut into small cubes
1 Little Gem lettuce heart
½ handful of flat-leaf parsley, chopped
sea salt flakes and freshly ground pepper
juice of ½ lemon

Pod the peas. Peel the baby onions but keep them whole.

Place the butter and bacon in a sauté pan and sizzle the bacon over low heat until lightly golden. Add the whole baby onions and sauté with the bacon for a few minutes so that they soften and absorb some of the fat.

Meanwhile, rinse the lettuce and parsley and let both drain thoroughly in a colander. Cut the lettuce into large chunks.

Check that the onions are soft inside before adding the peas and sautéing them for about 30 seconds. Then add the lettuce and parsley. Mix well and season with salt, pepper, and the lemon juice to finish off. Serve immediately to retain the beautiful color, crispness, and flavor of the peas.

....

TIP Braised peas with baby onions, bacon, and salad (or peas *bonne femme*), is a French classic that I love; it is no crime to replace the baby onions with any other onion. The braised green peas are wonderful with chicken, and I cannot eat a steak béarnaise without them. You can also omit the bacon if you like, to give you peas Française instead.

....

Poached chicken
with salad of peas, summer cabbage, and dill

SERVES 4 TO 6

1 organic chicken, about 2¾ to 3¼ lb
1 onion, peeled and halved
1 garlic clove, peeled
5 thyme sprigs
5 whole black peppercorns
sea salt flakes and freshly ground pepper

Check the chicken for any feather stumps and pluck them out. Remove any blood or intestine residues from the cavity and wipe with paper towels.

Place the chicken in a large pan, cover with water and add the halved onion, garlic, thyme, and peppercorns. Bring to a boil and skim off any foam or impurities that rise to the surface. Lower the heat and simmer for 30 minutes.

Turn off the heat and let the chicken sit in the hot broth until done—it will take about 15 to 20 minutes.

Remove the chicken and carve off the breast meat in large pieces. Season with a little salt and pepper. Serve the warm breast meat with the Salad of Peas, Summer Cabbage, and Dill (see below) and possibly some cooked grains or potatoes and good bread.

....

TIP Store the broth from the chicken either in the refrigerator or in the freezer. It is always good to have handy when making soup or risotto, or to use as a braising liquid.

....

Salad of peas, summer cabbage, and dill

½ summer cabbage
1 lb 2 oz peas in the pod (yielding about
 1⅓ cups peas when podded)
1 new-season onion
½ cup Greek yogurt
1 tablespoon honey
2 to 3 tablespoons apple cider vinegar
sea salt flakes and freshly ground pepper
1 handful of dill, coarsely chopped

Rinse the cabbage and drain thoroughly. Slice very finely and place in a bowl. Pod the peas, and peel and slice the onion very finely. Throw both in with the cabbage.

Mix the yogurt with the honey, vinegar, salt, and pepper in a bowl to make a dressing. Add to the salad bowl and toss around.

To finish, fold the dill into the salad. Serve immediately while it is crisp and delicious. I like to serve this salad with poached chicken, but it is also an excellent accompaniment to meatballs, kebabs, or patties as a kind of fresh, summery coleslaw.

Roast chicken »

Barbecued venison
and green potato salad with arugula, peas, radishes, and dill

SERVES 6

1 haunch (hind leg) of venison, about 3¼ lb
2 tablespoons honey
¼ cup apple cider vinegar
10 thyme sprigs, leaves picked
sea salt flakes and freshly ground pepper

Cut off the muscles from the leg bone, dividing the meat into the topside (top portion), silverside (middle portion), and thick flank (lower portion above the shin). Remove the shin and any other trimmings (save these for ground venison). You can ask your butcher to prepare the meat for you.

Cut away the tendons from the muscles. Combine the honey, vinegar, thyme leaves, salt, and pepper in a dish with the pieces of venison and let marinate in the refrigerator for 30 to 60 minutes.

Cook the meat on a barbecue or on a ridged grill pan over medium heat for about 30 to 35 minutes so that it is still slightly pink in the middle.

Remove the meat from the barbecue and let rest for 10 minutes before cutting into slices. Serve with the Green Potato Salad (see right) and some good bread.

....

TIP Run the shin meat and trimmings through a meat grinder or food processor and enjoy some venison meatballs the following day.

....

Green potato salad

2¼ lb new potatoes
sea salt flakes
1 lb 2 oz peas in the pod (yielding about 1⅓ cups peas when podded)
10 radishes
2 tablespoons white wine vinegar
2 tablespoons cold-pressed canola oil
1 tablespoon honey
freshly ground pepper
1 handful of chervil, coarsely chopped
1 handful of dill, coarsely chopped

Cook the new potatoes following the Potato Salad recipe on page 36, which gives a perfect result every time. Once drained and slightly cooled, cut the potatoes into quarters and add to a bowl.

Pod the peas. Rinse the radishes and cut into thin slices, then add to the bowl of potatoes, along with the peas.

Whisk the vinegar, oil, honey, salt, and pepper together in a bowl to make a vinaigrette and add the chopped chervil and dill.

Pour the vinaigrette over the still-warm potatoes and mix carefully—the vinaigrette will be absorbed much more effectively while the potatoes are warm, and they will even thicken it.

Season with more salt and pepper if necessary and serve warm or cold. This makes an ideal side for all kinds of barbecued and summer food.

Seared hanger steak
with frisée lettuce

1 lb 5 oz hanger steak (see tip)
10 thyme sprigs, chopped
2 tablespoons olive oil
sea salt flakes and freshly ground pepper
1 frisée lettuce (curly endive)
½ handful of parsley
1 small red onion
2 tablespoons apple cider vinegar
2 tablespoons cold-pressed canola oil

Remove the largest tendons and membranes from the hanger steak and rub the meat with the chopped thyme, olive oil, salt, and pepper.

Heat up a ridged grill pan and fry the steak for a short time over very high heat—give it about 2 to 3 minutes on each side so that it is still quite pink and juicy in the middle.

Meanwhile, cut off the root of the lettuce and divide it into large leaves. Wash the leaves and dry them in a salad spinner or with a clean dish towel. Pick the leaves from the parsley stems and wash and dry them as well. Peel and finely slice the red onion, then mix with the frisée and parsley. Toss with the vinegar, canola oil, salt, and pepper.

Remove the meat from the pan and let rest for 1 minute before cutting it into thin slices and serving with the salad. This makes enough for lunch for 4 people, but you can stretch it to 6 people if you serve it as an appetizer.

....

Tip Hanger steak, also known as butcher's steak and what the French call onglet, is so called because it hangs from the diaphragm, and is located just above the kidneys. You can order hanger steak at your butcher's, or just replace it with flank steak.

....

Beef patties
with baked new-season onions, parsley, and pearl barley

1 lb 5 oz ground beef, 6 to 8% fat
sea salt flakes and freshly ground pepper
1 tablespoon standard canola oil
2 teaspoons butter

Shape the meat into 4 equal-sized patties and give them a little squeeze so that they are flat. Then use a knife to score the surface of each patty in a criss-cross pattern. Season with salt and pepper.

Heat up a skillet with the oil and add the butter. When the butter is sizzling, start frying the beef patties over medium heat—they should be cooked for about 3 minutes on each side so that they are still pink in the middle. At least, that's how I like my beef patties, provided that the beef is freshly ground from the butcher's. Otherwise, in the interests of food safety you should cook the meat all the way through. Serve with Baked New-season Onions, Parsley, and Pearl Barley (see below).

Baked new-season onions, parsley, and pearl barley

2 large handfuls of coarse sea salt
18 new-season red onions
5 thyme sprigs
2 teaspoons butter
½ handful of flat-leaf parsley, chopped
2 to 3 tablespoons apple cider vinegar
⅔ cup cooked pearl barley
sea salt flakes and freshly ground pepper
3 tablespoons freshly grated horseradish, or to taste

Cover the bottom of an ovenproof dish with the coarse salt and place the whole unpeeled onions and thyme sprigs on top.

Bake the onions in a preheated oven at 325°F for 20 to 25 minutes until they are soft and sweet. Remove from the oven and let

cool slightly, then cut the root off each onion and squeeze the baked onion flesh out of the skin.

Melt the butter in a saucepan, add the baked onion flesh, chopped parsley, vinegar, and pearl barley and sauté for about 1 to 2 minutes over low heat or until heated up thoroughly.

Season the onion compote with salt, pepper, and horseradish to taste. Serve with the beef patties and some rye bread.

Sweet and sour lamb fricassee
with summer cabbage and dill

1 lb 5 oz boneless shoulder or breast of lamb
2 quarts water, or potato stock (see tip) and water
1 cup whole black peppercorns
1½ tablespoons allspice berries
20 bay leaves
1 handful of thyme
1 garlic clove, peeled
small handful (about 15) dill stems
4 carrots
2 onions
4 parsley roots
sea salt flakes
½ cup aged white wine vinegar
2 tablespoons jaggery
3 tablespoons heavy whipping cream
½ cup whole milk
freshly ground pepper
2 to 3 tablespoons cornstarch mixed with a little cold water
½ handful of finely chopped dill
½ summer cabbage, finely chopped

Cut the meat into 1¼-inch cubes and blanch them in a saucepan of boiling water for 4 to 5 minutes. Strain off the water and place in another saucepan with the 2 quarts water, or potato stock and water. Bring to a boil and skim off any foam or impurities that rise to the surface.

Make a bouquet garni by placing the peppercorns, allspice, bay leaves, thyme, garlic, and dill stems in the center of a square of gauze (or fill an empty teabag) and tie with a piece of thread to seal. Peel the carrots, onions, and parsley roots and throw into the pan. Season with 1 tablespoon salt and add the bouquet garni.

Cook the meat and vegetables over low heat for about 25 minutes until the vegetables are tender and have given off some flavor, then remove the vegetables and save them for the garnish.

Continue cooking the meat with the bouquet garni for about 1½ hours until very tender.

Pour about 4 cups of the broth through a sieve into another pan. Season with the vinegar, sugar, cream, milk, salt, and pepper. Stir in the cornstarch paste and simmer until thickened while you cut the reserved vegetables into large cubes. Add the meat and vegetables to the thickened sauce and heat through before seasoning once again.

Finally, add the finely chopped dill and summer cabbage and swiftly stir it all together so that the cabbage just warms through but is still quite raw and crunchy.

Serve immediately with some boiled potatoes and wholegrain bread.

....

TIP The potato stock that I use in this recipe is good old-fashioned water from boiling potatoes but of the more flavorful kind. When you cook new potatoes, just add lots of parsley to the boiling water, and when the water comes to a boil, skim off any foam or impurities. Once the potatoes are cooked, you can use the cooking water as a lightly parsley-flavored stock in soups or stews, for example.

....

Roast pork belly
with parsley sauce and refrigerator-pickled cucumbers

1 lb 10 oz pork belly, sliced
sea salt flakes and freshly ground pepper
2 tablespoons butter
3 tablespoons all-purpose flour
2 cups lowfat milk
freshly grated nutmeg, to taste
1 large handful of parsley, chopped

If the pork belly slices are thick, wrap them in a double layer of plastic and tenderize them a little using a meat tenderizer. Season the slices well with salt and pepper.

Place on a rack set in a roasting pan to catch the fat and juices and roast in a preheated oven at 350°F for 10 to 15 minutes or until very crisp and brown.

Melt the butter in a small saucepan and gradually add the flour, stirring, to make a smooth roux. Add the milk while stirring vigorously. Simmer for 5 to 10 minutes to cook out the flour, stirring occasionally. Season the sauce to taste with grated nutmeg, salt, and pepper, and then add lots of chopped parsley—you can't really add too much. At this point my mother would add the fat from the pork belly to the sauce, but you really shouldn't, as it would smother the distinct but lovely flavor of the parsley and would not enhance the sauce as a companion to the pork belly. Serve the pork belly and parsley sauce with some boiled new potatoes and Refrigerator-pickled Cucumbers (see below).

Refrigerator-pickled cucumbers

1 cup white wine vinegar
1 cup sugar
1 cup water
10 whole black peppercorns
4 bay leaves
1 teaspoon dill seeds
2 cucumbers
sea salt flakes

Combine the vinegar, sugar, water, peppercorns, bay leaves, and dill seeds in a saucepan and bring to a boil. As soon as it reaches boiling point, remove from the heat and let cool.

Wash the cucumbers and cut them into very thin slices—use a mandoline if you wish. Place the cucumber slices in a bowl, sprinkle with salt, and let stand for 10 to 15 minutes so that they give off a little liquid. Wring out as much liquid as possible from the cucumbers using your hands and then throw them into the cooled pickling vinegar. Let the cucumbers stand to pickle for at least a few hours before serving them.

The cucumbers can be stored in sterilized preserving jars in the refrigerator and will keep fresh for about 20 to 30 days.

Barley porridge
with a stew of chanterelles, baby onions, and pork sausages

1¼ cups chicken stock or water
1 cup beer
1¼ teaspoons sea salt flakes
⅔ cup coarse rye flour
⅔ cup coarse barley flour
⅓ cup freshly grated hard cheese, such as Høost, or aged Gouda or Grana Padano
2 teaspoons butter

Bring the chicken stock or water, beer, and salt to a boil in a saucepan and then add the flours in a steady stream while stirring. Cook for 20 to 25 minutes until all the flour taste has cooked away, stirring occasionally. While the porridge boils, you can make the Stew of Chanterelles, Baby Onions, and Pork Sausage (see right).

When the porridge is done, add the grated cheese and butter, and stir until smooth. Scoop a little porridge onto a plate, top with some of the stew, and serve immediately. This can be eaten as a lunch dish, appetizer, side, or garnish for poultry or light meat (veal or rabbit).

I am aware that serving porridge as a savory dish will be a novelty to many, but in reality it is no different from the polenta widely used in southern Mediterranean cuisine. In the Nordic countries, since ancient times, we have eaten lots of porridge and other spoon-friendly foods based on grains and flour. Before we fed on bread, we fed on porridge, so to speak. In fact, porridge has been on the menu for the past 6,000 years!

Stew of chanterelles, baby onions, and pork sausage

3½ oz chanterelles
1¾ oz baby onions
2 pork sausages
2 teaspoons cold butter
3 tablespoons water
sea salt flakes and freshly ground pepper
1 tablespoon olive oil
2 tablespoons apple cider vinegar
½ handful of flat-leaf parsley, chopped

Clean the chanterelles with a brush or a small vegetable knife. Peel the baby onions and cut the sausages into large chunks.

Put the onions in a small saucepan with the butter, 3 tablespoons water, salt, and pepper and sauté over low heat for 4 to 5 minutes or until tender.

Add the sausages and chanterelles to a hot pan with the olive oil and fry over high heat for 1 to 2 minutes until they are well done. Transfer to the pan of onions and sauté together for a few minutes. Season the stew with the vinegar, salt, and pepper. Finish off the stew with the chopped parsley.

Tip Serve a bowl of tender, ripe plums for dessert.

Making your own sausages

✳

Wash your hands. Hygiene is of the utmost importance when making sausages. Once the casing is stuffed and sealed, it is a closed system where aggressive bacteria can spread and thrive.

✳

Buy sausage casings made from animal intestines at your butcher's or from online retailers. Hog casings are the cheapest and will make a sausage the thickness of "medister," a traditional Danish pork sausage about 1 inch in diameter and flavored with allspice and cloves. Lamb casings have a smaller diameter, are thinner, and will therefore result in a crisper sausage. Beef casings will give you "ølpølse," a long, spicy Scandinavian sausage slightly resembling a salami in texture and taste, but usually the diameter of a middle finger. The casings are normally stored in brine, so make sure you rinse them in plenty of cold water before using them.

✳

Use good meat and fat. Choose the type of meat you like the best and add about 7 ounces hard pork back fat to 1¾ pounds of meat. Sausages are usually made with fat, and if you don't add enough, you will end up with a dry sausage with little flavor.

✳

Buy yourself a meat grinder with a sausage-stuffing attachment from a kitchenware supplier or an online retailer.

✳

Find some exciting recipes, and season them well to taste. For example, hot and spicy: finely grated lemon zest, chile, garlic, cumin, fresh cilantro (to take away some of the spiciness), ground ginger, salt, and pepper; for traditional: fresh mint, sage, white wine vinegar, garlic, beer, prunes, nutmeg, salt, and pepper.

✳

Always use meat that is as cold as possible—it will be easier to grind, and will bind with the liquid and spices more easily. If the meat gets too warm, the fat will split from the ground meat and form little "grains." This will impair the flavor, and result in a dry sausage. So, make sure you store your sausage ingredients in the refrigerator or freezer during the process. It is also a good idea to store your meat grinder and other utensils in the freezer before and during the process.

✳

Always let the filling sit for an hour or so for the flavors to meld and reach optimal taste and texture.

✳

Make a small test meatball. No matter how sure you are of your seasoning, when dealing with spices it is always a good idea to fry a small amount of the filling so that you can sample exactly how the sausage will taste when it is made.

✳

It is important not to seal the end of the casing when you begin to stuff the filling into it because then the air won't have anywhere to escape. Wait until the casing is fully stuffed before you seal both ends. Follow these steps:

1 Fit the casing over the end of sausage-stuffing attachment.

2 Fill the casing by running the finished filling through the feed tube of your grinder.

3 Make a knot in each end of the casing once it is full, but be careful not to fill it too much. You will need some room to divide it into smaller sausages, and when frying the sausages the casing will contract and may burst more easily if you have stuffed it too firmly.

4 Divide into smaller sausages by twisting the casing at equal intervals. This process is a little like making balloon animals, alternating the direction of the twisting each time by making one twist to the left and then the next twist to the right.

✳

Preboil your sausages if you wish. Regardless of whether you want to fry, barbecue, or smoke your sausages, it may be a good idea to preboil them for 10 to 15 minutes to reassure yourself that they are cooked through. Boiling also reduces the risk of the sausages bursting when you fry them. However, there are types of sausage that you normally wouldn't preboil, such as medister, for example (see left).

✳

Enjoy your homemade sausages while they are still warm. Sausages are more delicious when the fat is soft, so make sure your dinner guests are gathered around the table as soon as the sausages are cooked.

✳

Enjoy a good beer with your sausages. This last piece of advice is definitely worth remembering. Serve a stout beer with a stout sausage—a decent bitter ale to match the fatty sausage!

Homemade sausages

3½ oz potatoes
1 onion
1 garlic clove
1 lb 2 oz mixed ground pork and beef,
    8 to 10% fat (or 14 oz ground meat
    and 3½ oz hard pork back fat that
    you grind yourself)
sea salt flakes
1¼ cups lowfat milk
1 to 2 organic eggs
3 rosemary sprigs, chopped
1 teaspoon ground fennel
1 teaspoon ground allspice
freshly ground pepper
2 to 3 yards hog or lamb casings

Peel the potatoes, onion, and garlic, and chop coarsely. Add to a pan of water and cook for 20 to 25 minutes until they are soft.

Drain the vegetables, then mash thoroughly in a large bowl with a potato masher or whisk. Mix in the ground meat and salt. Continue mixing, adding the milk, eggs, rosemary, spices, and pepper.

Fry a small meatball of the filling until cooked through and taste to check the seasoning before proceeding. Now let the stuffing begin! The process in itself isn't difficult, but it requires some explanation for a first-time sausagemaker. Therefore I suggest you take a look at Making Your Own Sausages (see page 79) where I explain in detail how to stuff your sausages. When you have finished stuffing the sausages and have used up all the filling, put the sausages in the refrigerator to rest for 30 to 60 minutes. This gives the filling time to set.

Fry or barbecue the sausages for 3 to 4 minutes on each side until they have a beautiful crisp outside and are cooked through, but still juicy in the middle. If you like, you can preboil the sausages. This will help keep their shape when you fry them and they won't burst as easily.

You will soon discover that making your own sausages is surprisingly easy and fun, and I bet you will start making your very own variety of sausages with anything from pork and beef to lamb and duck.

TIP If you don't have a meat grinder with a sausage-stuffing attachment, you can wrap the filling in caulfat and still enjoy the homemade sausage experience. Caulfat is a thin membrane that surrounds a pig's stomach and can be ordered from your butcher. Soak the caulfat before using it, then wrap it in a thin layer around the filling that you have shaped into a sausage. Make sure the caulfat fits really tightly around the filling and is well sealed so that the juices won't leak out during the cooking process. As the sausage cooks, the caulfat is supposed to melt away, but this will only happen if the layer is thin enough. If there is a lot left, you may need to strip it off before serving the sausage. Now that you have engaged with the sausagemaking process, why not make double or triple the quantity and divide into portions in bags, and store in the freezer? They will make the perfect dinner and the kids will love them. Be sure to preboil the sausages before freezing them in the interests of food safety. Serve with a Classic Potato Salad (see page 36).

Homemade hotdogs

2 small baguettes
2 tablespoons olive oil
2 tablespoons prepared mustard
4 Homemade Sausages (see left)
Homemade Tomato Ketchup (see right)
1 shallot, peeled and finely sliced
    into rings
½ handful of chives, finely snipped

Cut the baguettes in half lengthwise, making sure not to cut them all the way through. Oil the cut sides with the olive oil and toast on a hot ridged grill pan or in a dry skillet until crisp and slightly golden.

Take the baguettes off the heat and spread the mustard on the cut sides before placing a sausage in each. Finish off with some Homemade Tomato Ketchup (see below) and scatter the shallot rings and chives on top. Serve immediately while the baguettes and sausages are still warm and crisp. You can comfortably serve a luxurious hotdog such as this as a main course, enjoy it for lunch, or as a royal midnight snack.

Homemade tomato ketchup

1 onion
1 garlic clove
1 tablespoon olive oil
¼ cup jaggery
1 star anise
1 teaspoon curry powder
sea salt flakes and freshly ground pepper
1 lb 2 oz tomatoes
3 tablespoons apple cider vinegar

Peel and chop the onion and garlic (it doesn't matter how finely, as the ketchup will be blended later). Sauté lightly in the olive oil in a saucepan. Add the sugar, star anise, curry powder, salt, and pepper to the pan and let the onion caramelize in the sugar.

Dice the tomatoes coarsely and add to the pan with the vinegar. Let simmer over low heat for about 45 minutes until it reaches a compote consistency.

Transfer the tomato mixture to a blender and blend to a smooth purée. Pass through a very fine sieve, using a spoon to facilitate the process if necessary. Pour the ketchup into a bowl ,then refrigerate.

If you are not planning on using it immediately, pour the ketchup into a sterilized preserving jar, seal, and store in the refrigerator. Unopened it will keep well for 50 to 60 days and, after opening, for about 10 to 15 days.

Pork chops
marinated in elderflower and apple cider vinegar

4 bone-in pork chops with fat, about 7 oz each
2 tablespoons elderflower concentrate or cordial
1 tablespoon apple cider vinegar
1 tablespoon cold-pressed canola oil
sea salt flakes and freshly ground pepper

Score the fat of the chops a few times so that it doesn't contract too much during the cooking process. Place the chops in a dish, add the elderflower concentrate or cordial, apple cider vinegar, canola oil, salt, and pepper. Let marinate at room temperature for 10 to 15 minutes.

Cook the chops on a very hot barbecue or in a ridged grill pan for 3 to 4 minutes on each side so that they have a beautiful crust but are still juicy in the middle. Remove the chops from the barbecue or grill pan and season with some more salt and pepper. Serve with the Crispy Salad of Cauliflower, Hazelnuts, and Celery (see page 100), some good bread, and boiled new potatoes.

Barbecued veal chops
with "burnt" summer leeks

4 bone-in veal chops with fat, 9 oz each
5 thyme sprigs, chopped
1 tablespoon olive oil
sea salt flakes and freshly ground pepper

Scrape the chops with a knife to remove any bone fragments and score the fat a few times so that it doesn't contract too much during the cooking process. Place the chops in a dish, add the thyme, oil, salt, and pepper and turn the chops over to coat them in the marinade.

Cook the chops on a very hot barbecue or ridged grill pan for 2 minutes on each side or until well browned on the outside but still juicy inside. Serve with "Burnt" Summer Leeks (see below).

"Burnt" Summer Leeks

8 young leeks
2 tablespoons apple cider vinegar
2 tablespoons cold-pressed canola oil
1 tablespoon jaggery
sea salt flakes and freshly ground pepper
1 handful of flat-leaf parsley, chopped
10 mint leaves, chopped

Cut off the root and tops of the leeks, then rinse them thoroughly in cold water.

Drain them and place on a medium-hot barbecue or ridged grill pan. Cook the leeks for 3 to 5 minutes on each side so that they are completely black and charred on the outside—you should eat the "burnt" parts as well, which bring a pleasing smoky flavor to the otherwise sweet summer leeks.

Mix the vinegar, oil, sugar, salt, pepper, parsley, and mint together in a bowl to make a dressing. Then slice the leeks open lengthwise. Place them on a platter with the soft and tender insides upward. Pour the dressing on top of the leeks and serve them while they are still warm with the veal chops.

Chargrilled liver
with warm salad of beets, horseradish, and dill

10½ oz lamb, veal, or venison liver
4 thyme sprigs, chopped
2 garlic cloves, minced
2 tablespoons olive oil
sea salt flakes and freshly ground pepper
8 beets
¼ cup jaggery
5 whole black peppercorns
15 fennel seeds
1 cup cherry vinegar
½ fennel bulb, finely sliced
1½ tablespoons freshly grated horseradish
½ handful of dill, chopped

Remove any outer membrane from the liver and wipe it lightly with paper towels. Cut the liver into thick strips and put them in a bowl. Add the thyme, garlic, oil, salt, and pepper. Place the liver in the refrigerator to marinate for 30 to 45 minutes.

Meanwhile, wash and place the whole beets in a saucepan of salted water. Cook over low heat, with the lid on, for about 15 to 20 minutes until tender but al dente.

Drain and rinse the beets in cold water, then gently rub the skins off with your hands (wear plastic gloves so that your hands are not completely stained red). Cut the beets into wedges and place them in a bowl.

Combine the sugar, peppercorns, fennel seeds, and cherry vinegar in a saucepan and cook until the mixture has reduced by half and begun to turn syrupy in consistency. Remove the peppercorns and fennel seeds. Add the beets to the hot syrup and cook for 1 to 2 minutes, stirring to make sure they are glazed on all sides. Remove from the heat, add the finely sliced fennel, horseradish, and dill and toss thoroughly. Season with salt and pepper, and sprinkle extra salt on top if necessary.

Cook the marinated liver on a hot barbecue or ridged grill pan for about 2 minutes on each side. They should still be pink and juicy in the middle.

Cut the liver into thin slices and serve immediately with the warm beets and some good bread.

Tip This dish can also be made with beef heart or, if you are able to obtain it, venison heart. If using heart, cut it in half and rinse thoroughly under cold running water, then let soak in cold water for 2 to 3 hours. Follow the method for the liver.

Fish

Pan-fried mackerel
with pickled tomatoes and thin and crunchy rye bread toast

2 large mackerel
1 tablespoon standard canola oil
sea salt and freshly ground pepper

Check that the mackerel are fresh—they should have glossy, bulging eyes, red gills and smell of the sea, not of the harbor. Clean the mackerel, scrape any scales off the skin with a knife, and wash in cold water. Remove the bones to create 4 fillets, using a pair of tweezers for the small ones, if necessary, or just ask your fish dealer to do the work for you.

Heat the oil in a skillet and start frying the mackerel fillets—first on the skin side for 2 to 3 minutes or until the skin is crisp and golden. Then flip them over and fry for 1 minute on the other side, seasoning with salt and pepper as you go. You will only fit 2 fillets in the pan at a time, so if you have an extra skillet, fire that one up as well and you will have all the fillets done at the same time.

Serve the warm mackerel fillets with Pickled Tomatoes and Thin and Crunchy Rye Bread Toast (see right). This is a glorious combination—oil-rich fried mackerel and crispy toast, with the sour-sweet tomatoes balancing the richness of the fish. The dish is as good for lunch as it is for dinner.

. . . .

TIP You can replace the crispy toast with cooked potatoes to serve with the mackerel and pickled tomatoes.

. . . .

Pickled tomatoes

12 cherry tomatoes
3 tablespoons olive oil
3 tablespoons apple cider vinegar or other white vinegar of your choice
2 shallots
10 fennel seeds
1 garlic clove, peeled
sea salt flakes and freshly ground pepper
sugar, to taste

Wash the tomatoes but keep the stalks on—they give off a lovely fresh tomato flavor when cooked. Put them in a Dutch oven and add the oil, vinegar, shallots, peeled and cut into fine wedges, and fennel seeds and garlic clove, lightly crushed to get more flavor out of them, with salt, pepper, and sugar to taste.

Gently heat up the tomato mixture, then transfer the pan to a preheated oven at 200°F and cook for about 30 to 45 minutes or until the tomatoes start to burst.

Take the dish out of the oven and let the tomatoes sit for at least 1 to 2 hours before you eat them. They are even better if you prepare them a few days in advance so that they have more time to sit and mature in the pickling juice.

Thin and crunchy rye bread toast

8 to 12 very thin slices of rye bread (see tip)
2 tablespoons cold-pressed canola oil
sea salt flakes

Place the bread slices on a cookie sheet lined with parchment paper—press them flat to the sheet by hand if needed. Drizzle with the canola oil and sprinkle some salt on top. Bake the bread slices in a preheated oven at 315°F for 10 to 12 minutes or until they are very crisp.

Take them out of the oven and transfer to a wire rack to cool, when they will become even crispier.

. . . .

Tip In order to slice the rye bread as thinly as possible, use bread that is a few days old and chill it in the refrigerator beforehand so that it is firmer and therefore easier to slice.

. . . .

MARSH SAMPHIRE
On salt marshes and tidal flats, samphire (saltwater baby asparagus) are at their best in summer and stand tall, ready for harvest.

Barbecued mackerel
with warm gooseberry compote

**4 small mackerel, about 9 oz each,
    or 2 large, about 14 oz to 1 lb 2 oz each**
1 organic lemon
5 dill stems, chopped
2 tablespoons mustard
1 tablespoon standard canola oil
sea salt flakes and freshly ground pepper

Check that the mackerel are fresh—they should have glossy, bulging eyes, red gills, and smell of the sea, not of the harbor. Clean the mackerel, scrape any scales off the skin with a knife, and wash in cold water (or ask the fish dealer to do the work for you). Cut the lemon into slices and place them in the cavity of the mackerel along with the chopped dill stems and mustard. Close up the cavity using a trussing needle, if you wish.

Score the skin of the mackerel a few times, rub it with the canola oil, and sprinkle with salt and pepper.

Cook the mackerel on a very hot barbecue for 3 to 5 minutes on each side, depending on the size. Ensure that you don't move the mackerel around or turn them ahead of time, because the skin breaks easily. If you have a little patience, both the skin and the fish will loosen from the grill after the requisite length of cooking time.

Eat the freshly cooked mackerel with Warm Gooseberry Compote (*see* below) and boiled new potatoes.

Warm gooseberry compote

10½ oz green gooseberries
2 shallots
½ cup jaggery
10 fennel seeds
5 whole black peppercorns
**½ cup apple cider vinegar or other light
    fruit vinegar**
sea salt flakes and freshly ground pepper

Snip off the stems and flower ends from the gooseberries with a pair of kitchen scissors and rinse the fruit in cold water. Peel the shallots and cut into thin rings.

Put the sugar, fennel seeds, and peppercorns in a saucepan over medium heat to warm up. When the sugar begins to bubble and caramelize, add the shallots, gooseberries, and vinegar and season with a pinch of salt. Simmer for 10 to 15 minutes with the lid on until you have a dense compote. Season, if you wish, with some extra sugar, vinegar, salt, or pepper.

Remove the peppercorns from the compote before serving if you prefer, or at least make your diners aware of them, as they are not very pleasant to chew on.

Barbecued sea trout
with cauliflower and asparagus in yogurt dressing

1 lb 5 oz sea trout fillet, skin on
sea salt flakes
½ cauliflower
12 green asparagus
1 cup low-fat plain yogurt
3 tablespoons apple cider vinegar
2 tablespoons cold-pressed canola oil
1 teaspoon acacia honey
freshly ground pepper
10 caraway seeds

Check that sea trout is fresh and smells of the sea, not of the harbor. Use a knife to scrape the scales off the skin and remove any bones, then divide into 4 pieces, about 5½ ounces each. Season the sea trout with a little salt and let sit at room temperature for 10 minutes before cooking them.

Meanwhile, start making the salad. Cut the cauliflower into large florets and break off the woody ends of the asparagus. Cut both the cauliflower florets and asparagus into small pieces, then rinse and drain the vegetables well in a colander.

Mix the yogurt with the vinegar, oil, honey, salt, and pepper in a bowl to make a dressing. Toast the caraway seeds in a dry skillet until they pop, then crush them using a mortar and pestle, and add to the dressing.

Pour the dressing over the vegetables and mix well. If necessary, season with more salt, pepper, vinegar, and honey to taste.

Cook the sea trout pieces on a hot barbecue for 2 to 3 minutes on each side—first on the skin side, until the skin is crisp and golden, then flip it over and cook until done. Turn the fish pieces over once only to avoid breaking them. Serve with the cauliflower and asparagus salad, boiled new potatoes, and some good bread.

Barbecued herring
with vinaigrette of mustard seeds, green strawberries, and cold-pressed canola oil

6 herrings
2 tablespoons prepared mustard
finely grated zest of 1 organic lemon
sea salt flakes and freshly ground pepper
½ handful of dill, chopped
2 tablespoons cold-pressed canola oil

Vinaigrette
1 tablespoon yellow mustard seeds
1 shallot
10 green strawberries
2 tablespoons elderflower vinegar
2 tablespoons cold-pressed canola oil
½ bunch of dill, chopped
sea salt flakes and freshly ground pepper

Check that the herrings are fresh—they should have glossy, bulging eyes, red gills, and smell of the sea, not of the harbor. Clean the herrings, scrape the scales off the skin with a knife, and remove the bones to create 12 individual fillets (or ask the fish dealer do the work for you).

Place the herring fillets, skin-side down, in a dish, spread the mustard onto the flesh side, and scatter with the lemon zest, salt, pepper, and chopped dill. Let the herrings marinate in the refrigerator for 20 to 25 minutes before grilling them.

Meanwhile, prepare the vinaigrette. Toast the mustard seeds lightly in a dry skillet, just until they start to release their wonderful aroma. Peel the shallot and chop it very finely, and cut the green strawberries into thin slices, and set aside.

Drizzle the canola oil over the herrings and cook them on a very hot barbecue, first on the skin side for about a minute, then for a minute on the other side.

Transfer the herring fillets to a deep dish and scatter them with the mustard seeds, shallot, and strawberries. Finish off by drizzling them with the elderflower vinegar, canola oil, and chopped dill, and season to taste with salt and pepper.

This is a summery, playful way of preparing fried herring and I am absolutely nuts about it. Serve the herring warm and fresh from the barbecue with some good wholegrain bread and a green salad for lunch, or with some boiled new potatoes for dinner—both combinations are utterly delicious.

Do put the elderflower vinegar and canola oil on the table so that your guests can help themselves to some extra dressing if they so wish.

Pan-fried herring
with stewed leeks

8 double herring fillets
2 tablespoons prepared mustard
2 tablespoons freshly grated horseradish
1 handful of dill, chopped
sea salt flakes and freshly ground pepper
1 cup rye flour
3 tablespoons standard canola oil
2 teaspoons butter

Check that the herring fillets are fresh and smell of the sea, not of the harbor. Clean the herrings and scrape the scales off the skin with a knife. Place in a dish, skin-side down, spread the flesh side with the mustard, and scatter with the grated horseradish, chopped dill, salt, and pepper. Fold the fillets together and dip them in the rye flour.

Heat a skillet and add the oil, and when that is hot, add the butter and let it bubble. Fry the herring fillets for about 3 minutes on each side until they are golden and crisp. It may be necessary to press down a little on the folded herring fillets with a lifter when you first add them to the pan so that they don't unfold.

Serve the freshly fried herring with Stewed Leeks (see right) and a pot of cooked potatoes.

● ●

Tip I love fried herring, but should there be leftovers after dinner, I cook up some pickling brine in just 5 minutes (see page 94, Pickled Mackerel) and let the fried herring spend the night in it. Then at lunchtime the next day I can enjoy pickled and fried herring with rye bread and raw onions, but the herring only gets better over the following days. I also tend to fry extra herrings deliberately, since I have the skillet going anyway.

● ●

Stewed leeks

6 large leeks
1 to 1¼ cups water, divided
sea salt flakes
3 tablespoons all-purpose flour
4 cups skim milk
juice of ½ lemon
freshly ground pepper
a little sugar, if needed
freshly grated nutmeg, to taste
½ handful of parsley, chopped

Cut off the root and tops of the leeks, then cut them into rings ¾ inch thick. Rinse them thoroughly in cold water so that all of the soil is washed away.

Put the leeks in a saucepan with the water and some salt and cook for 2 to 3 minutes over low heat. Mix the flour with 1 cup of the milk until smooth and stir into the leeks and boiling water, then add the rest of the milk. Let the stew cook for 4 to 5 minutes so that it thickens and the flour taste is cooked away.

Taste the stew and add lemon juice, salt, pepper, a little sugar if necessary, and grated nutmeg—as much as you like. Scatter the stew with the chopped parsley and it is ready to serve.

Besides being perfect with fried herring, these stewed leeks are also lovely with other classics such as fried eel, meatballs, and sausages.

Steamed mussels
with wheat beer, young leeks, and dill

4½ lb mussels
3 shallots
2 garlic cloves
white part of 1 large leek, rinsed
1 tablespoon butter
½ cup apple cider or tart apple juice
1¼ cups wheat beer, plus extra to season
3 tablespoons heavy whipping cream
12 to 16 small young leeks
sea salt flakes
½ handful of dill, chopped
1 tablespoon apple cider vinegar
2 tablespoons cold-pressed canola oil
freshly ground pepper

Follow the first three steps of the recipe for Steamed Mussels with Lovage, Chervil, and Beer on page 34 to prepare and steam the mussels, and to make the sauce with the mussel broth and cream.

Cut off the root and the tops of the small young leeks, then rinse them thoroughly in cold water. Blanch the leeks in salted boiling water for about 4 to 5 minutes, drain, then mix them with the chopped dill, vinegar, oil, salt, and pepper to make a fresh "salad." Pour the leeks onto the mussels.

Season the sauce with salt, pepper, and a little extra fresh beer. Pour it over the mussels as well and serve the dish immediately with some good wholegrain bread to soak up the delicious sauce.

Gravad turbot
and fennel crudités with mustard vinaigrette

7 oz very fresh skinless turbot fillets
10 coriander seeds
5 juniper berries
10 fennel seeds
5 whole black peppercorns
1 teaspoon sea salt
1 teaspoon jaggery

Check that the turbot is really fresh and smells of the sea, not of the harbor. Remove any remaining bones and skin fragments, and scrape away any stray scales and membranes if necessary.

Toast the spices in a dry skillet until they start to release their lovely aromas, then crush them using a mortar and pestle. Place the turbot in a dish and sprinkle with the salt, sugar, and spices. Cover the dish tightly with plastic wrap and let the turbot marinate in the refrigerator for 36 to 48 hours. Flip the fillets over a few times during the process, but remember to recover the dish with the plastic wrap each time so that the fish doesn't dry out.

Once the marinating time has elapsed, take the turbot out of the dish and lightly pat dry with paper towels while trying not to dislodge the spices. Cut the fish into thin slices and serve with some toasted rye bread and the Fennel Crudités with Mustard Vinaigrette (see right). It's a great dish for dinner parties.

Fennel crudités with mustard vinaigrette

1 fennel bulb
1 shallot
2 tablespoons apple cider vinegar
1 tablespoon prepared coarsely ground mustard
1 teaspoon honey
sea salt flakes and freshly ground pepper
2 tablespoons cold-pressed canola oil

Rinse the fennel thoroughly in cold water and slice it very finely, using a mandoline, if you wish.

Peel the shallot and cut it into chunks. Put in a blender with the vinegar, mustard, honey, salt, and pepper and blend into a smooth dressing. Then add the oil in a very thin stream with the blender running so that the dressing retains its consistency.

Toss the fennel with the vinaigrette and season with some more salt and pepper. Serve immediately while the fennel is fresh and crisp.

WILD THYME
The bright pink flowers of wild thyme are both decorative and taste nice.

Pan-fried plaice
with browned butter, parsley, and new potatoes

4 plaice
all-purpose flour, for dusting
sea salt flakes and freshly ground pepper
1 stick butter
2 tablespoons elderflower vinegar
1 handful of flat-leaf parsley, chopped
2¼ lb new potatoes, boiled (see method on page 36), to serve

Check that plaice is fresh, with beautiful clear, bulging eyes and a smell of the sea, not of the harbor. Clean the plaice, cutting off the head and fins, and remove the skin. Then rinse the fish thoroughly in cold water, cleaning off all the blood and guts (or ask your fish dealer to do all the work for you).

Cut an incision all the way along the line that the plaice naturally has down the middle (this will prevent the super-fresh fish from contracting too much and arching during cooking). This cut has a second important function; while frying, you can spoon some of the hot butter from the pan onto the thick end of the plaice (where the head was) so that it penetrates the flesh and enables both the thick and thin parts to be cooked evenly in the same time, instead of the thinner part drying out before the thicker part is properly cooked.

Dust the plaice with flour and season with salt and pepper. Melt the butter in a hot skillet and let it bubble, then fry the plaice for about 3 to 4 minutes on each side or until they are beautifully golden on both sides. You can probably only fit a single plaice in the pan at a time, unless you have a very large skillet, so it may be a good idea to use 2 pans at a time. A good trick to check whether the plaice are done is to find the pointed bone that sits just below where the head has been cut off. If it can be pulled out effortlessly, the plaice are finished; if not, they need a little more time in the pan.

Serve the plaice with the butter from the pan flavored with the vinegar and chopped parsley, along with the boiled potatoes. This dish is simple and exceptionally good.

A long history

Pan-fried plaice has been a constant feature of Danish food culture for centuries. In the first published recipe for the dish, which appeared in Marcus Loofts' cookbook in 1766, the flounder, as the fish was called, is skinned, dusted in flour, and fried at a high temperature, then served with browned butter and lemon juice and scattered with parsley. By the early 1800s, the fish was fully coated—C. Jacobsen recommends in his cookbook of 1815 that the fish be first dipped in beaten egg and then in bread crumbs mixed with flour before frying over high heat in browned butter.

Pan-fried mullet
with cucumber and peas in dill butter with aquavit

1 lb 5 oz grey mullet fillets, skin on
sea salt flakes
1 tablespoon olive oil
1 cucumber
1 tablespoon butter
1⅓ cups podded peas
1 shallot
freshly ground pepper
grated zest of ½ organic lemon
½ handful of dill
1 tablespoon aquavit

Check that the mullet is fresh and smells of the sea, not of the harbor. Use a knife to scrape the scales off the skin and remove any bones. Then divide the fish into 4 equal-sized pieces and score the skin lightly a few times. Sprinkle salt on both sides and let stand for 5 minutes.

Heat up a skillet with the oil and fry the mullet first on the skin side for 2 to 3 minutes or until the skin becomes beautifully crisp and golden, then flip the fish over and cook for 1 to 2 minutes on the other side.

Meanwhile, peel the cucumber, cut it in half lengthwise, and scrape out the seeds with a teaspoon, then slice it into wedges ½ inch thick. Melt the butter in a pan, add the cucumber and peas, and sauté for about 2 minutes over low heat.

Peel and chop the shallot finely, then add to the pan with the cucumber and peas. Season with salt, pepper, and the lemon zest. Chop the dill and add to the pan along with the aquavit and mix well. Serve immediately with the fried mullet fillets, with some boiled new potatoes and a green salad as side dishes.

TIP Buy 3½ ounces extra mullet fillet, but ask your fish dealer to remove the skin, and use for the Salt and Sugar-cured Mullet to serve the following day with the Cold Cucumber Soup (see page 66).

Light dishes

Omelet
with new potatoes, spinach, and hot-smoked salmon

1 onion
14 oz new potatoes, boiled
   (*see* method on page 36)
2 tablespoons butter
sea salt flakes and freshly ground pepper
1½ cups fresh spinach
3½ oz hot-smoked salmon
6 organic eggs
1 cup lowfat milk

Peel and slice the onion finely, and cut the boiled potatoes into large cubes. Sauté the onion and potatoes in the butter in an ovenproof skillet (*see* tip), then season to taste with salt and pepper. Rinse the spinach well, drain, and add it to the pan.

Divide the hot-smoked salmon into smaller pieces, add to the skillet, and mix well. Crack the eggs into a bowl, one at a time so that you can check that they are fresh. Add the milk and whisk together, then pour the mixture into the pan. Fry the omelet for a few minutes in the pan so that it just sets before transferring it to a preheated oven at 400°F.

Bake the omelet for 8 to 10 minutes or until it has set fully and is slightly golden on top. Serve while it is warm with some wholegrain rye bread. Pickled beets (*see* page 195) are also a good accompaniment, and I personally have a weakness for mustard whenever there is an egg dish on the table.

Tip If you don't have an ovenproof skillet, you can make the omelet on the stove and cover with the lid of a large saucepan so that the eggs get a little heat from above as well.

Lightly salted sea trout
with cucumber and dill in smoked curd cheese dressing

7 oz very fresh skinless sea trout fillet
1 teaspoon sugar
2 tablespoons sea salt flakes
1 cucumber
2 teaspoons Smoked Curd Cheese
   (*see* page 14)
1 tablespoon apple cider vinegar
1 tablespoon standard canola oil
3 tablespoons Greek yogurt, 2% fat
sea salt and freshly ground pepper
½ handful of dill

Day 1
Check that the sea trout is really fresh and smells of the sea, not of the harbor. Check the fish for bones and scrape off any remaining scales with a knife so that the fillet is nice and clean, then place it in a small dish.

Mix the sugar and salt together and sprinkle the mixture evenly over the sea trout fillet. Cover the dish with plastic wrap and chill in the refrigerator for 12 hours.

Day 2
Peel the cucumber, cut it in half lengthwise, and scrape out the seeds with a teaspoon. Then cut it into cubes. Mix the smoked curd cheese with the vinegar, oil, yogurt, salt, and pepper in a bowl to make a dressing. Toss the cucumber pieces in the dressing. Rinse and chop the dill finely, and add it to the cucumber mixture. Season with more salt and pepper if necessary.

Take the sea trout out of the dish and pat dry with paper towels. Cut into thin slices and serve with the cucumber and dill mixture, along with some good white bread. Serve the dish as a light meal or as part of a special lunch.

Salad of white and green asparagus
with shrimp

6 white asparagus
6 green asparagus
sea salt flakes and freshly ground pepper
½ fennel bulb
2 tablespoons elderflower vinegar or
   light fruit vinegar
1 tablespoon jaggery
1 hard-boiled organic egg, shelled
   and chopped
1 tablespoon prepared mustard
2 tablespoons cold-pressed canola oil
3½ oz small cooked, peeled shrimp
   (*see* page 45)
½ handful of chervil, chopped

Peel the white asparagus and break off the woody stem ends, but simply rinse the green ones in cold water before breaking off the stem ends.

Cook the white asparagus in a saucepan of boiling salted water for 2 to 3 minutes, depending on thickness, then immediately transfer them to cold water to stop the cooking process. They should be tender but still quite crisp.

Cut the white asparagus on a slight diagonal into pieces 1¼ to 1½ inches long, and slice the raw green asparagus quite finely, then add both to a bowl. Slice the fennel very finely with a sharp knife or a mandoline, rinse it in cold water, and then let it drain for a while before adding it to the asparagus.

Mix the vinegar, sugar, hard-boiled egg, mustard, salt, pepper, and oil together in a bowl to make a dressing. Pour it onto the salad and toss well. Scatter with the peeled shrimp and chopped chervil, and eat the salad with some good bread.

Mackerel pickled in apple cider vinegar
with sweet cicely

4 mackerel, about 10½ to 14 oz each
2 tablespoons sea salt flakes
½ organic lemon, cut into wedges
4 carrots
2 red onions
2 garlic cloves
2 cups water
1¼ cups apple cider vinegar
10 fennel seeds
2 star anise
10 whole black peppercorns
2 tablespoons sugar
1 handful of sweet cicely

Day 1
Clean and fillet the mackerel as in the Pan-fried Mackerel recipe on page 84. Make a few diagonal cuts in the skin, then place the fillets in a deep dish, sprinkle them with the salt, scatter with the lemon wedges, and let chill in the refrigerator for 30 minutes.

Meanwhile, peel the vegetables and garlic cloves, then cut the carrots into slices and the onions into wedges, but leave the garlic cloves whole.

Put the vegetables in a pan with the 2 cups water, vinegar, spices, sugar, and the stems from the sweet cicely (reserve the leaves for later). Bring to a boil and, as soon as the liquid reaches boiling point, pour it evenly over the mackerel fillets. Remove the sweet cicely stems (they have already added their flavor). Cover the dish with plastic wrap and place the fillets in the refrigerator until the following day.

Day 2
Take the dish out of the refrigerator and serve the mackerel fillets and vegetables just as they are, with the cicely leaves, freshly boiled potatoes, and rye bread. The dish can be served both for lunch and at dinner.

Tip You can also heat the mackerel and vegetables in the dish in a preheated oven at 315°F for 8 to 10 minutes and then enjoy them warm.

Rye salad
with blackberries, beets, and horseradish

1¼ cups pearled rye
2½ cups water
3 tablespoons cherry vinegar, or to taste
3 tablespoons cold-pressed canola oil
1 teaspoon acacia honey
sea salt flakes and freshly ground pepper
6 to 8 small beets
3 tablespoons freshly grated
   horseradish, or more to taste
½ handful of chervil, chopped
⅔ cup fresh blackberries

Rinse the rye grains in cold water and place in a saucepan with the water, or enough to cover them. Bring the water to a boil, skim off any foam or impurities that rise to the surface, then lower the heat. Cook the rye for 20 minutes or until tender, but al dente. Let stand, covered, for 5 to 10 minutes.

Strain any excess water off of the rye grains and add the vinegar, oil, honey, and salt and pepper to taste so that they absorb all the flavors, then let them cool slightly.

Take the skin off of the beets, cut them in half, and then slice them very thinly. Add the rye to the beets, horseradish, chervil, and blackberries in a bowl and gently toss the salad. Season with more salt, pepper, and vinegar if needed. With a piece of cheese and some good bread, this grain salad would easily fill me up. You could also serve the dish as a side for *steak à la Lindström* or a piece of pink-roasted veal liver.

Stew of chanterelles on toast

14 oz chanterelles
1½ tablespoons butter
3 tablespoons hard cider or sherry
½ cup heavy whipping cream
sea salt flakes and freshly ground pepper
1 shallot
finely grated zest and juice of
   ½ organic lemon
8 slices of white bread
1 tablespoon olive oil

Cut off the root end of the chanterelles and clean the mushrooms with a brush or a small vegetable knife. If they are very dirty, you can wash them gently. Cut the chanterelles into smaller pieces and set them on some paper towels to dry if necessary.

Melt the butter in a saucepan, add the chanterelles, and sauté over medium heat for 3 to 5 minutes. Add the hard cider, or sherry, and cream and cook the chanterelles until they have absorbed the liquid and the mixture has begun to thicken. Season with salt and pepper. Peel and mince the shallot, then add it to the chanterelles toward the end of cooking—it makes them firmer and adds a sharp contrast to the cream. Season with the lemon zest and juice.

Drizzle the bread slices with the olive oil and toast them under the broiler, in a ridged grill pan, or in the oven.

Spoon the stewed chanterelles onto the crisp bread and serve as a small appetizer or for lunch with a good salad. I think this is terrific food!

Tip You can of course use other wild or cultivated mushrooms in the stew.

Eggs in pots
with chanterelles and grated cheese

4 organic eggs
1 tablespoon olive oil
sea salt flakes and freshly ground pepper
2 teaspoons butter
3½ oz cleaned chanterelles (*see* left)
¾ oz Comté cheese
2 chervil sprigs, chopped

Crack the eggs one at a time into individual cups to check them for freshness. Oil 4 ovenproof glass dishes or small bowls with the olive oil and then put one egg into each. Season the eggs with salt and pepper and bake them in a preheated oven at 325°F for about 10 to 12 minutes or until the eggs are firm but still soft in the middle.

Melt the butter in a skillet and fry the chanterelles for 2 to 3 minutes over high heat, then season with salt and pepper.

Place the fried chanterelles on top of the baked eggs. Grate the cheese on top and scatter with the chervil. Serve the eggs while they are warm. This works wonderfully as a brunch dish or as a different kind of lunch.

Chicken salad
with baked shallots and chanterelles

6 shallots
sea salt flakes
1 teaspoon prepared mustard
1 teaspoon honey
2 tablespoons apple cider vinegar
2 tablespoons cold-pressed canola oil
freshly ground pepper
about 5½ oz poached chicken (*see* tip)
3½ oz cleaned chanterelles (*see* left)
2 tablespoons standard canola oil
½ handful of parsley, chopped

Place the whole unpeeled shallots in an ovenproof dish, sprinkle them with a little salt, and bake them in a preheated oven at 350°F for 15 to 20 minutes or until they are fully cooked.

Remove the shallots from the oven and set aside to cool. When the shallots have cooled, cut the root off and slip them out of their skins. Cut the shallots into chunks and put them in a bowl.

Mix the mustard, honey, vinegar, cold-pressed canola oil, salt, and pepper together in a bowl to make a dressing and pour it evenly over the shallots. Place the chicken on top of the shallots.

Heat up a skillet and fry the chanterelles in the canola oil over medium heat for 3 to 4 minutes or until they have shrunk a little. Season with salt and pepper, remove the mushrooms from the heat ,and let them cool slightly.

Add the chanterelles and chopped parsley to the salad, toss well, and season with more salt and pepper. Serve on a slice of toasted rye bread or white bread as an appetizer, or serve for lunch with a good salad.

Tip If you don't have any cooked chicken on hand, then cook 2 chicken legs (the thigh and drumstick) following the directions for Poached Chicken on page 72, let cool, and then pick the meat off of them. This should yield the equivalent of the 5½ ounces chicken meat that you need for the salad.

WILD BLUEBERRIES
On heaths and in well-lit pine forests, wild blueberries will be starting to sprout.

Stew of chanterelles »

Tartlets
with summer vegetables in béchamel sauce

1½ tablespoons butter
2½ tablespoons all-purpose flour
2 cups warm chicken stock
1 organic egg yolk
3 tablespoons heavy whipping cream
sea salt flakes and freshly ground pepper
finely grated zest and juice of
   1 organic lemon
4 white asparagus
4 green asparagus
½ summer cabbage
1 lb 2 oz peas in the pod (yielding about
   ⅔ to 1 cup peas when podded)
½ handful of sweet cicely or chervil,
   freshly torn
12 Tartlet Shells (*see* right)

Melt the butter in a saucepan and add the flour, stirring, to make a smooth roux. Add the warm chicken stock and stir vigorously while it comes to a boil to stop any lumps from forming. Let simmer for 7 to 8 minutes.

Mix the egg yolk and cream together, then whisk into the sauce and simmer for a further 2 to 3 minutes. Pass the sauce through a sieve and season to taste with salt, pepper, and lemon zest and juice. The sauce should be light, creamy, and velvety.

Peel the white asparagus and break off the woody stem ends, but simply rinse the green ones in cold water before breaking off the stem ends. Slice the asparagus and cabbage finely, shell the peas, and add all the vegetables to the sauce. Cook for 1 to 2 minutes, remove from the heat, and mix the freshly torn sweet cicely or chervil into the stewed vegetables.

Warm the tartlet shells in a preheated oven at 400°F for 2 minutes, then fill them with the stewed vegetables. Serve the tartlets as an appetizer or a light main course, depending on the number of diners.

Tartlet shells
MAKES 12 TARTLET PASTRY SHELLS

2 to 3 tablespoons standard canola oil
10½ oz puff pastry (defrosted if frozen)
all-purpose flour, for dusting

You will need 24 tartlet pans or molds, each about 4 to 4½ inches in diameter. Oil 12 on the inside and 12 on the outside thoroughly with the canola oil.

Roll the puff pastry out thinly on a floured work surface. Cut out 12 circles about 4½ to 5½ inches in diameter and use them to line the internally oiled pans. Make sure the pastry is pressed in firmly, with no air bubbles caught under the dough, then place the externally oiled pans on top of the pastry shells, to keep the dough pressed against the bottom pans. Let them rest in the refrigerator for 20 to 25 minutes.

Bake the tartlet shells in a preheated oven at 400°F for 12 to 14 minutes. Let them cool slightly in the pans before gently turning them out.

Tip The tartlet shells can also be made with "dull pastry," which is puff pastry that has been kneaded so that the butter layers have been removed, typically the rekneaded trimmings left over from cutting out the dough. Pastry cases made with "dull pastry" will keep their shape a little better, but they are not quite as crisp and flaky.

Tartlet traditions

Pies or small cups of pastry served with stews or sweet fillings have been popular for centuries in Europe. With the birth of classic French cuisine in the 18th century, these dishes were refined with the use of puff pastry or shortcrust pastry. In the 1700s, the term "tartlets" referred only to sweet dishes, and it was not until the subsequent century that savory recipes were introduced. Tartlets had their heyday in the 20th century, when they were served between the appetizer and main course at the great dinners of the bourgeoisie, but soon they became a beloved part of menus at festive occasions at all levels of society. As a child, I had enough margarine-based industrial tartlets to last a lifetime, so if you don't have the opportunity to make croustades or tartlet shells using proper butter-based pastry, I would recommend toasted bread instead.

Vegetable accompaniments

Pea purée
with almonds and mint

**1⅓ cups podded peas (1 lb 2 oz to
    1 lb 5 oz unpodded weight)**
2 tablespoons whole blanched almonds
2 tablespoons olive oil
**2 tablespoons fresh cheese, such as
    cream cheese or ricotta**
**3½ tablespoons freshly grated
    Parmesan cheese**
4 mint leaves, chopped
sea salt flakes and freshly ground pepper
**juice of ½ lemon or a little apple cider
    vinegar, or a little finely grated
    lemon zest**

Blanch the peas in a saucepan of boiling
water for 30 seconds and then immediately
drain and plunge them into cold water to
stop the cooking process.

Roast the almonds in a dry skillet until they
are slightly golden.

Put the peas in a food processor with
the roasted almonds, oil, fresh cheese,
Parmesan, and chopped mint. Process to
a coarse purée. Season with salt, pepper,
and the lemon juice or apple cider vinegar.
You can also use a little grated lemon zest
instead if you want to stop the purée from
turning a more khaki-colored green due to
the acid of the lemon juice or vinegar. Eat
the purée with a piece of toasted bread or
some crackers as a snack, or as a side for
barbecued or grilled meat.

Cauliflower purée
with a crispy salad of cauliflower, hazelnuts, and celery

1 cauliflower, green leaves discarded
3 celery stalks
3 tablespoons hazelnuts
2 tablespoons standard canola oil
sea salt flakes and freshly ground pepper
**finely grated zest and juice of
    ½ organic lemon**
2 teaspoons butter
**some mixed herbs, such as chervil and
    flat-leaf parsley, rinsed**

Cut off the outermost small florets of
the cauliflower and put them in a bowl.
Cut the rest of the cauliflower into large
chunks and place in a saucepan with a
little water. Steam the cauliflower, with
the lid on, for about 10 to 12 minutes. The
cauliflower should be tender, but not
overcooked or else it might start to smell
and taste a little "soggy" (that lingering
smell of cauliflower filled the air in every
staircase in my childhood).

Meanwhile, make the salad. Wash the
celery and cut it into very fine strips, and
crush or chop the hazelnuts lightly. Add
the celery and hazelnuts to the small
cauliflower florets in the bowl and marinate
them in half the oil, salt, pepper, and a little
of the lemon juice.

Put the steamed cauliflower and ½ cup of
the cooking water in a blender, add the
butter, the remaining oil, and lemon juice
and the zest and blend to a smooth purée.
Season with salt and pepper.

Serve the warm purée scattered with the
crisp salad and garnished with the herbs as
an appetizer with some good bread, or use
it as a side. The creamy purée is almost like a
mayonnaise, and I am absolutely nuts about
combining it with fish and shellfish, for
example, as an accompaniment to boiled
langoustines, shrimp, or squid.

Griddled vegetables
with sprinkle of smoked pork fat, dill seeds, and sorrel

10 freshly harvested carrots with tops
8 freshly harvested onions
1 handful of green asparagus
1 zucchini
2 tablespoons olive oil
sea salt flakes and freshly ground pepper
1 oz smoked pork fat (lard)
**finely grated zest and juice of
    1 organic lemon**
1 teaspoon dill seeds
a little parsley and chervil, chopped
**1 small handful of sorrel (wood sorrel or
    lemon balm can also be used)**

Wash and peel the carrots and onions, and
chop the carrots in half lengthwise and the
onions into quarters. Break off the woody
stem ends of the asparagus and cut the
zucchini into slices ½ inch thick.

Roll all the vegetables in the oil, salt, and
pepper, then cook on a hot ridged grill
pan for a few minutes on each side until
they begin to color and are lightly cooked
(they should still be crunchy). Arrange the
vegetables on a serving platter.

Cut the smoked pork fat into thin slices
and fry them in a dry skillet for about 2 to
4 minutes on each side so that they become
golden and crisp. Remove from the pan and
let drain on paper towels to absorb
the excess fat.

Add 1 tablespoon of the rendered fat from
the pan to a bowl with the lemon zest and
juice, salt, and pepper. Toast the dill seeds
in a dry skillet until they begin to pop, then
remove from the pan and crush them lightly
with the flat side of a chef's knife. Add to
the dressing and pour it evenly over the
vegetables. Sprinkle the crispy fat on top
along with the chopped herbs and sorrel.
Eat the vegetables as an appetizer or as a
side to fish, meat, or poultry.

Salt-baked potatoes

2¼ lb new potatoes
¼ cup sea salt flakes

Rinse the potatoes in cold water. Put the potatoes in a heavy saucepan and add water to barely cover them. Add the salt and bring to a boil. Cook the potatoes, with the lid on, for about 10 minutes or until they still have a little bite.

Pour almost all the water out, leaving ¼ inch of water behind in the pan. Let the potatoes steam, uncovered, while shaking the pan continuously to keep them moving in the salty water. When the water has evaporated, a thin layer of salt will have formed on the outside of the potatoes. Cover and let the potatoes sit for 10 minutes off the heat. Take the lid off and place the pan back on the heat for 1 to 2 minutes, shaking the pan again.

This method of cooking potatoes makes them wrinkly and gives them a unique texture with a chewy exterior and a lovely taste from the salt layer. Eat the wrinkled potatoes with the Lovage Dip and Cream Cheese with Chervil and Lemon (see below) as a snack or appetizer before dinner. You can also use them as an accompaniment to shellfish and fish dishes—create a wonderful and easy summer meal by simply adding some smoked herring from your fish dealer and serving with a crisp green salad.

Lovage Dip

½ handful of lovage
1 handful of parsley
½ cup standard canola oil
1 shallot, peeled
3 tablespoons apple cider vinegar
1 oz fresh wheat bread, crust removed
sea salt flakes and freshly ground pepper
a little jaggery or honey

Wash and tear the lovage and parsley, then add to a food processor along with the oil, shallot, vinegar, and bread. Blend to a coarse dip. Season with salt, pepper, and sugar or honey so that the balance is just right and serve with the Salt-baked Potatoes.

This dip is also great with ordinary boiled new potatoes or as a green sauce for crisply cooked summer vegetables.

Cream cheese with chervil and lemon

3 tablespoons cream cheese
1 teaspoon prepared mustard
finely grated zest and juice of
½ organic lemon
sea salt flakes and freshly ground pepper
1 tablespoon olive oil
½ handful of chervil, chopped

Mix the cream cheese and mustard together in a bowl, then stir in the lemon zest and juice, salt, pepper, oil, and, lastly, the chopped chervil.

In addition to being a lovely dip for potatoes and other summer vegetables, this is excellent in a sandwich or on a slice of rye bread.

Barbecued new potatoes
with two kinds of herb butter

2¼ lb new potatoes
sea salt flakes
1 to 2 tablespoons olive oil

Soak 8 to 10 wooden skewers in cold water for about 30 minutes to prevent them from burning on the barbecue.

Scrub the potatoes in cold water to remove all the soil. Put the potatoes in a saucepan of salted water so that it just covers them, bring to a boil, and cook for 6 to 8 minutes over low heat until soft but al dente. Drain and plunge them into cold water to stop the cooking process.

Drain the potatoes again and thread 4 to 6 onto each skewer. Brush with the olive oil and sprinkle with salt. Cook on a hot barbecue for a total of 3 to 5 minutes, remembering to turn them occasionally so that they get some color and are crisp on all sides.

Eat the hot potatoes with some herb butter (see below). Select the butter you like the best, or make a little of each kind. Serve as an accompaniment to barbecued food, such as the Barbecued Veal Chops with "Burnt" Summer Leeks on page 82, or as a small barbecue snack or appetizer.

Herb butter with parsley, garlic, and lemon

1 stick softened butter
1 handful of flat-leaf parsley
1 garlic clove, minced
finely grated zest and juice of
½ organic lemon
1 tablespoon soy sauce
sea salt flakes and freshly ground pepper

Put all the ingredients in a bowl and mix together well so that all the flavorings are evenly distributed in the butter. Transfer the herb butter to a clean bowl, or seal it in plastic wrap, form it into a small roll, and place in the refrigerator until it is completely cold. The butter will keep fresh for 2 months in the freezer or 1 week in the refrigerator.

Herb butter with Parmesan cheese and sweet basil

1 stick softened butter
2 tablespoons freshly grated
Parmesan cheese
1 handful of basil
1 tablespoon apple cider vinegar
sea salt flakes and freshly ground pepper

Make, chill, and store the herb butter as above.

Stuffed tomatoes
with wheat berries, herbs, and fresh goat cheese

8 tomatoes
1 onion
4 celery stalks
2 tablespoons olive oil, divided
1⅓ cups cooked grains, such as
    pearl barley
½ handful of parsley, chopped
½ handful of chervil, chopped
½ handful of basil, chopped
sea salt flakes and freshly ground pepper
1¾ oz fresh goat cheese

Cut a lid off the top of each tomato and scrape the flesh out with a teaspoon. Push the tomato flesh through a sieve placed over a bowl to extract the juice and remove the seeds. Peel and chop the onion, slice the celery finely, and sauté both vegetables briefly in 1 tablespoon of the oil. Remove from the heat, mix in the cooked grains, and add a little of the tomato juice as well as the chopped herbs. The grain filling should not be swimming in the juice, so add just enough to be absorbed. Season with salt and pepper.

Place a small dollop of goat cheese in each tomato, then some grain filling on top, and finish with a little more goat cheese. Put the tomatoes in an oiled ovenproof dish, drizzle with the remaining oil, and season with salt and pepper. Bake the tomatoes in a preheated oven at 425°F for 15 to 20 minutes or until they are baked through and beautifully "au gratin" on top.

Serve the tomatoes immediately. With a rich salad and some good bread, they will make a great main course, but you can also serve them as an accompaniment to a main course, especially lamb.

Crispy salad of summer cabbage
with peas and scallions

½ summer cabbage
2 tablespoons prepared mustard
2 tablespoons apple cider vinegar
sea salt flakes and freshly ground pepper
3 tablespoons cold-pressed canola oil
1 teaspoon sugar
4 scallions
⅔ cup freshly podded peas
1 handful of dill, coarsely chopped

Remove the stalk and, if necessary, the outer leaves of the cabbage and discard them. Slice the cabbage as finely as possible and place in cold water so that it becomes even more crisp.

Mix the mustard, vinegar, salt, and pepper together in a bowl. Whisk in the oil until the mixture is smooth and adjust the flavor with the sugar.

Slice the scallions very finely. Drain and dry the cabbage in a salad spinner, then place in a salad bowl and toss it with the scallions, peas, the vinaigrette, and the chopped dill. Finally, season with more salt and a little more pepper if you wish.

Young summer beets
with cottage cheese, smoked pork fat, and tarragon

12 small young beets
sea salt flakes
1 tablespoon cherry vinegar or other
    fruit vinegar
1 tablespoon cold-pressed canola oil
1 teaspoon acacia honey
freshly ground pepper
1 oz smoked pork fat (lard)
½ cup cottage cheese
½ handful of tarragon, chopped

Cut off the long green leafy tops from the beets as well as the roots. Wash the beets thoroughly in cold water so that you get all the soil off. Put them in a pan of salted water so that the water just covers them and bring to a boil for 7 to 8 minutes until soft but al dente. Drain and then plunge the beets into cold water to stop the cooking process.

Rub off the skin of the beet to uncover their silky interior (put on a pair of plastic gloves if necessary so that your hands are not completely stained red). Add the whole beets to a bowl with the vinegar, oil, honey, salt, and pepper and let them marinate for 10 to 15 minutes.

Cut the smoked pork fat into ½-inch cubes. Put the fat cubes in a cold skillet and fry them gently until they are crisp and the fat has rendered. Drain them in a sieve to remove the excess fat.

Serve the beets with a scoop of cottage cheese, and scatter with some crispy fat cubes and freshly chopped tarragon. Season finally with a little salt and pepper. Eat with bread as a small lunch dish, a juicy appetizer, or as part of a main course.

Baking and sweet things

Quick and easy rye bread

MAKES 1 LOAF

1 cup buttermilk
2½ cups cold water
⅔ cup beer
1 tablespoon sea salt flakes
¼ oz (1 tablespoon) fresh compressed
    yeast (baker's yeast)
1¾ cups chopped rye kernels
1½ cups flaxseed
1 cup sunflower seeds
¾ cup sesame seeds
2 cups wholemeal flour
3 cups rye flour
canola oil, for oiling

Put all the ingredients into the bowl of an electric stand mixer fitted with a dough hook and knead the dough for 10 minutes. Alternatively, give your arms a workout and knead the dough by hand in a large bowl.

Transfer the dough to an oiled rye bread pan with a 3½-quart capacity, cover the pan with plastic wrap, and place in the refrigerator for at least 12 hours before baking, preferably longer. The longer the dough sits, the more flavor the bread develops, but the maximum you can leave it is 6 days, otherwise the acidity of the finished bread will be too high.

Bake in a preheated oven at 350°F for 1½ hours. Invert the bread onto a wire rack to cool thoroughly before you slice it.

Almond and chocolate cake
with strawberries and lightly whipped cream

SERVES 6

Meringue layers
1 cup whole blanched almonds
2 organic egg whites (about ⅓ cup)
1 cup confectioners' sugar
3½ oz good-quality dark chocolate, such
    as Valrhona Manjari 64%

Filling
2 cups fresh strawberries
1 cup heavy whipping cream, lightly
    whipped
a few lemon balm tips

For the meringue, spread the almonds on a cookie sheet lined with parchment paper and roast them in a preheated oven at 315°F for 8 to 10 minutes or until golden and fragrant. Let the almonds cool, then chop them in a food processor or with a knife.

Whisk the egg whites until stiff, then whisk in the confectioners' sugar a little at a time and beat until you have a glossy and smooth meringue mixture. Chop the chocolate coarsely and fold into the meringue along with the chopped almonds.

Draw 2 circles, each about 10½ inches in diameter, on a piece of parchment paper placed on a cookie sheet . Spread the meringue mixture over them using a spatula for a neat result. Bake in a preheated oven at 325°F for about 15 minutes until crisp and golden on the outside but still slightly soft in the center.

Let the meringue layers cool, then carefully remove them from the parchment paper and place them on a cake plate.

For the filling, rinse the strawberries only if necessary, and then hull (see page 114).

Cut them in half and spread them out on the meringue layers, decorating with lightly whipped cream and a lemon balm tips. You can either make 2 open-faced cakes or place the layers on top of each other so that you have a single cake. Serve immediately while the meringue is still lovely and crisp.

WILD STRAWBERRIES
Commonly found in the wild and woodlands in summer—you'll need to hunt for a secret spot to find them!

Mirabelle plums

Mirabelle is the common name for small, early-ripening red and yellow plums, often found in the wild or planted in thickets, hedges, and cottage gardens. Mirabelles grow on robust bushes or as trees up to 30 feet in height with clear thorns at the ends of the branches and smooth, glossy leaves 1½ to 3¼ inches wide. The white blossom appears at the earliest time for fruit trees, in April to May. The individual trees cross-pollinate one another and produce a wealth of varying flavors.

Where to find mirabelles

Research your hunting ground for wild mirabelles in April to May when you should be able to see the first tiny fruits on the trees so that you can just go out and collect the fruit once they ripen in August. Occasionally you will find trees with fruits so

sweet and juicy that they resemble grapes. Mark their location on your GPS! Other mirabelles may not be as exciting in flavor, but they can still be used in marmalades or for pickling. Some mirabelles lack acidity, so you should always add a little apple cider vinegar or lemon juice to taste when cooking with the fruit, regardless of what the recipe calls for. Mirabelles can replace plums in most recipes.

Mirabelle marmalade

For this easy marmalade recipe, you will need 2¼ pounds mirabelles, 2½ cups sugar, 1 cup water, and ½ cup plum vinegar or other dark fruit vinegar.

Wash the mirabelles and remove the stalks. Add the fruit to a saucepan with the sugar and measured water, cover,

and bring to a boil. Once boiling point is reached, remove the lid and let simmer over low heat for 20 to 25 minutes, giving the mixture the occasional light stir, until you have a dense compote. Add the vinegar and cook the marmalade for another 10 to 15 minutes. Once the mirabelles are tender and blending together, the pits will float to the surface and you can then skim them off effortlessly. This way, you can avoid the tedious task of removing all the pits beforehand. The pits also contribute both flavor (bitterness) and pectin to the marmalade. Pour the marmalade into sterilized glass jars and seal tightly. This will keep fresh in the refrigerator for 4 to 6 weeks. You can vary the flavor by adding different fresh herbs, for example rosemary, thyme, mint, or tarragon.

Almond cake
with blackberries and white chocolate

SERVES 8

5 organic egg yolks
1 cup sugar
½ vanilla bean, split lengthwise and
    seeds scraped out
1½ sticks butter, plus extra for greasing
3½ oz good-quality white chocolate,
    such as Valrhona Ivoire 35%, chopped
1⅓ cups fresh blackberries
1⅔ cups whole blanched almonds
2 tablespoons all-purpose flour
2 organic egg whites

Beat the egg yolks, sugar, and vanilla seeds together until the mixture turns white and creamy with a consistency like egg nog.

Melt the butter and white chocolate gently in a bain-marie or a heatproof bowl set over a pan of barely simmering water. Stir the blackberries into the egg mixture and add the chocolate mixture. Chop the almonds finely—you can use a food processor for a finer texture—and fold into the batter with the flour.

Whisk the egg whites in another bowl until completely stiff and fold them into the batter.

Grease a springform cake pan, 9½ to 10½ inches in diameter, with butter and pour the batter into it. Bake in a preheated oven at 350°F for 30 to 35 minutes or until golden brown on the top and firm in the center. Remove the cake from the oven and let it cool on a wire rack before serving.

This is one of my favorite almond cakes. It is very moist and stays delicious for several days if you store it in a cool place. You can warm it before serving, but this is not necessary. In spring and early summer I make it with rhubarb and gooseberries, then later in summer with raspberries or, as here, with blackberries. It is not a light cake so, even though vanilla ice cream pairs well with just about everything, I actually prefer Yogurt Ice Cream with this (see page 246) or Homemade Sour Milk (see page 116).

Plum muffins
MAKES 12 TO 15 MUFFINS

1 stick softened butter, plus extra
    for greasing
1 cup jaggery
2 large organic eggs
1 cup all-purpose flour
¼ cup walnuts, finely chopped
10 ripe plums

Grease 12 to 15 holes of 1 to 2 muffin pans with butter.

Beat the butter and sugar together thoroughly until pale and fluffy, then add the eggs one at a time (don't add the second egg until the first one has been absorbed completely, to prevent the batter from splitting. Finally, add the flour and the walnuts and mix until well combined.

Cut the plums in half, discard the pits, slice the flesh into large cubes, and mix them into the batter.

Pour the batter evenly into the greased muffin holes and bake in a preheated oven at 400°F for about 15 minutes or until the muffins are completely golden and crispy on top. Serve warm.

Gooseberry trifle

Compote
1 lb 2 oz green or red gooseberries
¾ cup jaggery
½ vanilla bean, split lengthwise and
    seeds scraped out, bean reserved
finely grated zest and juice of
    ½ organic lemon

Custard
3 pasteurized egg yolks
½ cup confectioners' sugar
½ vanilla bean, split lengthwise and
    seeds scraped out
3 tablespoons heavy whipping cream

To finish
3½ oz Almond Macaroons (see page 114)
3 tablespoons sherry

For the compote, snip off the stems and flower ends from the gooseberries with a pair of kitchen scissors and rinse the fruit in cold water. Place the gooseberries in an ovenproof dish and toss them with sugar, vanilla seeds and bean, and lemon zest and juice. Bake in a preheated oven at 300°F for 20 to 25 minutes, tossing them around during the baking time so that the berries are well mixed with the vanilla and lemon. Let the baked gooseberries cool and then they are ready to join the trifle.

To make the custard, beat the egg yolks, sugar, and vanilla seeds together until white and with the creamy consistency of egg nog. Whip the cream to soft peaks, then fold it gently into the egg mixture so that both the whipped cream and the egg mixture retain their airiness. I usually add a single spoon of the whipped cream first and give it a proper stir, to completely mix it with the egg mixture, then it will be easier to fold in the rest of the whipped cream carefully to create an airy and well blended custard.

Assemble the trifle in layers in 4 glass dessert dishes, alternating between the compote, custard, and macaroons, sprinkling the macaroons with a little sherry along the way. It is now up to you whether you serve the trifle immediately or let it rest in the refrigerator so that the macaroons soften and combine with the compote. Personally, I prefer the latter method, but as with other classics, there are different schools of thought within the field of trifles.

Almond macaroons
MAKES ABOUT 25 TO 30 MACAROONS

⅔ cup whole blanched almonds
2 organic egg whites
½ cup sugar

Spread the almonds on a cookie sheet lined with parchment paper and roast them in a preheated oven at 315°F for 10 to 12 minutes. Let the almonds cool, then grind them as finely as possible in a food processor. Lower the oven temperature to 300°F.

Whisk the egg whites until stiff, adding 2 tablespoons of the sugar while whisking. Then fold the remaining sugar and the ground almonds gently into the egg whites.

Place the mixture in a wide, heavy saucepan and "roast" it over low heat until it is smooth. Let the batter cool slightly, then pour it into a pastry bag and pipe small blobs onto a cookie sheet lined with parchment paper, keeping an ample distance between them, because they will spread significantly. Bake the macaroons for about 15 minutes or until crisp on the outside and still slightly soft in the center. Transfer them to a wire rack to cool and then store them in a cake can until it is empty!

Elderflower granita
with strawberries

1 cup elderflower concentrate
    or cordial
1 cup water
2 tablespoons jaggery
1 tablespoon apple cider vinegar
6 to 8 fennel seeds
5 whole black peppercorns
3½ cups fresh strawberries, to serve

Bring all the ingredients except the strawberries to a boil in a saucepan. Once the mixture has reached boiling point, remove from the heat and let infuse for 30 minutes.

Pass the mixture through a sieve into a bowl and place the bowl in the freezer. Freeze for at least a few hours prior to use.

Rinse the strawberries only if necessary and then hull (*see* panel). When you are ready to serve, cut them into quarters and put them in a bowl or glass dish. Remove the granita from the freezer and, working quickly, scrape out the frozen mixture with a spoon to form elderflower "snow" or granita. Scrape as much as you need and serve immediately on top of the prepared strawberries, since the sour granita melts quickly.

Strawberries
with tarragon sugar and milk

4¼ cups fresh strawberries
¼ cup sugar
½ handful of tarragon, leaves picked
1¾ cups cold lowfat milk

Rinse the strawberries as little as possible, and only if they are very dirty, then snip the hulls (calyxes) off (*see* panel).

Divide the strawberries among large wide soup bowls. Use a hand-held stick blender to blend the sugar and tarragon leaves into a delicious green-flavored sugar and then sprinkle it over the strawberries. Pour the cold milk over the berries and serve immediately.

Tip Sweet cicely also has subtle notes of licorice, as does tarragon, so it makes a good substitute, and it grows wild in many places. Mint and lemon balm are also great alternatives to tarragon in this recipe.

Strawberries

Freshly picked strawberries are a delicacy—and they can be just as delicious when they reach the plate. After strawberries are picked, avoid rinsing them if they look clean, but if they should need washing, always do so with the hull (calyx) on, as the berries easily absorb water and even more so after hulling. As a result, the strawberries will lose some of their flavor and won't keep fresh for long. Strawberries at room temperature taste far superior to cold strawberries, so if you store the berries in the refrigerator, remember to take them out a few hours before serving or, even better, let them sit in the sun for a short time. Best of all is eating the berries directly from the plants while they are fresh and taste of the summer and sunshine.

I don't only encourage you to do this because of romantic notions of summer vacations, children with berry-stained smiles, and endless strawberry fields. It is a simple fact that the strawberries' natural sugar content is highest at the time they are picked and the sweet strawberry flavor will diminish from that moment onward.

Homemade sour milk
with strawberries and honey

SERVES 6

35 fl oz carton fresh organic whole milk
½ cup fresh organic buttermilk

To serve
1⅓ cups fresh strawberries
¼ cup liquid honey, to serve

Day 1
Pour ½ cup of the milk from the carton into a glass and drink it or use it for something else. Now replace the milk you have poured out with the buttermilk, close the carton, and shake it well so that the milk and buttermilk blend together. Let the mixture sit for 18 to 24 hours in the kitchen so that it thickens and turns sour. Don't shake the mixture while it is souring; it won't do the fermentation process any good. Once sour, store the sour milk in the refrigerator so that it is cold and fresh for serving.

Day 2
Rinse the strawberries only if necessary and then hull (see panel on page 114), and cut them into quarters. Pour the sour milk into 6 breakfast bowls or large, wide flat soup bowls and eat it with the strawberries and a drizzle of honey. Serve as part of a brunch or as a light summer dessert.

Raspberry sorbet
with vanilla and black pepper

4 cups fresh raspberries
4 cups water
2 cups jaggery
½ vanilla bean, split lengthwise and seeds scraped out, pod reserved
10 whole black peppercorns
finely grated zest of 1 organic lemon and the juice of 2

1 organic egg white and 2½ tablespoons superfine sugar (optional)

Put the raspberries in a pan with the 4 cups of water, sugar, vanilla seeds and bean, and peppercorns. Bring to a boil and cook for 3 to 4 minutes. Remove the pan from the heat and season with the lemon zest and juice. Let stand to infuse for 20 minutes.

Remove and discard the peppercorns and vanilla bean. Blend the raspberry syrup in a blender or with a hand-held stick blender. Strain the blended syrup through a coarse sieve, allowing a little of the raspberry flesh to pass through. Now follow the recipe for Rhubarb Sorbet on page 60 from step 3 to finish making the sorbet.

Enjoy the sorbet with fresh raspberries and maybe a little cold whipping cream.

Rødgrød
(red berry compote)

3½ fresh mixed berries, such as strawberries, currants, blueberries, and blackberries
⅔ cup fresh raspberries or blackberries
½ cup water
¾ cup sugar, plus extra for sprinkling
½ to 1 tablespoon potato flour mixed with a little cold water

Rinse the berries in cold water (but see panel on page 114 if using strawberries) and then remove the stems and hulls. Put all the berries except the raspberries or blackberries in a pan with the ½ cup water and sugar, stir well, and let steep for a few hours so that they give off some of their juices.

Place the pan over low heat and bring to a boil, skim off the foam, and cook the berries for 2 to 3 minutes. Remove the pan from the heat and gently stir in the raspberries so that they remain as whole as possible.

Thicken the compote with the potato-flour paste by adding it when the berries are just below boiling point; it is important that the compote is still warm, but if it boils after the potato flour has been added, the texture will be gooey.

Sprinkle the compote with a thin layer of sugar to prevent a skin from forming and let cool in the refrigerator. Serve the berry compote with milk, cream, or a scoop of good vanilla ice cream (see page 60)

Rødgrød with milk

Although many Danes today rarely eat *rødgrød*, we all agree that it is truly a national dish, perhaps most of all because it is what we torture foreigners with when we can't resist demonstrating their inability to pronounce our difficult language in the phrase *rødgrød med fløde*—red berry compote with cream. In fact, we have only cooked this type of fruit compote for the past hundred years or so, since it wasn't until the advent of domestic sugar-beet production in the late 1800s that sugar became affordable enough for fruit compotes to be a common summer dish on Danish dinner tables. A perfectly cooked, smooth compote with a mixture of mild and intensely flavored berries served with ice-cold milk and crunchy sugar is royal dining indeed.

FOREST RASPBERRIES
If you find yourself in a humid forest glade, you may be lucky enough to find wild raspberries hiding under the leaves!

Raspberry sorbet »

« **Refrigerator preserved redcurrants**

Refrigerator preserved redcurrants

1 lb 2 oz (about 4½ cups) fresh redcurrants
1 cup sugar

Rinse the redcurrants in cold water and remove them from their stems. Alternatively, opt for the rustic solution of leaving the stems on (it looks so beautiful, too). Drain the currants well in a colander, then layer them with the sugar in a dish. Be careful not to stir the currants too much, otherwise you risk them bursting. Let the currants chill in the refrigerator for an hour.

Serve the preserved currants with ice cream, a cake, or just with lightly whipped cream, or with skyr that has been softened with a little milk.

Blackberry trifle

Custard
½ vanilla bean
2 organic egg yolks
3 tablespoons sugar
1 tablespoon cornstarch
1¼ cups lowfat milk

To assemble
3½ oz Almond Macaroons (*see* page 114)
3 tablespoons sherry
1⅓ cups blackberries
½ cup heavy whipping cream, lightly whipped
finely grated zest of ½ organic orange

First make the custard. Split the vanilla bean lengthwise, scrape the seeds out, and, using the flat side of your knife, crush them with a little of the sugar on a cutting board. Add the vanilla seeds and bean and the remaining ingredients to a pan, stir well, and bring to a boil while whisking vigorously. Boil the custard for 2 to 3 minutes or until it is thick and smooth.

Pour the custard into a small bowl and place in the refrigerator to cool completely.

When the custard is cold, it is time to build your trifle. Crumble the macaroons lightly and place in the base of a serving bowl or individual serving glasses, reserving some for a final sprinkling, then drizzle with the sherry. Place the blackberries on top and then a little custard. Repeat until you have used up the blackberries and custard. Finish with a topping of lightly whipped cream and a sprinkling of crushed macaroons and grated orange zest. Let the trifle soften in the refrigerator for 30 to 60 minutes before serving.

....

TIP Trifle is easy to vary according to the season—the combination of macaroons, fruit, and custard is eternally good, whether it is hot or cold outside (I can always squeeze down a small trifle), and you can make it with all manner of fruits or berries, for example, gooseberries (*see* page 113), plums, stewed apples and quinces, pickled cherries, rhubarb in spring, and so on. I alternate between using the cream in the form of a cooked vanilla custard, as here, or an uncooked vanilla cream, as in the aforementioned Gooseberry Trifle recipe.
....

Blackberry parfait
with aquavit and homemade almond macaroons

SERVES 6 TO 8

⅔ cup fresh blackberries
1 tablespoon aquavit
2 cups heavy whipping cream
5 pasteurized egg yolks
½ vanilla bean, split lengthwise and seeds scraped out
⅓ cup sugar
3 to 5 grains of coarse salt
Almond Macaroons (*see* page 114), to serve

Make sure all the ingredients are cold—and the bowls as well. Put the blackberries in a small bowl, drizzle with the aquavit, and let steep in the kitchen for 10 minutes.

Whisk the remaining ingredients together using an electric stand mixer or an electric hand mixer until softly whipped.

Mash the aquavit-soaked blackberries lightly with a fork and mix them into the parfait cream. Pour the cream into a loaf pan or into small ramekins and place in the freezer. Freeze the parfait for 2 to 3 hours before serving. You can leave it in the freezer for 2 to 3 days before it gets too hard and forms large ice crystals. Remove the parfait from the freezer about 30 minutes before serving (a little less if you have used ramekins) and serve with the macaroons.

The addition of aquavit in the parfait affects both the flavor and the texture—the parfait will be softer, since the alcohol prevents the mixture from freezing really hard. You can, however, also make the dessert without it.

....

TIP This parfait doesn't require an ice-cream maker, just a bowl, a whisk, and a freezer and, unlike other parfaits, you don't need to whisk the cream and egg yolks separately. It is simply an ultra-easy ice cream! I always add a little salt to my parfait mixtures, because it accents the sweetness and enhances the flavor of cream, eggs, and vanilla. And I vary the recipe extensively—this parfait can be made with virtually any berry.
....

Blackberries
with sugar-roasted rye bread and whipped cream

4 slices of day-old rye bread
2 tablespoons sugar
1 tablespoon melted butter
1 cup heavy whipping cream
2¾ cups fresh blackberries

Cut the bread into very small cubes. Spread the bread cubes out in an ovenproof dish, sprinkle with the sugar, and drizzle with the melted butter. Bake the bread cubes in a preheated oven at 325°F for 10 to 15 minutes until they are perfectly crisp, stirring a couple of times during baking.

Whip the cream to a light foam. Divide the blackberries between 4 individual bowls, top with the whipped cream and toasted rye bread cubes, and enjoy as an effortless and lovely dessert.

We have blackberries in our garden, so we often eat them for breakfast with rye bread croutons, and yogurt, but our children often ask for a scoop of whipped cream on top, too!

Buttermilk dessert

3 pasteurized egg yolks
¾ cup sugar
seeds from ½ vanilla bean
2 cups buttermilk
2 cups Homemade Sour Milk
 (see page 116)
finely grated zest and juice of 1 lemon
1 handful of lemon balm, chopped
Toasted Oat Flakes (see right)

Whisk the egg yolks and sugar together until pale and the sugar has dissolved.

Mix the vanilla seeds into the egg mixture, reserving the vanilla bean. Gently add the buttermilk, sour milk, vanilla bean, and lemon zest and juice. Stir well until thoroughly combined.

Place the buttermilk dessert in the refrigerator and let infuse for at least 2 to 3 hours before serving. When it is time for dessert, sprinkle the buttermilk with the chopped lemon balm and Toasted Oat Flakes, and serve immediately.

Toasted oat flakes

2 cups rolled oats
3 tablespoons honey
12 teaspoons butter
10 sea salt flakes

Toast the oats lightly in a dry skillet until golden and crisp. Add the honey, butter, and salt to the pan and stir well with a wooden spoon until the oats are evenly caramelized, which usually takes just a few minutes.

Pour the oats onto a cookie sheet lined with parchment paper and let them cool. They are now ready to use.

Cream dessert
with elderflower gelatin

SERVES 6

Cream dessert
3 gelatin sheets
2 cups heavy whipping cream
1½ tablespoons jaggery
½ vanilla bean, spit lengthwise and
 seeds scraped out, bean reserved
3 tablespoons elderflower concentrate
 or cordial

Elderflower jelly
1 gelatin sheet
½ cup elderflower concentrate or cordial

For the cream dessert, soak the gelatin sheets in cold water for 5 minutes. Put the cream, sugar, vanilla seeds and bean, and elderflower concentrate or cordial in a saucepan and bring to a boil. As soon as the mixture reaches boiling point, remove from the heat and add the well drained gelatin. Let the cream mixture sit in the pan for 30 minutes. Pour it into a pitcher, and then divide among 6 glass dessert dishes. Chill for at least 6 hours before serving.

To make the elderflower gelatin, soak the gelatin sheet in cold water for 5 minutes, drain it well, and place in a small saucepan along with the elderflower concentrate or cordial. Heat the mixture carefully so that the gelatin sheets melt, then let cool until the mixture begins to stiffen a little.

Spread the cooled but still liquid gelatin on top of the cream dessert in the serving glasses and return them to the refrigerator for a few hours until serving. You now have a small dessert that is sweet enough as it is, but may be accompanied by a bowl of ripe strawberries. For extra flair, you can throw a few slices of strawberry or some fresh elderflowers into the gelatin mixture—my girls love it.

Tip This tastes wonderful too if you replace the elderflower gelatin with pink rhubarb gelatin, made exactly the same way but using Rhubarb Cordial (see page 57).

Cream dessert

Gelatin-based dishes have been known for centuries and even by the late Middle Ages it was highly regarded to serve a clear gelatin inlaid with various beautiful ingredients. Desserts using gelatin such as *risalamande* (Danish rice pudding), mousses, and cream desserts, such as the one above, grew in popularity in the second half of the 1800s. At their peak in the 20th century, every self-respecting kitchen had a ring mold in which to set cream desserts. In this recipe, I have cut down on the gelatin to achieve a more delicate consistency. You can substitute half of the cream with milk if you prefer a lighter dessert.

Fall

Seasonal ingredients

Cultivated produce

apples
beets
Belgian endive
blackberries
Brussels sprouts
cabbage
carrots
cauliflower
celery root
cod
corn
eel
elderberries
garfish
green beans

green tomatoes
haddock
hare
herring
horseradish
Jerusalem artichoke
kale
kohlrabi
leeks
lingonberries
lobster
nuts
onions
parsley
pears

plums
pumpkin
quince
salsify
sea trout
venison
weever
wild duck

In the wild

chanterelles
ceps
rowan berries
quince
apples
hazelnuts
chestnuts
cranberries
oyster mushrooms
woodcocks
horn of plenty

yellowfoot mushrooms
sea beet
sloes
sheathed woodtuft
blue stalk mushrooms

Soups and appetizers

Onion soup
with cheese on toast

5 large onions
2 garlic cloves
2 teaspoons butter
8 thyme sprigs
sea salt flakes and freshly ground pepper
1½ quarts water or light chicken stock
2 tablespoons apple cider vinegar

Peel the onions and garlic cloves. Cut the onions in half and slice them finely.

Melt the butter in a large saucepan, add the onions, whole garlic cloves, and thyme sprigs and sauté gently until the onions begin to caramelize and take on a little color. Add salt and pepper to taste and sauté for a further 2 to 3 minutes. Add the water or stock and let the soup simmer over low heat for 20 minutes.

Season the soup with the vinegar and possibly a little more salt and pepper if necessary. Eat the soup piping hot, with warm Cheese on Toast (see below).

Cheese on toast

8 slices of day-old white bread
1 tablespoon standard canola oil
1 cup freshly grated hard cheese,
    such as Høost or Grana Padano
sea salt flakes and freshly ground pepper

Brush the bread slices with the oil, place them on a broiler rack, and toast them under the broiler for about 1 minute each side or until the bread is crisp and golden. Remove the bread slices from the broiler, scatter with the grated cheese, and put them back under the broiler for a further 30 seconds so that the cheese melts. Season to taste with salt and pepper and serve immediately while warm and crisp.

Yellow split pea soup
with parsley and horseradish

1¼ cups dried yellow split peas
2 quarts water
2 onions
2 garlic cloves
1 lb 2 oz pork belly
8 sausages from Southern Jutland
    or any smoked pork sausage
½ handful of thyme sprigs
3 carrots
½ celery root
5 to 7 large potatoes
3 leeks
10½ oz baby onions
sea salt flakes and freshly ground pepper
2 to 3 tablespoons apple cider vinegar
½ handful of parsley
1 oz fresh horseradish root

Drain the split peas and put them in a pan with the measured water. Peel the onions and garlic, then cut them into fairly large chunks. Add them to the pan along with the pork belly, sausages, and thyme sprigs and bring the soup to a boil. Skim off any foam or impurities, then simmer for about 45 minutes until the split peas are tender.

Lift the pork belly and sausages out, then blend the split peas and onions, thyme, and broth in the pan with a hand-held stick blender to a coarse purée (remove the thyme sprigs first, if you like).

Peel the carrots, celery root, and potatoes, then cut the vegetables into ½-inch cubes. Cut off the roots and tops of the leeks, then cut them into rings and wash them thoroughly in a bowl of cold water so that you get all the soil off. Peel the baby onions but keep them whole. Add all the vegetables to the pea soup along with the pork belly and sausages and simmer for a further 20 minutes until the vegetables are tender. Dilute the soup with a little extra water if it is too thick, and season to taste with salt, pepper, and the vinegar.

Finally, rinse the parsley, let drain thoroughly, then coarsely chop it. Peel and grate the horseradish, then mix it with the chopped parsley and stir into the soup. Serve the steaming hot yellow split pea soup in bowls and scattered with extra thyme leaves. Serve the pork belly and sausages as sides, and put some bread and mustard on the table as well. You may also want to consider beer and aquavit as accompaniments.

. . . .

Tip Old-fashioned yellow split peas are perfect with pork, but you can just as readily make a vegetarian version of this soup. Simply omit the pork belly and sausages and follow the recipe opposite.

. . . .

Creamy kale soup

9 oz curly kale, stalks removed
sea salt flakes and freshly ground pepper
4 cups chicken stock
3 tablespoons heavy whipping cream
2 to 3 tablespoons apple cider vinegar
2 apples

Check the kale for any bits of stalk, discard them, and wash the kale thoroughly in cold water. Let drain in a colander. Reserve about 1¾ ounces of the kale, then blanch the rest in a pan of boiling salted water for 2 to 3 minutes. Drain and immediately plunge it into a bowl of cold water to stop the cooking process, then drain in a colander.

Heat the stock up in a saucepan. Chop the blanched kale coarsely and put it in a blender, pour in the hot stock, and blend until the soup is completely smooth. Season with the cream, salt, pepper, and finally the vinegar. It is important that the vinegar is added just before serving, otherwise the soup will lose its bright green color.

Pour the soup back into the saucepan. Cut the apples into quarters, remove the cores, and cut into small pieces. Cut the reserved raw kale into thin strips and add to the soup with the apple as a garnish. Heat the soup and serve with some good bread.

Potato soup

2 baking potatoes
3½ to 4 cups water
1 shallot, peeled and minced
½ garlic clove, peeled and minced
9 oz fresh spinach, washed
1 tablespoon standard canola oil
sea salt flakes and freshly ground pepper

Peel and slice the potatoes thinly. Put them in a saucepan and add the water, then cook for about 15 to 20 minutes until tender.

Lightly sauté the shallot and garlic in the oil in a separate saucepan without browning. Chop the spinach coarsely, throw it into the pan, and sauté for about 30 seconds. Pour the cooked potatoes with their cooking water into the pan and simmer the soup for a maximum of 2 minutes so that it stays fresh and green. Blend in a blender or with a hand-held stick blender until smooth, then pass it through a coarse sieve, if necessary, to make sure there are no lumps.

Season with salt and pepper to taste, then serve piping hot scattered with Crispy Croutons (see below). You can serve it as an appetizer, or as a main course with a nice salad, some cooked grains, or cold meat.

Crispy croutons

2 slices of day-old white bread
2 tablespoons standard canola oil
sea salt flakes

Cut the bread slices coarsely into pieces and toss them in the oil and some salt.

Spread the bread pieces out on a cookie sheet lined with parchment paper and bake in a preheated oven at 325°F for 5 to 6 minutes until crisp and golden.

. . . .

TIP Have some lovely pears for dessert—they are in their prime right now. In my family we love to peel the pears at the table, and then drizzle them with a little lemon juice, which enhances their flavor.

. . . .

Creamy root vegetable soup
with crisp bacon and chopped parsley

1½ lb mixed root vegetables, such as
    celery root, carrots, parsley roots,
    and parsnips
1 apple
2 garlic cloves, peeled
3 thyme sprigs
1 tablespoon standard canola oil
2 quarts water
3 tablespoons heavy whipping cream
sea salt flakes and freshly ground pepper
2 to 3 tablespoons apple cider vinegar
1 oz bacon
½ handful of parsley

Wash and peel the root vegetables, then cut them into large cubes. Core the apple, but leave the peel on, and cut it into large cubes as well. Add the root vegetables, apple, whole garlic cloves, and thyme sprigs to the hot canola oil in a large saucepan, and sauté over low heat for 5 minutes until the root vegetables begin to brown and caramelize. Add the measured water and let the soup simmer, with a lid on, for 15 minutes, then add the cream and cook for a further 5 minutes.

Blend the mixture to a smooth and even consistency with a hand-held stick blender, and season to taste with salt, pepper, and the vinegar. A note here on using vinegar: it is a basic seasoning component in line with salt, pepper, and sugar, and if you haven't yet tried adjusting the taste of your food with vinegar, you will discover that the flavors unfold and come into balance. I would not dream of making a soup of heavy, sweet-tasting root vegetables without giving it a splash of acid. Taste the soup before and after you add the vinegar, then you will know what I am talking about.

When the soup is cooked and seasoned to perfection, cut the bacon into small cubes and fry it in a skillet until crisp.

Chop the parsley. Heat the soup up again and serve with the crisp bacon and chopped parsley on top with some good bread on the side. Toast is certainly not a bad idea!

Smoked salmon
with pearl barley, walnuts, and apples

¾ cup pearl barley (uncooked)
1¼ cups water
sea salt flakes and freshly ground pepper
1 tablespoon standard canola oil
finely grated zest and juice
    of ½ organic lemon
1 teaspoon acacia honey
2 celery stalks
1 oz fresh baby spinach
1 apple
1½ tablespoons walnuts
5¾ oz thinly sliced smoked salmon
    (or sea trout)

Rinse the pearl barley well in cold water. Put it in a saucepan, add the 1¼ cups of water and a little salt, and bring to a boil. Simmer with the lid on for about 20 minutes. Take the pan off the heat and let the barley stand, covered, for 5 to 10 minutes.

When the barley is done—it should be tender but still al dente—season to taste with salt and pepper.

Whisk the oil, lemon zest and juice, honey, salt, and pepper together in a bowl to make a dressing and let stand for 5 to 10 minutes to allow the flavors to develop.

Rinse the celery and spinach. Slice the celery very finely and mix with the spinach in a large bowl. Cut the apple into quarters, remove the core, and slice it very finely. Add it to the bowl, along with the cooked pearl barley and the walnuts, coarsely chopped. Mix the dressing into the salad and serve it with thin slices of smoked salmon (or sea trout) and some good bread.

Marinated herring
with carrots and onions

2 red onions
3 carrots
½ cup cold-pressed canola oil
½ cup apple cider vinegar
½ cup jaggery
½ cup water
4 bay leaves
1 tablespoon whole black peppercorns
1 tablespoon juniper berries
1 tablespoon coriander seeds
2 tablespoons prepared mustard
10 good-quality marinated herring fillets
1 large handful of dill

Peel the onions and carrots, then cut the onions into wedges and the carrots into slices. Place the vegetables in a saucepan along with the rest of the ingredients, except the herrings and dill, and cook until you have a syrupy consistency. Take the pan off the heat and let cool completely.

Put the herring fillets in a large, sterilized preserving jar, pour the cold syrup over them, and, finally, add the dill. Seal the jar tightly, put it in the refrigerator, and let stand for at least 3 days before you eat the herring.

Serve the herring on rye bread, topped with raw onions and possibly some fresh dill. The marinated herring will keep fresh, unopened and refrigerated, for 2 to 3 months and about 20 to 25 days once opened.

ROWANBERRIES
Remember to put a few bags of rowanberries in the freezer now to feed the wild birds in winter.

Pan-roasted herrings
with beets and apple vinaigrette

10 double herring fillets
a little wasabi paste or
    3 to 4 tablespoons freshly
    grated horseradish
sea salt flakes and freshly ground pepper
½ cup rye flour
1¼ cups apple cider vinegar
1¼ cups water
1⅓ cups jaggery
2 beets
2 apples
1 tablespoon standard canola oil
2 teaspoons butter

Check that herring fillets are fresh and smell of the sea, not of the harbor. Spread a very thin layer of wasabi paste on the flesh side of the herring fillets (it is super strong, so be careful with the amount) or sprinkle the fillets with the freshly grated horseradish. Season with salt and pepper, fold the fillets together, and dust the skin side with the rye flour.

Add the vinegar, 1¼ cups of water, and the sugar to a saucepan and bring the mixture to a boil. Peel the beets and cut them into small cubes. Core the apples and cut them into thin wedges—the apple pieces should be bigger than the beets because their cooking time is not the same. Add the apple and beets to the hot syrup and simmer for 2 minutes so that the syrup takes on both flavor and color.

Heat up a skillet and add the oil, and when that is hot, add the butter. When the butter has stopped bubbling, fry the herring fillets for about 3 minutes on each side until golden and crisp. It may be necessary to press down a little on the folded fillets with a lifter just after you have put them in the pan so that they don't unfold.

Transfer the fried herrings to a dish and pour the hot syrup over them. Let stand in the refrigerator for a few days to soak before you enjoy them (they will keep fresh for up to 1 week). Serve the pan-roasted herrings with the beets and apple vinaigrette on rye bread, preferably topped with capers and dill.

TIP Store the broth from the chicken, either in the refrigerator or in the freezer. It is always good to have on hand for making soup or risotto, or to use as a braising liquid.

Crudité of turnip, pears, and Savoy cabbage

½ turnip
2 pears, such as Conference or Doyenne
    du Comice
¼ Savoy cabbage
3 to 4 tablespoons apple cider vinegar
2 tablespoons standard canola oil
2 tablespoons acacia honey
sea salt flakes and freshly ground pepper
3½ tablespoons sunflower seeds

Peel the turnip, grate it on the coarse side of the grater, and place it in a bowl. Cut the pears into quarters and remove the cores, then cut them lengthwise into very thin wedges and add them to the bowl. Separate the leaves of the Savoy cabbage and wash them in cold water. Drain thoroughly and slice very finely, then add them to the bowl with the turnip and pears.

Mix the vinegar, oil, honey, salt, and pepper together in a separate bowl to make a dressing, then pour it over the turnip, cabbage, and pears.

Toast the sunflower seeds in a dry skillet until they are golden and beginning to pop. Season the crudités with additional salt and pepper, if needed, and scatter the toasted sunflower seeds on top. Serve as a small everyday appetizer.

Rillette of pheasant
with mustard and pickled squash with dill

SERVES 8

2 cleaned pheasants
1 tablespoon canola oil
2 carrots
2 onions
sea salt flakes and freshly ground pepper
2 garlic cloves
5 thyme sprigs
12 fl oz bottle dark beer
½ cup apple cider vinegar,
    plus extra to season
3 cups water or chicken stock

Check the pheasants for any feather stumps and pluck them out. Pat the cavities dry with paper towels. Follow the instructions in the tip on page 146 for cutting up the birds, saving the breasts for that recipe and the carcass for making stock.

Brown the pheasant legs and any leftovers from the breast in the oil in a large, hot Dutch oven. Peel the carrots and onions, cut into large chunks, and throw them into the pan as well. Season with salt and pepper and let the vegetables brown with the pheasant for a few minutes.

Peel the garlic cloves, add to the pan whole with the thyme sprigs, beer, vinegar, and stock, and bring to a boil. Then simmer over low heat, with the lid on, for 45 minutes to 1 hour until the meat is very tender.

Lift the pheasant legs out of the pan and place on a cutting board. Let the rest of the stew reduce until one-third of the broth remains.

Meanwhile, carve the meat off the legs, discarding the skin and bones. Make sure you remove the big tendons in the thighs as well and also check that there is no shot left in the meat. Add the meat to the stew again and mash around lightly with a whisk. That way, the broth, meat, and vegetables integrate much better with one another to form a delicate and rustic rillette. You should probably fish the thyme sprigs out first, especially if they are coarse and hard to chew. Season with salt, pepper, and a little extra vinegar, then pour the rillette into sterilized preserving jars where it will keep for 30 to 40 days if stored in the refrigerator.

Serve the pheasant rillette with toast and Pickled Squash with Dill (see below) as an appetizer or for lunch. If you want to make this a slightly larger dish, add a small green salad with walnuts, parsley, and some good apple balsamic vinegar.

Pickled squash with dill
MAKES 2 JARS

1 winter squash, such as Hokkaido or
    butternut
2 tablespoons coarse sea salt

Pickling brine
2 cups apple cider vinegar
2 cups water
2 cups jaggery
1 cinnamon stick
4 star anise
15 whole black peppercorns
3 dill stems

Day 1
Peel and halve the squash, then scrape out the seeds with a spoon. Cut the squash into slices about ½ inch thick, place them in a dish, and sprinkle them with the coarse salt. Let stand in the refrigerator for 12 hours.

Day 2
Rinse the squash slices in cold water and divide them between 2 sterilized preserving jars. Put the ingredients for the pickling brine in a saucepan and bring to a boil. Then pour the boiling mixture over the squash slices and seal the jars tightly. Place the jars in the refrigerator, in a cellar, or another cool place and let stand for about a week before eating. The pickled squash will keep fresh, refrigerated, for 6 months, and meanwhile you can enjoy it with virtually anything that simply lacks a little acidity.

Tip This pickling recipe also works really well with root vegetables like celery root, parsley roots, and parsnips, which you can prepare in exactly the same way as the squash. If using beets, they will need to be cooked first.

APPLES
Save a surplus of windfall apples for feeding wild birds in winter.

Marinated venison fillet
with kale purée and salad with refrigerator-pickled lingonberries

SERVES 8 TO 10

3 whole venison fillets (filet mignon or tenderloin), about 10½ oz each (or use lamb fillets)
½ cup sea salt flakes
1 cup unrefined brown sugar, not packed
2 tablespoons coriander seeds
2 tablespoons juniper berries
10 whole black peppercorns
1½ tablespoons fennel seeds
7 to 8 allspice berries
1 star anise

Trim off any tendons from the fillets and put the meat in a deep dish. Mix the salt, brown sugar, and spices together, then cover the meat completely in the mixture. Cover the dish with plastic wrap and let stand in the refrigerator, at a temperature of about 41°F, for 2 to 3 days. Turn the meat every day so that it is marinated evenly—it is important that the meat is covered in liquid throughout the process.

Remove the meat from the refrigerator when it feels firm but is still red inside. Strain off the liquid and discard it, reserving the spices. Crush them coarsely using a mortar and pestle. Wipe the meat lightly with paper towels and cover it again with the spices. Put it in a clean dish and place in the refrigerator for a further 24 hours, but this time without the plastic wrap so that the surface of the meat dries out a little.

Slice the meat very thinly with a very sharp knife and serve it with Kale Purée and Salad with Refrigerator-pickled Lingonberries (see right). Put some wholegrain bread on the table as well. Enjoy as an appetizer or lunch dish.

Tip The meat will keep fresh for 10 to 12 days in the refrigerator if it is tightly sealed in plastic wrap or in a container with a lid, so it does pay to marinate a few fillets all at once. If you don't have the opportunity to eat it all in that time, you can also store it in the freezer.

Kale purée and salad with refrigerator-pickled lingonberries

2 tablespoons fresh or frozen lingonberries (see tip below)
1 tablespoon jaggery
3½ oz curly kale, stalks removed
sea salt flakes and freshly ground pepper
finely grated zest and juice of ½ organic lemon
1 tablespoon olive oil

Sprinkle the lingonberries with the sugar in a bowl and let them marinate for 10 minutes. Meanwhile, check the kale for bits of stalk and discard, then wash it thoroughly in cold water and set in a colander to drain.

Throw two-thirds of the kale into a pan of salted boiling water and cook for about 5 minutes until tender but still retaining its green color. Transfer the kale to a blender with just the cooking water that is clinging to it, add salt, pepper, and the lemon zest and blend to a smooth purée. Transfer the purée to a bowl.

Chop the remaining raw kale very finely, dress it with the olive oil and lemon juice, and let marinate for 2 minutes. Season with salt and pepper. Serve with the kale purée and lingonberries to accompany the marinated venison fillet.

Tip If you can't get hold of fresh or frozen lingonberries, replace them with some good-quality and not-too-sweet lingonberry jam.

FALL GAME
Fall is game season and the hunt is now on!

Meat

Meatloaf
with lingonberries and homemade "sauerkraut"

2 slices of day-old white bread
⅔ cup lowfat milk
3½ oz mixed root vegetables, such as carrots, celery root, and parsley roots
1 small onion
9 oz ground veal, 5 to 7% fat
9 oz ground pork, 5 to 7% fat
sea salt flakes and freshly ground pepper
1 organic egg, lightly beaten
3 thyme sprigs, chopped
3½ oz bacon, divided

Sauce
1 tablespoon butter
1 tablespoon all-purpose flour
2½ cup lowfat milk
2 bay leaves
sea salt flakes and freshly ground pepper
3 tablespoons heavy whipping cream
2 tablespoons fresh or frozen lingonberries (*see* tip on page 134)
⅛ to ¼ oz blue cheese

Cut the bread slices into small cubes and let them soak in the milk for 10 to 15 minutes. Meanwhile, wash and peel the root vegetables, then grate them finely. Peel and dice the onion as finely as you can.

Put the ground meat in a bowl and add the root vegetables, onion, salt, pepper, egg, thyme, and finally the soaked bread and mix well. Cut half of the bacon into small cubes and incorporate it into the mixture. Let the mixture stand in the refrigerator while you make the sauce.

Melt the butter in a saucepan and add the flour, stirring, to make a smooth roux. Turn the heat down and add the milk, a little at a time. Stir continuously so that the sauce cooks evenly, then add the bay leaves, salt, and pepper. Simmer the sauce for 5 to 6 minutes.

Form the meat mixture into a loaf, place in an ovenproof dish, and place the remaining bacon slices on top. Pour the sauce into the dish with the meatloaf and bake in a preheated oven at 325°F for 50 minutes to 1 hour. Check whether the meatloaf is done by inserting a metal skewer into it. If the skewer is hot when you pull it out again and the liquid that trickles out is clear, it is ready.

Take the meatloaf out of the oven and pour the sauce into a saucepan. Heat the sauce up, add the cream, and season with the lingonberries, salt, pepper, and the blue cheese. Slice the meatloaf up and serve with the sauce, potatoes, and fresh Homemade "Sauerkraut" (*see* right).

A history of meatloaf

When Denmark was a major producer of bacon for the UK market around 1900, Danish housewives were duty bound to use more pork when cooking. At that time, the industry was lobbying for adding half ground pork to the traditional veal and beef in the ground-meat dishes that had already become fashionable in the first decades of the 20th century. This trend was aided by the meat grinder, with which most kitchens in Denmark had been equipped during this period. The combination of pork and veal or beef appeared not least in the many substitutes for a roast that were created at the time. One of them was the meatloaf, first mentioned in the last edition of A. M. Mangor's cookbook from 1910 under the name "Chinese hare," but later renamed as "meatloaf" by Miss Jensen, who also supplemented the dish with brown gravy, browned potatoes, and currant or lingonberry jelly. I have made a lighter version by adding root vegetables and also some crunchy cabbage, since the loaf itself doesn't have a lot of bite to it.

Homemade "sauerkraut"

1 small white cabbage
10 caraway seeds
10 dill seeds
8 juniper berries
1 cup hard dry cider
1 cup apple cider vinegar
1 tablespoon sea salt flakes
2 tablespoons honey, plus extra to season
freshly ground pepper
4 shallots

Cut the white cabbage into quarters, shred it very finely using a knife, and put it in a large bowl.

Crush the spices using a mortar and pestle and add them to a saucepan along with the cider, vinegar, salt, and honey. Bring to a boil and then pour the mixture over the cabbage. Mix well so that all the cabbage is marinated, and season with pepper.

Peel the shallots, slice them very finely, and add them to the bowl as well, tossing everything to coat thoroughly. Now season with more honey, salt, and pepper to taste. Let the cabbage marinate for 1 hour at room temperature before serving.

The cabbage will keep fresh for 10 to 12 days in the refrigerator. In fact, the flavor is actually enhanced after a few days.

TIP If you don't have any hard cider, use some good apple juice instead. I often make this same fresh sauerkraut with red cabbage instead, using a cherry or plum vinegar and a little cherry juice instead of apple cider vinegar and hard cider.

Braised beef ribs
with potato and squash purée

4½ lb forerib of beef
sea salt flakes and freshly ground pepper
3 garlic cloves
2 onions
2 carrots
3 large parsley stems
2 thyme sprigs
5 bay leaves
3 rosemary sprigs
1¾ cups strong red wine
1 cup water
2 tablespoons apple cider vinegar
a little sugar
2 teaspoons to 1 tablespoon cold butter

Score the ribs by making small cuts through the meat and fat, and season with salt and pepper. In an ovenproof dish, make a bed using the whole garlic cloves, onions, and carrots, peeled and cut into chunks, parsley stems, thyme sprigs, bay leaves, and rosemary sprigs. Place the forerib on top and pour the red wine and the measured water into the dish. Roast the forerib in a preheated oven at 325°F for 1½ hours, regularly basting the meat with the sauce. Add a little extra water, if necessary, to prevent too much of the sauce from evaporating.

Take the dish out of the oven and strain the sauce into a saucepan. Skim off the fat and adjust the flavor with the vinegar, salt, pepper, and sugar. Pour the sauce into a blender, add the parsley stems and rosemary sprigs (discarding the thyme and bay leaves), and blend it with the cold butter into a smooth, creamy sauce. Remove the bones from the meat (they should come away easily), then cut the meat into thick slices and pour the sauce over it. Serve immediately with the Potato and Squash Purée (see right) and some wholegrain bread.

Potato and squash purée

2¼ lb baking potatoes
14 oz winter squash, such Hokkaido
   or butternut
1 cup lowfat milk
3½ tablespoons butter
sea salt and freshly ground pepper

Peel the potatoes and squash. Halve the squash and scrape out the seeds with a spoon. Cut the potatoes and squash into 1¼- to 1½-inch chunks and place them in a saucepan with enough water to cover. Bring to a boil and cook for 25 to 30 minutes until they are tender. Drain and let sit in the pan for 2 to 3 minutes to cool slightly.

Heat up the milk in a small saucepan. Cut the butter into small cubes. Mash the vegetables with a potato masher or whisk, add the hot milk and butter, and beat until completely smooth and soft. Then season with salt and pepper. The purée is now ready to be served.

HAZELNUTS
If you are lucky enough to find crisp, fresh hazelnuts, they are a real delicacy at this time of year.

Roasted veal rump
with potato and root vegetable rösti and beet sauce

SERVES 4 TO 6

2¼ lb veal rump
sea salt flakes and freshly ground pepper
5 thyme sprigs, leaves picked
2 garlic cloves, peeled

Trim the rump, removing the tendons and some of the fat. Score a criss-cross pattern into the fat side and sprinkle with salt, pepper, the thyme leaves, and whole garlic cloves.

Put the rump in an ovenproof dish and roast it in a preheated oven at 500°F to brown for 5 minutes. Then lower the temperature to 325°F and roast the rump for a further 20 to 25 minutes. If you have a meat thermometer, you can check the core temperature of the meat, which should be about 136 to 140°F when you remove it from the oven. At that temperature it will be beautifully pink and juicy inside.

Let the veal rest for 7 to 8 minutes before you cut it into thin slices. Serve it with Potato and Root Vegetable Rösti (see below) and Beet Sauce (see right).

Tip Save 7 oz of the veal rump for the Beet Tartare with Horseradish and Cold Veal Rump (see page 199).

Potato and root vegetable rösti

14 oz baking potatoes
1 lb 2 oz mixed root vegetables, such as celery root, parsley roots, and carrots
sea salt flakes and freshly ground pepper
3 thyme sprigs, chopped
1 garlic clove, chopped
½ cup olive oil

Wash and peel the potatoes and other root vegetables, then grate them on the coarse side of the grater and squeeze out as much moisture as possible. Put the grated vegetables in a bowl and season with salt, pepper, and the chopped thyme and garlic.

Heat up a medium-sized skillet with the olive oil (if you have a nonstick skillet, this is the time to use it). Add the grated vegetables to the pan and press to form a firm pancake. Fry the rösti over medium heat for about 10 minutes on each side until it becomes golden and crisp. If you find it too hard to control the cooking process on the stove, you can finish the rösti in the oven— transfer it to a baking pan (if your skillet isn't ovenproof) and bake in a preheated oven at 350°F for 10 to 15 minutes. Slide the finished rösti onto a plate and cut it into wedges, like a cake, before serving.

Beet sauce

2 large shallots
2 garlic cloves
a little standard canola oil
5 to 6 thyme sprigs
2 bay leaves
2 cups beet juice (see tip)
1 cup cherry vinegar or other fruit vinegar, plus extra if needed
2 cups chicken or beef stock
3½ tablespoons cold unsalted butter, cut into cubes, plus extra if needed
sea salt flakes and freshly ground pepper

Peel the shallots and garlic, then coarsely chop them. Sauté them in a hot pan lightly greased with oil for a few minutes, taking care not to burn them. Add the thyme sprigs and bay leaves and then the beet juice and vinegar, and cook the mixture until reduced to one-third of its original volume.

Add the stock and let the sauce boil until it has a dense, shiny texture and the taste is intense, maybe still with a slight rawness to it.

Strain the reduced sauce through a fine sieve into a small saucepan. Add the cubes of cold butter while whisking vigorously.

Season to taste with salt and pepper and add a little more butter if needed and perhaps a little vinegar.

Tip Beet juice can be purchased at a health food store. Or, make it yourself by putting 1¼ to 1½ lb beets through a juicer.

Braised pork knuckle
with spicy sugar-browned cabbage

2 onions
3 carrots
1½ tablespoons butter
1 teaspoon sea salt flakes
1 teaspoon whole black peppercorns
1 teaspoon cumin seeds
1 teaspoon juniper berries
3 rosemary sprigs
1 garlic clove, peeled
3 tablespoons plum vinegar or other fruit vinegar
1 tablespoon brown sugar
1 tablespoon tomato paste
3 tablespoons standard canola oil
2 cups chicken stock
12 fl oz bottle dark beer
2 pork knuckles (hocks or shanks), about 3¼ to 4½ lb in total

Peel the onions and carrots, then cut them into chunks. Sauté them in the butter in a pan until they just start to soften, then transfer them to a large ovenproof dish or roasting pan. Add the rest of the ingredients, except the pork, to a food processor and blend into a smooth braising liquid.

Rub the pork knuckles with the braising liquid, set them on top of the vegetables, and pour the excess liquid over the meat. Cover the dish or pan with foil so that the knuckles are well covered and place in a preheated oven at 300°F to braise for 3 to 3½ hours until they are very, very tender. Remove the foil when 30 minutes of cooking time remain, scoop the braising liquid from the bottom of the dish or pan, and pour it over the pork about every 5 minutes to create a beautiful caramelized crust.

Serve the knuckles and braised vegetables with Spicy Sugar-browned Cabbage (see below). Make sure you put a jar of good-quality strong mustard on the table as well as some rye bread. Add some nice cold beer, and everyone should be more than satisfied.

Spicy sugar-browned cabbage

½ cup sugar
1 white cabbage
2 tablespoons sea salt flakes
freshly ground pepper
2 bay leaves
2 crushed allspice berries
2 thyme sprigs
½ cup dark beer
1¼ cups chicken stock
a little apple cider vinegar

Melt the sugar to a lightly golden caramel in a saucepan. Shred the cabbage finely and add it to the pan along with the salt, pepper, spices, and thyme, then sauté for 5 minutes.

Add the beer and chicken stock. Simmer, with the lid on, over low heat for about 45 minutes to 1 hour until the cabbage is very soft and all the liquid has evaporated. Season to taste with salt, pepper, and a few drops of apple cider vinegar until your cabbage has just the right flavor.

Burning love

2¼ lb baking potatoes
14 oz smoked bacon in one piece
6 onions
sea salt flakes and freshly ground pepper
1 cup whole milk
1 stick butter

Peel and halve the potatoes, then put them in a pan with water to just cover them. Bring to a boil and cook for 25 to 30 minutes until tender. Meanwhile, prepare the bacon. Cut the whole piece of bacon into

½-inch cubes and put them in a sizzling-hot sauteuse pan so they begin to fry the instant they hit the pan. Fry over medium heat until golden and crisp.

Peel and halve the onions, then slice them very finely. Lift the fried bacon out of the pan with a slotted spoon, leaving the rendered fat behind in the sauteuse pan. Place the bacon in a bowl on the side. Add the sliced onions to the sauteuse pan and fry over low heat until they are golden and tender—be careful not to burn them. Return the cubes of smoked bacon to the pan and let it all heat up and mingle, then season with salt and pepper.

Drain the potatoes when they are tender and let cool slightly in the pan for 2 to 3 minutes. Meanwhile, heat the milk up in a small saucepan and cut the butter into small cubes. Mash the potatoes (see tip) and add the hot milk and butter cubes until the mashed potatoes are heavenly smooth and soft. Season with salt and pepper.

Prepare portions of the mashed potatoes with a good scoop of onion and fried bacon on top, and serve the Burning Love sizzling hot, possibly with a palliative spoonful of plum chutney or lingonberry jam.

Tip When making mashed potatoes, it is important not to mash them for too long. If you use an electric stand or hand mixer, you risk ending up with a consistency like wallpaper glue, which happens as a result of overworking the naturally occurring starch in the potatoes. The best way is actually to fold the butter and milk into the mashed potatoes with a spoon or spatula.

The story of burning love

This beautiful name appeared for the first time in the early 1900s, referring to a dish made from leftovers: mashed potatoes with roasted, possibly salted and smoked pork belly and roasted onions. But a similar dish, a kind of thick potato soup served with fried pork belly, had previously been served in Southern Jutland in the 1800s, and on the island of Lolland it was common to have "picked pork," the name for the delicious meat left on the bones when the pork belly had been cut off. Even before the potato secured a foothold in the Danish South Sea Islands, this meat was fried, served with roasted onions, and perhaps supplemented with "extenuating circumstances," which was stikkelsbær or rhubarb compote. So the story of burning love is actually an old tale.

Apart from bacon, any kind of rich pork leftovers can be used in your burning love. Some leftover roast pork or the last remains of meat carved from the bones of a bone-in roast, fried in some fat with onions—that is true love!

Pork tenderloin medallions
with caramelized onions

6 onions
1½ tablespoons cold butter, divided
2 thyme sprigs, leaves picked
sea salt flakes and freshly ground pepper
2 tablespoons apple cider vinegar
1 trimmed pork tenderloin, about 1¼ lb

Peel the onions, cut them in half, and slice them finely. Add the onions to a sauté pan along with 2 teaspoons of the cold butter, the thyme leaves, salt, and pepper and sauté over medium heat for 15 to 20 minutes until they start to soften. Season to taste with salt, pepper, and the vinegar once the onions begin to caramelize, then sauté for a further few minutes until they have lightly browned.

Cut the tenderloin into 8 small medallions and press them slightly so that they flatten out a little.

Throw the rest of the butter into a very hot skillet and let it bubble away. Fry the medallions for 2 to 3 minutes on each side until they have a gorgeously golden surface, then season with salt and pepper. Put them in an ovenproof dish, cover with the onions, and cook in a preheated oven at 325°F for 6 to 7 minutes. Serve the tenderloin medallions with Pickled Squash with Dill (see page 132) and boiled potatoes.

> ### The making of a Danish classic
>
> Historically, tenderloin was one of the cuts from the pig that wasn't suitable for salting and therefore ended up as sausage meat along with the knuckle, among others. However, when fresh meat was more readily available in the latter half of the 1800s, dishes featuring fresh tenderloin started appearing. For many years pork muscle was used only as a substitute for more expensive meats, for example, by stuffing it with lard and serving it with a cream sauce, in the same way that game meat is stuffed with apples and prunes to mimic roast goose. Pork tenderloin can also be stuffed with parsley and served in a cream sauce, as a pork version of roast chicken. In this recipe, pork is a substitute for beef, which is traditionally served as medallions with caramelized onions. This pork dish is now a Danish classic that appears among the hot dishes on a smorgasbord. The vinegar added to the onions takes them to a whole new level.

Braised pork knuckle
with cabbage and apples

8 pork knuckles (hocks or shanks), about 7 oz per person (see tip)
2 tablespoons standard canola oil
sea salt flakes and freshly ground pepper
8 shallots
3 apples
½ Savoy cabbage
5 thyme sprigs
3 garlic cloves, peeled
¾ cup lager or wheat beer
3 tablespoons apple cider vinegar, plus extra to season
2 cups water, poultry or light veal stock
a little sugar
½ handful of parsley

Cook the pork knuckles in the oil in a large ovenproof sauté pan or Dutch oven until well browned on all sides. Season with salt and pepper. Meanwhile, peel and halve the shallots, cut the apples into quarters and remove the cores, and cut the cabbage into large chunks.

When the knuckles are browned, add the thyme sprigs, whole garlic cloves, shallots, apple, and cabbage to the pan and sauté for another minute. Add the beer, vinegar, and measured water or stock, bring to a boil, and skim off any foam or impurities. Cover the pan with a lid, place it in a preheated oven at 300°F, and braise for about 1½ to 2 hours. Stir the knuckles around a few times during the braising so that they are beautifully glazed on all sides.

Remove the pan from the oven and season the sauce with salt, pepper, a splash of vinegar, and a little sugar. You don't need to reduce the sauce any further, as it should be fine the way it is—not too thick but intense in flavor. Serve the knuckles with the parsley on top. They are lovely with mashed potatoes, or you can serve them with the Jerusalem Artichoke and Apple Purée (see page 142).

Tip The knuckle (also called the hock or shank) is part of the pig's leg, and is an inexpensive cut. It is absolutely delightful stewed for hours until the meat is so tender that it falls off the bone. Remember to preorder the knuckles at the butcher's; it may not be something they keep in stock.

Karbonader (Veal and pork patties)

2 slices of day-old white bread, crusts removed
3 tablespoons lowfat milk
1 lb 2 oz mixed ground veal and pork, 5 to 7% fat
sea salt flakes and freshly ground pepper
¼ cup mashed potatoes
1 organic egg, beaten
1½ cups fresh bread crumbs
1 tablespoon standard canola oil
2 teaspoons butter

Soak the bread in the milk for 10 minutes. Mix the ground meat with salt, pepper, the mashed potato, and soaked bread in a bowl. Knead the mixture thoroughly and then form into 4 equally sized patties.

Press the patties out to a thickness of approximately ¾ inch. Dip them in the beaten egg and then in the bread crumbs. Heat up a skillet and add the fat—first the oil and, when that is hot, then the butter. When the butter has finished bubbling, add the patties and fry over medium heat for 3 to 4 minutes on each side until golden and crisp on the outside and cooked through but still juicy on the inside.

Serve the patties with Glazed Carrots and Shallots (see below) and boiled potatoes, if you like, or just a fresh salad, maybe of grated raw carrots, apples, and oranges.

Glazed carrots and shallots

10½ oz carrots
7 oz shallots
2 teaspoons butter
3 tablespoons water
1 rosemary sprig
sea salt flakes and freshly ground pepper
½ cup apple cider vinegar, plus extra to taste
1 tablespoon honey, plus extra to taste

Peel the carrots and shallots, then cut the carrots into chunks and the shallots in half lengthwise. Put the carrots and shallots in a pan with the butter, measured water, and rosemary, and season with salt and pepper. Let the vegetables steam, with the lid on, for 3 to 4 minutes, then remove the lid and add the vinegar and honey. Cook for a further 5 to 6 minutes until the liquid is absorbed by the onions and carrots, which should start to look quite glossy and beautifully glazed.

Season the vegetables with salt, pepper, honey, and vinegar to achieve just the right balance of flavor. Serve with the patties, or with any dish that could use a sweet and sour garnish. Other dishes it goes well with are Pan-fried Garfish (see page 36) or braised meat or game dishes.

Braised shoulder of venison

with Jerusalem artichoke and apple purée

1 shoulder of venison, about 3¼ lb
½ cup apple cider vinegar
½ handful of thyme
sea salt flakes and freshly ground pepper
5 onions
3 red onions
5 shallots
2 garlic bulbs
2 cooking apples
1¼ cup ale or other dark beer
2 cups apple juice
½ handful of parsley, chopped

Score the shoulder a few times so that it absorbs the seasoning better, and rub it with some of the vinegar, thyme, and salt and pepper.

Peel the onions and shallots, then cut them into chunks. Peel all the garlic cloves but leave them whole. Put the onions, shallots, and garlic into a roasting pan. Core the apples, cut into wedges, and add to the roasting pan, then toss all the ingredients in the beer, the rest of the vinegar, the apple juice, the remaining thyme, and salt and pepper. Place the shoulder on top of the vegetables, cover with foil, and braise in a preheated oven at 315°F for 2½ to 3 hours until it is so tender that it is almost falling off the bone. Remember to glaze the meat by scooping up some of the liquid in the roasting pan and basting the shoulder with the delicious broth a few times during the cooking process.

When it is cooked, let the meat rest for 10 minutes before you carve into it (in fact, the meat should be so tender that you can just lift it from the bone). Serve the braised shoulder of venison with the baked onions in the glorious braising liquid, together with the Jerusalem Artichoke and Apple Purée (see below). Finish off by scattering it with the freshly chopped parsley.

Jerusalem artichoke and apple purée

2¼ lb Jerusalem artichokes
1 apple, such as Belle de Boskoop or Cox
2½ tablespoons skinned hazelnuts (see method on page 171)
1½ tablespoons butter
1 to 2 tablespoons apple cider vinegar
sea salt flakes and freshly ground pepper

Wash and scrub the Jerusalem artichokes thoroughly with a sponge so that all the dirt is removed, then cut them into large cubes. Cut the apple into quarters, remove the core, and cut it into large cubes. Add both the artichokes and apple to a saucepan of boiling water and cook for about 15 minutes until tender. Drain and then let the apples and artichokes sit in the pan until slightly cooled.

Transfer the artichokes and apple to a food processor, add the hazelnuts, butter, and 1 tablespoon of the vinegar and blend to a coarse purée. Season the purée with salt, pepper, and a little extra vinegar to taste, and serve immediately.

Roast chicken and carrot purée
with dill seeds and vinegar

SERVES 4 TO 6

1 large organic chicken, about 3¼ lb
5 thyme sprigs
5 rosemary sprigs
2 tablespoons cold-pressed canola oil
2 tablespoons apple cider vinegar
sea salt flakes and freshly ground pepper
1 handful of parsley, chopped

Check the chicken for any feather stumps and pluck them out. Remove any blood or intestine residues from the cavity and wipe with paper towels. Stuff the chicken with the whole thyme and rosemary sprigs. Rub the skin with the oil, vinegar, salt, and pepper.

Place the chicken in an ovenproof dish and roast in a preheated oven at 350°F for 50 minutes. Then turn the oven off but leave the chicken in the oven for 10 to 15 minutes.

Take the chicken out and cut it into 8 pieces—breasts, wings, thighs, and drumsticks. Serve with the Carrot Purée with Dill Seeds and Vinegar (see below) and the chopped parsley, along with some good bread and cooked grains or roast potatoes.

Carrot purée with dill seeds and vinegar

7 to 8 large carrots
10 dill seeds
¼ cup standard canola oil
3 to 4 tablespoons apple cider vinegar
1 tablespoon acacia honey, plus extra if needed
sea salt flakes and freshly ground pepper

Peel the carrots, cut them into smaller pieces, and cook in a pan of water with the dill seeds for about 20 minutes until tender.

Drain the carrots and place with the dill seeds in a food processor or blender. Add the oil, vinegar, honey, salt, and pepper and blend to a smooth purée. The sweetness of carrots varies with the season, so it is important to taste the purée when it is finished—but that is the case for pretty much all the food you make! There is a good chance that the purée could do with a bit more vinegar or honey before there is perfect harmony between acidity and sweetness. Serve the purée while it is warm.

Tip Any leftovers can be used as a spread in a sandwich or similar. Should you also happen to have some leftover cold chicken, you can make yourself quite a luxurious sandwich. Scatter some crunchy walnuts or crispy bacon on top and then scatter with chopped parsley to finish the snack off.

Griddled pheasant breast
with squash, mushrooms, and mushroom velouté

4 pheasant breasts (see tip)
1 tablespoon standard canola oil
sea salt flakes and freshly ground pepper
3½ oz mixed wild mushrooms, such as penny bun, chanterelle, boletus, horn of plenty, and funnel chanterelle
1 Hokkaido squash
2 teaspoons butter
1 rosemary sprig, chopped
finely grated zest and juice of ½ organic lemon

Marinate the pheasant breasts in the oil, salt, and pepper for 10 minutes.

Clean the mushrooms with a brush or a small vegetable knife. If they are very dirty, you can wash them gently. Cut them into smaller pieces. Peel and halve the squash, then scrape out the seeds with a spoon. Cut the squash into ¾-inch cubes. Sauté the mushrooms and squash in the butter in a hot sauté pan for a few minutes—the mushrooms should shrink quite a lot and the squash cubes should become tender. Add the chopped rosemary and lemon zest and juice, and season to taste with salt and pepper.

Cook the pheasant breasts on a very hot ridged grill pan for 3 to 4 minutes on each side. Remove the breasts from the pan and let them rest for 3 to 4 minutes. Slice them and serve with the squash and mushrooms, along with the Mushroom Velouté (see right) and, if you desire, some boiled or fried potatoes or boiled wheat grains.

Tip Buy two whole pheasants and carve them up yourself so that you have the breasts to grill in this recipe, the legs for the Rillette of Pheasant (see page 132), and a pair of carcasses to make stock. To cut up the pheasants, first slice off the legs by cutting between the thigh and the body all the way down to the thigh joint. Break the leg off at the joint and then finally cut through the skin so that the thigh is completely released from the body. Carve off the pheasant breasts by cutting down either side of the breastbone and loosening the fillets from the body, then divide the carcass into smaller pieces with a large, heavy knife.

Mushroom velouté

14 oz mixed wild mushrooms, such as
    penny bun, chanterelle, boletus,
    horn of plenty, and funnel chanterelle
2 tablespoons butter
⅓ cup all-purpose flour
2½ to 3 cups chicken stock
sea salt flakes and freshly ground pepper
2 tablespoons apple cider vinegar

Clean the mushrooms with a brush or a small vegetable knife. If they are very dirty, you can wash them gently. Cut them into smaller pieces if you want to. Sauté the mushrooms in half the butter in a sauté pan until lightly golden. Pour the mushrooms and any juice they may have given off into a bowl (the juice is perfect for flavoring the sauce later).

Melt the remaining butter in a pan over low heat, add the flour, and cook, stirring, until the mixture turns golden brown and smooth. Stir the chicken stock into the roux a little at a time, then bring the sauce to a boil and simmer for about 15 minutes, giving it the occasional stir to make sure it is completely smooth and all the flour taste has cooked away.

Add the mushrooms and their juice and let the sauce simmer for another couple of minutes. Season with salt, pepper, and the vinegar before serving your velvety mushroom velouté.

· ·

Tip Velouté is one of French cuisine's "mother sauces"; it forms the base of other sauces and thus can be flavored with virtually anything. The options include herbs, mushrooms, mustard, or a nice bouillon that goes with the dish you want to serve the sauce with. Velouté means "velvety" or "mellow," and that is just what this dish is.

· ·

Game stew
with white barley risotto

1lb 5 oz boneless shoulder of venison
    with fat removed
1 tablespoon olive oil
2 onions
4 carrots
5 thyme sprigs
1 garlic clove, peeled
4 juniper berries, lightly crushed
sea salt flakes and freshly ground pepper
1 cup red wine, plus extra if needed
4 cups venison or beef stock
1 tablespoon cold butter, cut into cubes
½ oz dark chocolate, grated

Check the meat for tendons and remove them, then cut the meat into ¾-inch cubes (or ask your butcher or supplier to do the work for you). Cook the meat over high heat in the olive oil in a large pan so that it is beautifully browned on all sides.

Peel the onions and carrots, then cut them into pieces the same size as the meat. Throw the vegetables into the pan along with the thyme sprigs, whole garlic clove, and lightly crushed juniper berries, and brown them as well until they are lightly golden. Season with salt and pepper. Add the red wine and cook until reduced to half its original volume. Add the stock and bring the stew to a boil. Skim off any foam or impurities that rise to the surface and then simmer for about 1½ hours over low heat until the meat is tender.

Just before serving, add the cubes of cold butter and grated chocolate—this will round off the taste of the stew and give it a delicious thick and "sticky" texture. Don't allow the stew to boil after the chocolate has been added, or it may result in a slightly grainy texture. Season with salt and pepper and, if necessary, a splash of fresh red wine. Serve with the White Barley Risotto (*see* right) and a good-quality lingonberry jam.

White barley risotto

1 shallot
2 tablespoons butter
1 cup pearl barley (uncooked)
½ cup white wine
4 cups boiling chicken stock or water
sea salt flakes
2 tablespoons sour cream, 18% fat
½ cup freshly grated hard cheese, such
    as Høost or Grana Padano
freshly ground pepper
2 tablespoons apple cider vinegar
½ handful of flat-leaf parsley, chopped

Peel and chop the shallot, then sauté it in half the butter in a saucepan until it is translucent but has not taken on any color. Rinse the pearl barley well in cold water, then add it to the pan and sauté for a few minutes. Add the white wine and cook until the grains have absorbed it. Then add the boiling stock or water little by little so that the grains are covered at all times, and stirring occasionally to stop them from sticking to the bottom of the pan. It is important to season it with salt during cooking so the pearl barley can absorb it. Cook the grains for 25 to 30 minutes until they are tender but still al dente.

Remove the pan from the heat and add the sour cream, the remaining butter (cut into cubes), and the grated cheese, so that the barley risotto has a more liquid and creamy consistency. Season with salt, pepper, and the vinegar. Scatter with the chopped parsley and serve immediately.

In this recipe, where the creamy barley is matched with a potent game stew, I have chosen not to garnish it with wild mushrooms and a little squash or celery root purée, which could otherwise be a nice accompaniment to the dish.

Chanterelles

The chanterelle is a firm-fleshed fungus with a cap ¾ to 4 inches in diameter and a characteristic apricot fragrance. The stem is 2½ to 3¼ inches in length and usually slightly pointed at the base. Chanterelles don't have gills on the underside, as button or flat mushrooms do, but instead have ridges that run down to the stem. The chanterelle is easy to recognize, with its color varying from pale yellow to bright orange. It can only be confused with the false chanterelle, which often has a stronger orange color, no smell, and a more velvety surface.

The chanterelle grows in acidic soil in deciduous as well as coniferous forests. There are many different species to be found in uplands and lowlands, along trail edges or dirt roads in rural areas with mixed woodland and lots of shade. They can be picked from midsummer to mid-November.

How to pick chanterelles

Pick the mushrooms gently, cut off the root, and give them a quick clean on the spot. Finish cleaning them at home without using water, because that will wash away some of the flavoring substances. Gently tear the bigger chanterelles into smaller pieces and fry them in a skillet until they begin to sizzle. Chanterelles are good in sauces but have enough flavor to give a distinctive character to a homemade stock, and they are fantastic stewed in cream and served on a piece of bread.

Dried chanterelles

If you find a lot of chanterelles or other wild mushrooms during the summer and fall, and you have collected more than you can eat, drying them is a great idea. Clean the mushrooms without using water to avoid washing away some of the flavor. Cut them into small pieces or thin slices, and place them on a baking pan lined with parchment paper. Place them in a preheated oven at 140°F (you can leave the oven door slightly ajar) for about 1 to 1½ hours or until they are completely dry—this is important, otherwise they will quickly rot once you store them. Let the mushrooms cool, then pack them into sterilized glass jars, seal tightly, and store in a cool, dry place. You can dry most mushrooms in this way and thus enjoy them well beyond their normal season. Use your dried mushrooms in risottos, sauces, and soups or as a tasty sprinkle on top of a good stew.

Fish

Boiled lobster
with lemon mayonnaise

1 tablespoon salt
1 teaspoon sugar
2 live lobsters, about 1½ to 1¾ lb each

Bring a large pan of water with the salt and sugar added to a boil. Kill the lobsters by inserting a large kitchen knife into the neck of the lobster and then quickly cutting down straight through the head so that the lobster dies instantly. Then plunge the lobster into the boiling water and boil for 5 minutes. Take the pan off the heat and put the pan and its contents in the refrigerator for the lobster to cool in the cooking brine. When the lobster has cooled, you should aim to remove the flesh from the shell in whole pieces as far as possible. The easiest way to do this is to cut the lobster in half with a large knife, then crush the claws with the side of the knife or use a pair of seafood scissors. A hammer could also be used, but just be careful that you don't smash the claws altogether. Once all the lobster meat has been removed, check the meat for any remnants of shell, and remove the dark vein (intestinal tract) running all the way down the tail.

Serve the lobster meat with Lemon Mayonnaise (*see* right) and good bread, and remember to put the pepper mill on the table too. Freshly ground pepper is mandatory when there is seafood on the menu.

Lemon mayonnaise

2 pasteurized egg yolks
½ tablespoon French mustard
finely grated zest of ½ organic lemon, and juice of 1
sea salt flakes and freshly ground pepper
⅔ cup cold-pressed canola oil

Using an electric hand mixer or a balloon whisk, whisk the egg yolks, mustard, half the lemon juice, salt, and pepper together in a bowl until thick and white. Slowly add the oil in a thin stream while whisking vigorously. It is of the utmost importance to add the oil gently and slowly so that the mayo doesn't curdle. Should it begin to do so, you can try and save it by adding a few drops of cold water while still whisking vigorously. Season the finished mayonnaise with the lemon zest and extra juice and, if needed, additional salt and pepper.

Orange and fennel-marinated cod

14 oz cod fillets
1 teaspoon sea salt flakes
1 tablespoon sugar
1 red onion
1 fennel with feathery tops
3 tablespoons apple cider vinegar
finely grated zest and juice of 1 organic orange
6 fennel seeds, coarsely crushed
5 juniper berries
2 tablespoons standard canola oil
freshly ground pepper

First, check that the cod fillets are nice and fresh and smell of the sea, not of the harbor. Remove the skin and any bones from the fillets, put them in a dish, and sprinkle with salt and the sugar. Cover the dish with plastic wrap and let stand in the refrigerator for 2 hours.

Cut the fillets into very thin slices and place them on a platter.

Peel the onion. Cut the fennel in half, rinse it thoroughly in cold water, and drain. Chop both the onion and fennel very finely (save the feathery leaves from the fennel for the garnish). Put the vegetables in a saucepan, add the vinegar, orange zest and juice, coarsely crushed fennel seeds, juniper berries, and oil and bring it to a rapid boil. Turn off the heat and let the marinade cool slightly, then pour it evenly over the thin slices of cod while it is still warm. Let the cod soak for about 10 minutes before serving.

Finish the cod off by scattering it with some chopped fennel fronds and some freshly ground black pepper. The marinated cod is a delightful appetizer or lunch served with good bread, but it could also be part of a main dish together with a few other small dishes, such as the Mushroom and Savoy Cabbage Pie (*see* page 155) or the Brussels Sprout Salad with Orange, Walnuts, and Pearl Barley (*see* page 238).

BLUE STALK MUSHROOMS
In fall, these mushrooms light up the forest floor.

Fish and chips

8 large baking potatoes
1 lb 5 oz skinless haddock or cod fillet
sea salt flakes
1 cup all-purpose flour, plus extra for
**   sprinkling**
1 teaspoon fine salt
2½ cup dark beer
3 quarts canola oil, for deep-frying

Peel the potatoes, cut into batons about ½ inch thick and 4 inches long and add them to a bowl of cold water. Let soak for about 30 minutes, then let drain thoroughly.

Check that the fish is fresh and smells of the sea, not of the harbor. Remove any bones or stray scales and cut the fish into 8 evenly sized pieces. Sprinkle with salt and a little flour, then let rest in the refrigerator for 10 minutes.

Meanwhile, mix the flour, fine salt, and beer together in a bowl to make a sticky batter. Transfer the batter to the refrigerator and let rest for 10 minutes.

Pour the oil into a large pan. Heat it up to 170 to 180°C, or until the wooden end of a match sizzles when you drop it in the oil. Dip the pieces of fish in the batter, then put them straight into the hot oil 3 to 4 pieces at a time so the oil doesn't lose too much heat. Fry the fish for about 3 to 4 minutes until golden and crisp. Remove with a slotted spoon, place on paper towels to drain, and sprinkle with sea salt flakes.

Double-cook the chips in the sizzling oil so that they become deliciously crisp and golden. First cook them at a lower temperature, around 260 to 285°F, for about 4 to 5 minutes until they become tender but without taking on any color, then remove from the oil. Fry a second time at a higher temperature, around 350°F, for about 3 to 4 minutes until crisp and golden. Lift the chips out, drain on paper towels, and season with sea salt. Eat the fish and chips while they are hot. Serve with Homemade Mayonnaise (*see* page 68) for dipping and beer to wash it down.

Fish cakes
with quick tartare sauce

1 lb 5 oz skinless cod or haddock fillet
1 teaspoon sea salt flakes
2 organic eggs
2 tablespoons all-purpose flour
⅔ cup heavy whipping cream
1 carrot
1 baking potato
½ handful of dill, chopped
freshly ground white pepper
2 teaspoons butter
1 tablespoon canola oil, for frying

Check that the fish is fresh and smells of the sea, not of the harbor. Put the fish in a food processor and grind coarsely. Add the salt and pulse the ground fish until it is sticky. This way, it will bind with the liquid much better and the cakes will be less likely to fall apart. Place the fish in a mixing bowl.

Add the eggs, flour, and then the cream, a little at a time, and stir well until the ground mixture has a good, firm consistency.

Peel the carrot and potato, then grate them finely. Squeeze the moisture out of the vegetables with your hands, then stir them into the fish-cake mixture. Finally, add the chopped dill and white pepper. Refrigerate the mixture for 30 minutes before frying.

Fry large spoonfuls of the mixture in the butter and oil over medium heat—it is important to be patient so that they form a beautiful crust on the underside before you turn them. That way they will also keep their shape and become firmer, producing a better end result. Serve the golden fish cakes with a bowl of boiled potatoes or good rye bread, as well as a green or more rustic salad and a generous dollop of Quick Tartare Sauce (*see* right).

••

TIP It is important that all the ingredients are at the same temperature, because they will combine a lot more easily.

••

Quick tartare sauce

1 fennel bulb
2 carrots
½ cauliflower
2 tablespoons standard canola oil
sea salt flakes and freshly ground pepper
1½ tablespoons jaggery
3 tablespoons apple cider vinegar
2 pasteurized egg yolks
1 tablespoon prepared mustard
1 tablespoon apple cider vinegar,
**   plus extra to season**
1¼ cups cold-pressed canola oil
⅓ cup chopped gherkins
½ handful of chervil, chopped

Prepare and wash all the vegetables. Grate the outer parts of the cauliflower on the coarse side of the grater and place in a bowl. Then cut the rest of the cauliflower (discarding any tough stalk) and the other vegetables into ¼-inch cubes.

Put the vegetables in a saucepan along with the standard canola oil, salt, pepper, sugar, and vinegar, cover with the lid and let them steam for 3 to 4 minutes until slightly soft but still with a bite. Stir a few times during the steaming so that the vegetables are evenly cooked. Take the pan off the heat and let the contents cool.

While the vegetables are cooling, it is time to make the mayonnaise. Using an electric hand mixer or a balloon whisk, whisk the egg yolks, mustard, vinegar, salt, and pepper together in a bowl until thick and white. Slowly add the cold-pressed canola oil in a thin stream while whisking vigorously—be careful not to make the mayo curdle. When all the oil has been added, adjust the flavor with a little additional salt, pepper, and vinegar. Finally, fold the steamed vegetables, grated cauliflower, and chopped gherkins into the mayonnaise, and finish with the freshly chopped chervil.

Baked potatoes
with salmon tartare and dill yogurt

4 large baking potatoes
coarse sea salt
1 cup Greek yogurt, 10% fat
finely grated zest and juice
  of 1 organic lemon
½ handful of dill, chopped
sea salt flakes and freshly ground pepper
2 anchovy fillets
1 tablespoon capers
1 small shallot
7 oz very fresh skinless salmon fillets

Wash the potatoes and put them in an ovenproof dish on a little bed of coarse salt. Bake the potatoes in a preheated oven at 350°F for 45 minutes to 1 hour until tender.

Meanwhile, combine the yogurt with the lemon zest and juice, chopped dill, salt, and pepper in a bowl. Finely chop the anchovies and capers, and peel and finely chop the shallot. Cut the salmon into very small cubes with a sharp knife. (When making tartare, it is important to cut the fish, not chop it.) Put the salmon in another bowl and season with the anchovies, capers, and shallot. Mix well so that the ingredients are evenly distributed, and season with salt and pepper.

Take the potatoes out of the oven and cut a cross in the top of each potato. Squeeze them a little so that they open up and serve with the salmon tartare and dill yogurt to enable diners to garnish their own potato. Remember to set teaspoons on the table so people can scrape out the delicious potatoes!

Tip If you want to serve baked potatoes as a main course, allow 1½ to 2 potatoes per person, and preferably make an additional filling: maybe one of my herb butters on page 102 or perhaps some stewed mushrooms. Earlier in the year, in the transition between late winter and early spring, baked potatoes with lumpfish roe and crème fraîche are a real treat.

Pan-fried herrings
marinated in apple cider vinegar

10 double herring fillets
½ cup prepared wholegrain mustard
sea salt flakes and freshly ground pepper
1 cup rye flour
1 tablespoon standard canola oil
2 teaspoons butter
1¼ cups apple cider vinegar
1¼ cups water
1¼ cups jaggery
5 bay leaves
10 whole black peppercorns

Check that the herring fillets are fresh and smell of the sea, not of the harbor. Place the herring fillets in a dish, skin-side down, rub the flesh side with the mustard, and season with salt and pepper. Fold the fillets together and dip them in the rye flour to coat.

Heat a skillet and add the fat—first the oil and, when that is hot, the butter. When the butter has stopped bubbling, fry the herring fillets for about 3 minutes on each side until golden and crisp. It may be necessary to press down a little on the folded fillets with a lifter just after you have added them to the pan so that they don't unfold.

Combine the rest of the ingredients in a saucepan and bring to a boil. Pour the hot syrup evenly over the fried herrings to cover and let cool slightly before you transfer the dish to the refrigerator to marinate for a couple of days.

Eat the pan-fried marinated herrings on good rye bread with thin slices of raw onion on top.

Tip You can heat up the herring and marinade a little by briefly placing it in a preheated oven at 300°F, then serve warm with some boiled potatoes and fried onions—another great way to enjoy the dish.

OYSTER MUSHROOMS
In fall, the forest is full of the delicate, translucent-stemmed caps of oyster mushrooms cascading from the surface of dead hardwood trees.

Light dishes

Salted cod sandwich
with mustard cream and pickled Jerusalem artichokes

Salted cod
- **7 oz skinless cod fillet (or use another codlike fish, such as pollack, hake, lingcod, or cusk)**
- **1 teaspoon sugar**
- **2 tablespoons sea salt flakes**

Mustard cream
- **1 cup Greek yogurt, 2% fat**
- **2 tablespoons prepared mustard**
- **1 teaspoon acacia honey**
- **sea salt flakes and freshly ground pepper**

To serve
- **8 slices of good wheat bread**
- **1 tablespoon olive oil**
- **8 small cocktail tomatoes**
- **3½ oz Pickled Jerusalem Artichokes (see page 167)**
- **2 handfuls of mixed herbs, such as flat-leaf parsley, chervil, and chives**

Check that the cod fillet is nice and fresh and smells of the sea, not of the harbor. Check the fish for bones and use a knife to scrape off any stray scales. Put the cod fillet in a dish and sprinkle with the sugar and salt. Cover the dish with plastic wrap and let stand in the refrigerator for at least 2 to 3 hours, preferably longer. Alternatively, the cod can be left to salt over a few days, if that fits better with your schedule.

When ready to serve, brush the sugar and salt mixture from the cod and cut the fish into thin slices.

For the mustard cream, mix all the ingredients together in a bowl until smooth and a good consistency for spreading onto the toasted bread.

Oil the bread slices with the olive oil and toast them in a preheated oven at 425°F for 5 to 6 minutes until crisp and golden. Let the toasted bread cool slightly, then spread 4 slices with the mustard cream and top with the thin slices of salted cod, the tomatoes, halved, and the pickled artichokes. Finish off with a good scattering of herbs and then place the remaining toasted bread slices on top. Serve the warm sandwiches with a green salad.

Mushroom and Savoy cabbage pie

Pastry
- **1¼ cups all-purpose flour, plus extra for dusting**
- **½ cup spelt flour**
- **a little salt**
- **1 stick softened butter, plus extra for greasing**
- **1 organic egg**

Filling
- **10½ oz mixed mushrooms, such as button, oyster, or chanterelle**
- **10½ oz Savoy cabbage**
- **2 teaspoons butter**
- **3 thyme sprigs, freshly chopped**
- **sea salt flakes and freshly ground pepper**
- **3 organic eggs**
- **¾ cup cottage cheese**
- **½ cup lowfat milk**
- **a little grated nutmeg**
- **⅓ cup freshly grated hard cheese, such as Høost, or ripe Gouda or Grana Padano**

First, make the pastry. Put the flours and salt in a bowl, add the softened butter, cut into small pieces, and rub in with your fingertips until the mixture resembles bread crumbs. Stir in the egg and knead into a smooth dough. Transfer the dough to a floured bowl, cover it with plastic wrap, and let rest in the refrigerator for 30 minutes.

Roll the dough out on a lightly floured surface to a thickness of about ¼ inch and place in a greased 9½-inch diameter pie plate. I usually transfer the dough from the table to the pie plate by rolling the dough around the rolling pin and then rolling it out into the dish. Press the dough into the pie plate and trim the excess dough from the edges. Place a piece of parchment paper on top of the pie crust and add coarse salt, rice, dried beans, or other heavy ingredients that will keep pressure on the crust while it is prebaking.

Prebake the pie crust in a preheated oven at 350°F for 10 to 15 minutes until it is firm and slightly golden.

While the pie crust is in the oven, clean the mushrooms with a brush or a small vegetable knife, then cut them into small pieces. Rinse the cabbage, drain thoroughly, and then slice finely. Sauté the mushrooms in the butter in a skillet until softened slightly, then add the cabbage. Season with the freshly chopped thyme, salt, and pepper, and remove the pan from the heat.

Remove the pie crust from the oven and remove the parchment paper and weights. Pour the mushroom and cabbage mixture into the pie crust. Mix the eggs, cottage cheese, and milk together in a bowl, and season with salt, pepper, and nutmeg, then pour the mixture over the vegetables and scatter with the grated cheese. Bake the pie in the oven at 325°F for 30 to 35 minutes until the filling has set and the pie is golden on top. Take the pie out of the oven and let it rest for 5 minutes before you slice it.

Serve the pie on its own or with the Orange and Fennel-marinated Cod (see page 150). If you want to serve it as a more substantial meal, supplement it with some boiled wheat grains flavored with a little apple cider vinegar and canola oil.

Tip The pie can be made the day before and served cold.

Fynbo
with pear mostarda and homemade crispbread

7 oz firm yellow cheese, such as
   Danish Fynbo or Vesterhavsost,
   or aged Gouda
Pear Mostarda (*see* below)
Homemade Crispbread (*see* right)

Cut the cheese into blocks or batons and serve it with the Pear Mostarda (*see* below) and Homemade Crispbread (*see* right) after a nice dinner.

Pear mostarda
MAKES 1 SMALL JAR

3 ripe pears, such as Clara Frijs
   or Grise Bonne, or Williams
3 tablespoons water
2 tablespoons wholegrain mustard
1 tablespoon honey
a little apple cider vinegar
1 tablespoon standard canola oil
sea salt flakes and freshly ground pepper

Peel the pears, cut them into quarters, and remove the cores. Cut them into large cubes. Put the cubes in a saucepan with the measured water, cover with a lid, and steam over low heat for about 15 to 20 minutes until tender. Then remove the lid and let the water evaporate.

Put the pears in a blender with the mustard and honey and blend to a purée. Season with a little vinegar, the oil, salt, and pepper. Pour the mostarda into a small sterilized preserving jar and store it in the refrigerator, where it will keep for 30 to 40 days unopened and 15 to 20 days once you have opened it.

• •

Tip Although the name is Italian, the spicy-sweet fruit condiment mostarda is not unknown in ancient Nordic cuisine. Pear mostarda is also fabulous with Nordic cheeses, cold meats, and most smoked products.

• •

Homemade crispbread
MAKES ABOUT 35 TO 40 CRISPBREADS

½ cup wholemeal flour
1 cup lowfat milk
2 tablespoons fennel seeds, plus extra
   for sprinkling, coarsely crushed
2 cups all-purpose flour
coarse sea salt, for sprinkling

Mix the wholemeal flour and milk together in a bowl.

Toast the fennel seeds in a dry skillet until they begin to pop, then crush them using a mortar and pestle. Add them to the wholemeal flour and milk mixture. Let stand for 10 minutes in the kitchen.

Mix the all-purpose flour into the milk mixture, a little at a time, until you have a smooth dough (save a little of the flour for rolling out the dough). Let the dough rest in the refrigerator for 15 minutes.

Roll the dough out thinly on a lightly floured surface, cut into long strips about 1¼ x 8 inches and place on baking pans lined with parchment paper. Brush the crispbreads with water and sprinkle with coarse sea salt and some extra fennel seeds. Bake in a preheated oven at 170°F for about 6 to 8 minutes until golden and crisp. Let the crispbreads cool, then store in an airtight container for up to 2 to 3 months.

Apple, Jerusalem artichoke, and bacon compote

1 lb 2 oz Jerusalem artichokes
1 lb 2 oz apples
1 tablespoon apple cider vinegar, plus
   extra to season
8 thick slices of bacon, preferably
   dry-salted
sea salt flakes and freshly ground pepper
3 tablespoons water
2 to 3 thyme sprigs, leaves picked
1 teaspoon sugar

Wash and peel the Jerusalem artichokes, then cut them into smaller pieces. Core the apples, dice them into small cubes, and toss them with the vinegar.

Cook the bacon either on a baking pan in a preheated oven at 300°F or in a skillet on the stove over very low heat for 40 to 50 minutes or so that the bacon is crisp and releases most of its fat (you will need to use the fat, so reserve it). Remove the bacon from the pan and keep it warm.

Sauté half the Jerusalem artichokes and apples in a little of the bacon fat in a sauté pan until slightly softened. Then add salt, pepper, and the measured water and let steam, with the lid on, over medium heat for about 10 to 15 minutes until the apples and artichokes are tender but still retain some structure.

You can now choose to either fry the remaining apples and artichokes over high heat in a little of the bacon fat for a beautiful, golden exterior, then scatter with the thyme, or you can add the rest of the Jerusalem artichokes to the compote along with the thyme leaves. In the latter case, steam the compote for a further 3 to 4 minutes until the Jerusalem artichokes are tender, and finish by mixing the raw apple pieces into the hot compote so that there is a crispy element to the dish and the compote is not too soft. Add salt, pepper, the sugar, and extra vinegar to taste.

Serve the compote in the pan, with the bacon on top and, if you like, the roasted apples and artichokes on the side. Serve with plenty of great rye bread. This is also a very nice dinner for the apple season.

Warm pheasant salad
with scorzonera and carrots

1 cleaned pheasant
2 tablespoons standard canola oil
sea salt flakes and freshly ground pepper
10½ oz mixed root vegetables, such as carrots, celery roots, parsley roots, and parsnips
3 thyme sprigs
2 bay leaves
5 whole black peppercorns
2 to 2½ cups water
2 to 3 scorzonera (black salsify), or regular salsify
2 carrots
½ cup fruity vinegar, such as raspberry, sherry, or red wine
¼ handful of flat-leaf parsley, leaves only
1 tablespoon cold-pressed canola oil

Brown the pheasant thoroughly on all sides in 1 tablespoon of the standard canola oil in a skillet. Season with salt and pepper. Transfer the pheasant to a roasting pan and roast in a preheated oven at 325°F for 35 to 40 minutes until it is well done but still juicy. Remove from the oven and let rest for 10 to 12 minutes.

Remove the pheasant meat from the bones and put it in a bowl (save the bones to make the stock you need for the dressing).

Wash and peel the mixed root vegetables, then cut them into large cubes, and brown them in the remaining 1 tablespoon standard canola oil in a sauteuse pan along with the pheasant carcass, chopped into smaller pieces. When the vegetables are golden, add the thyme, bay leaves, peppercorns, and enough of the measured water to cover, then bring to a boil and skim off any foam or impurities that rise to the surface. Lower the heat and simmer the broth for 1 to 1½ hours.

Strain the broth through a fine sieve, then reduce down to an intense stock of only about 3 tablespoons.

Wash and peel the scorzonera and carrots, then cut them into long, thin strips with a vegetable peeler. Pour the vinegar into a small saucepan and boil it until it has a syrupy consistency, then mix with the hot, reduced broth. Toss the vegetable strips, pheasant meat, and parsley leaves in the broth, and season with salt, pepper, and the cold-pressed canola oil. Serve immediately while it is warm.

Tip You can make this salad with quail instead—two small quail will yield the same amount of meat as one pheasant.

Open-faced rye bread sandwich
with smoked haunch of venison and compote of turnip, apples, and horseradish

½ turnip, about 7 oz
sea salt flakes
1 tablespoon cold-pressed canola oil
1 tablespoon apple cider vinegar
1 tablespoon acacia honey
freshly ground pepper
2 apples
¼ cup freshly grated horseradish
1 handful of chives, chopped
7 oz thinly sliced smoked haunch of venison (order at the butcher's)
4 slices of rye bread

Peel the turnip and cut it into ½-inch cubes, then rinse them in cold water. Bring a saucepan of salted water to a boil and cook the turnip for about 2 minutes until tender but still with a bite.

Drain the turnip and put the warm cubes in a bowl, then marinate them in the oil, vinegar, honey, salt, and pepper.

Cut the apples into quarters, remove the cores, and dice into cubes the same size as the turnip. Add to the turnip along with the

horseradish, mix well, and let cool slightly. Finish by adding the chives.

Put the smoked venison slices on the rye bread, pile a generous portion of the warm turnip compote on top, and serve immediately.

Omelet
with crispy Jerusalem artichokes

14 oz Jerusalem artichokes
1½ oz bacon
1 tablespoon cold-pressed canola oil
1 zucchini
2 thyme sprigs, leaves picked
sea salt flakes and freshly ground pepper
6 organic eggs
⅔ cup lowfat milk

Wash and peel the Jerusalem artichokes, then dice them into large cubes. Cut the bacon into cubes as well, and put both the artichokes and bacon in a hot ovenproof skillet with the oil. Fry for 4 to 5 minutes over medium heat until the artichokes are tender and lightly golden and the bacon is crisp.

Cut the zucchini into cubes and add them to the pan along with the thyme leaves, salt, and pepper.

Crack the eggs into a bowl one at a time so that you can check that they are fresh. Add the milk and whisk together, season with salt and pepper, and pour the egg mixture into the pan. Stir around lightly so that the artichokes, zucchini, and bacon are evenly distributed, then let the egg mixture stand for a few minutes to become firm.

Transfer the pan to a preheated oven at 500°F and bake the omelet for about 5 to 6 minutes. You may want to use the broiler function in the oven at the end so that the omelet is nice and golden on top. Remove the omelet from the oven, transfer to a platter, and serve as part of a brunch.

Vegetable accompaniments

Pearl barley salad

¾ cup pearl barley (uncooked)
1¼ cups water
sea salt flakes and freshly ground pepper
2 tablespoons apple cider vinegar, plus extra if needed
2 tablespoons olive oil
1 tablespoon acacia honey, plus extra if needed
1 turnip
2 apples
½ handful of chervil

Rinse the pearl barley well in cold water. Put it in a saucepan, add the measured water, and bring to a boil. Simmer with the lid on for about 20 minutes. Take the pan off the heat and let the barley stand for 5 to 10 minutes, still with the lid on.

Put the barley in a bowl and season with salt, pepper, vinegar, oil, and honey so that the hot grains absorb all the nice flavors. Place the bowl in the refrigerator.

Peel the turnip and cut it into very thin slices using a mandoline or a sharp knife, then put the slices in a bowl. Cut the apples into quarters and remove the cores. Cut the wedges into very thin slices and mix with the turnip. Add the cooked pearl barley and season, if necessary, with a little extra vinegar, salt, and pepper.

Chop the chervil coarsely and mix it into the salad. Taste again and add salt, pepper, vinegar, or honey to taste. Mix well once more and serve.

Serve this salad as an alternative to potatoes, rice, cooked grains, or other hearty side dishes. It has the crunchiness, acidity, and sweetness to accompany heavier meat dishes, and I am particularly fond of it as a side to pork; the combination of turnip, apple, and the anise-flavored chervil is absolutely delicious with, for instance, roast pork.

Baked beets
with yogurt and dill

2¼ lb beets
¼ cup coarse sea salt
1 cup Greek yogurt, 2% fat
1 tablespoon apple cider vinegar
2 tablespoons acacia honey
10 dill seeds, crushed
1 handful of dill, chopped
sea salt flakes and freshly ground pepper

Wash the beets clean of soil, place them in an ovenproof dish, and sprinkle with the coarse salt. Bake the whole beets in a preheated oven at 325°F for 1 hour 10 minutes to 1 hour 20 minutes until tender and wrinkled (the baking time can vary, of course, if the beets are very large or very small).

Remove the beets from the oven and scrape the skin off with a small, sharp knife as soon as they are cool enough to handle. Cut them into chunks and put them in a bowl.

Mix the yogurt with the vinegar, honey, crushed dill seeds, chopped dill, salt, and pepper in a bowl. Pour the dressing over the beets when they have cooled but are still slightly warmer than room temperature and mix well. Let the beets stand to absorb the flavors of the dressing for 10 minutes before serving. It is a good idea to give them one last round of seasoning—the balance often changes once the flavors of the beets and dressing have blended.

The beets pair well with fish, light meats, and poultry. And if you fancy a meat-free day, serve them with cooked grains and a salad of raw, grated vegetables or fruits, such as carrots, apples, cabbage, and so on.

Baked carrots

12 carrots
1 oz smoked bacon
2 tablespoons standard canola oil
½ cup apple juice
3 tablespoons apple cider vinegar
1 basil sprig, leaves picked
1 tablespoon dark brown sugar
sea salt flakes and freshly ground pepper

Peel the carrots and cut them into coarse batons, then place in an ovenproof dish. Cut the bacon into cubes and put in a bowl with the rest of the ingredients. Stir everything together and pour the mixture over the carrots. Toss around a few times so that the batons are well coated.

Bake in a preheated oven at 425°F for 6 to 8 minutes. The temperature is very high in order for the carrots to get a nice caramelized exterior.

Remove the carrots from the oven and let cool slightly, then serve as a side dish to grilled pork, meatloaf, meatballs, or poultry.

Salad of squash, lingonberries, bacon, and chestnuts

1 large butternut or Hokkaido squash
2 tablespoons apple cider vinegar
2 tablespoons cold-pressed canola oil
sea salt flakes and freshly ground pepper
1 tablespoon acacia honey
2½ oz fresh or frozen lingonberries, defrosted if frozen
1 tablespoon jaggery
3 tablespoons whole blanched almonds
1 handful of chervil, chopped
8 baked chestnuts
1¾ oz bacon

Peel the squash (I think it is easiest to use a knife) halve it, then scrape out the seeds with a spoon. Cut it into chunks or wedges, place them in a large roasting pan lined with parchment paper, and toss them well in the vinegar, oil, salt, pepper, and honey. Bake in a preheated oven at 350°F for 7 to 8 minutes until tender but still al dente.

The squash will give off a little liquid during cooking. Pour this liquid into a small saucepan and reduce to half its original volume. Blend it with a hand-held stick blender so that it becomes thick and smooth, then pour it evenly over the baked squash. Put the dish in the refrigerator.

Mix the lingonberries with the sugar and let stand for 10 minutes in the kitchen.

Roast the almonds in a dry skillet until golden, then transfer them to a cutting board and chop them coarsely. Mix the almonds with the baked squash, then add the lingonberries and chopped chervil, and maybe a little extra salt and pepper to taste.

Peel the baked chestnuts, then cut them into slices as thin as possible without them crumbling apart. Scatter the salad with the chestnuts. Dice the bacon and fry in a hot skillet until crisp. Scatter the salad with the crispy bacon and serve.

The squash salad can be served with fish or seafood or as an independent appetizer or a main course accompanied by some good-quality bread.

Baked mushrooms
with hard cider and garlic

1 lb 2 oz button or Portobello mushrooms
3 garlic cloves, lightly crushed
3 rosemary sprigs, plus extra, finely chopped, to serve
2 tablespoons olive oil, plus extra to serve
sea salt flakes and freshly ground pepper
½ cup hard cider

Clean the mushrooms with a brush or a small vegetable knife, then place them in an ovenproof dish with the lightly crushed garlic, rosemary sprigs, olive oil, salt, and pepper. The pour in the hard cider.

Bake in a preheated oven at 300°F for 12 minutes. Eat the mushrooms warm with a little finely chopped rosemary, giving them a light drizzle of olive oil just before serving.

The mushrooms can be served as a small dish on its own or as an accompaniment to most meats and fish.

CHESTNUTS
Take a walk in the forest and you may be lucky enough to find genuine sweet chestnuts.

Baked parsley roots
with salsa of Savoy cabbage and almonds

2¼ lb parsley roots
2 to 3 tablespoons apple cider vinegar
5 thyme sprigs, chopped
1 tablespoon standard canola oil
sea salt flakes and freshly ground pepper

Salsa
¾ cup chopped Savoy cabbage in chunks
1 shallot, peeled
½ handful of parsley
¼ cup whole blanched almonds
½ cup standard canola oil
3 tablespoons apple cider vinegar, plus extra if needed
sea salt flakes and freshly ground pepper
a little jaggery or honey

Peel the parsley roots and cut them into chunks. Put the roots in an ovenproof dish and toss them with the vinegar, chopped thyme, oil, salt, and pepper. Bake the parsley roots in a preheated oven at 350°F for 7 to 8 minutes until the roots are tender but still have a bite to them. Take the roots out of the oven and let them cool.

Now make the salsa. Add the cabbage, shallot, parsley, almonds, oil, and vinegar to a food processor and blend to a coarse dip. Season with salt, pepper, and the sugar or honey, then toss the salsa with the parsley roots. Add extra salt, pepper, sugar, or vinegar to taste.

The baked parsley roots are a great side to a variety of dishes, especially classic pork dishes, such as sausages, meatballs, fillet steaks, and pork collar, but they are also quite delicious with a piece of steamed fish or as a (lunch) side dish with charcuterie.

Brussels sprouts salad
with chickpeas, apple, and capers

½ cup dried chickpeas, soaked in cold
    water for 12 hours
1 garlic clove, peeled
½ handful of flat-leaf parsley
2 tablespoons olive oil
finely grated zest and juice of 1 organic
    lemon, plus extra juice if needed
sea salt flakes and freshly ground pepper
10 Brussels sprouts
2 apples
2 tablespoons capers

Drain the soaked chickpeas and rinse them thoroughly in clean water. Put the chickpeas in a pan, cover with water, and add the whole garlic clove and the parsley stems. Bring to a boil, then simmer the chickpeas gently for 35 to 45 minutes until tender.

Drain the chickpeas, pour them into a bowl, and, while they are still hot, season with the olive oil, lemon zest and juice, salt, and pepper so that they absorb the flavors.

Wash the Brussels sprouts, drain, and chop very finely. Cut the apples into quarters, remove the cores, and slice into thin wedges. Wash the parsley thoroughly and chop it coarsely. Add the sprouts, apples, parsley, and capers to the bowl of chickpeas and toss well. If necessary, season with more pepper, salt, or lemon juice to taste. Now the salad is ready to serve.

"Burnt" leeks and lemon in oil
with dill flowers and coriander and fennel seeds

MAKES 1 JAR

4 winter leeks
1 organic lemon
4 dill flower heads
1 tablespoon coarse sea salt
1 tablespoon coriander seeds
1 tablespoon fennel seeds
1 bay leaf
about 2 quarts good olive oil

Cut off the roots and tops of the leeks, then rinse them thoroughly in cold water. Drain them well and cut them into pieces about 4 inches in length (or any length that will suit the preserving jar you want to use). Heat a ridged grill pan until it is sizzling hot, place the leeks on it, and cook them for about 3 to 4 minutes on each of their four "sides" so that they have beautiful grill marks all around. Cut the lemon into quarters and grill the lemon wedges on the flesh sides until they have a golden color.

Put the leeks, lemon, dill flower heads, salt, and spices in a sterilized preserving jar and add the olive oil to cover. Seal tightly, place the jar in the refrigerator, and let stand to pickle for about 14 days before you serve the leeks. If the jar is kept chilled and the leeks and lemons are covered by the oil, the shelf life is 2 to 3 months. Both leeks and lemons (thinly sliced) can be used as a garnish for almost any dish, but I would suggest in particular grilled chicken and Fried Flounder with Braised Belgian Endive (*see* page 218) or the Seared Hanger Steak with Frisée lettuce (*see* page 75), where you can cut the leeks into thin slices and mix them into the salad.

Tip When you have eaten all the leeks and lemons, you can reuse the oil for frying or use it as a dressing for salads as well as cooked and steamed vegetables so that nothing is wasted.

SHEATHED WOODTUFT
This mushroom can be commonly foraged as late as November.

Pickled squash
with onions and bay leaves

MAKES 4 LARGE JARS

2 winter squash, such as butternut or Hokkaido
½ cup coarse sea salt
4½ oz shallots
¾ oz fresh horseradish root
5 bay leaves
2 teaspoons whole black peppercorns
2 teaspoons mustard seeds (any type)
2 quarts apple cider vinegar
2¼ lb sugar
4 cups water

Day 1
Peel and halve the squash, then scrape out the seeds with a spoon. Cut the squash into slices, place them in a bowl, and sprinkle with the coarse salt. Let the squash sit for 12 hours in the refrigerator.

Day 2
Wipe the squash slices free of salt and put them in sterilized preserving jars. Peel and coarsely chop the shallots, and peel and slice the horseradish. Insert them, along with the spices, between the squash slices.

Bring the vinegar, sugar, and the measured water to a boil in a saucepan, then pour the boiling syrup over the squash in the jars. Seal the jars and let the squash stand to pickle in the refrigerator or in a cool cellar or other cool place for about a week, before enjoying them with boiled, fried, or braised meats and poultry, or as a condiment in a sandwich. The pickled squash will keep fresh, stored in the refrigerator, for up to 6 months.

Pickled cabbage
with juniper, chervil, and pears

½ white cabbage, about 1 to 1½ lb
sea salt flakes
1 teaspoon cumin seeds
10 juniper berries, chopped
½ cup apple cider vinegar
freshly ground pepper
2 pears, such as Conference or Doyenne du Comice
1 handful of chervil, chopped

Remove the outer leaves of the cabbage and chop the rest of the cabbage very finely. Bring a large pan of lightly salted water to a boil and throw the cumin seeds and chopped juniper berries into the water. Cook the cabbage for 2 to 3 minutes until it is tender but still has some bite. Drain the cabbage and flavor with the vinegar, salt, and pepper. Then let cool.

Cut the pears into quarters, remove the cores, and cut them into long, thin strips. Mix the cooled cabbage with the pears and chopped chervil just before serving.

Serve the pickled cabbage as an accompaniment to the Braised Shoulder of Venison with Jerusalem Artichoke and Apple Purée (see page 142) and other dishes with game, or with the Braised Pork Knuckle with Spicy Sugar-browned Cabbage (see page 139) as an alternative to the browned cabbage.

Pickled Jerusalem artichokes

3 tablespoons cold-pressed canola oil
3 tablespoons apple cider vinegar
1 tablespoon clear honey
sea salt flakes and freshly ground pepper
7 oz Jerusalem artichokes
½ bunch flat-leaf parsley

Put the oil, vinegar, honey, salt, and pepper a small saucepan and bring to a boil.

Wash the Jerusalem artichokes thoroughly and slice them into very fine slices using a mandoline or a sharp knife. Spread the slices in the bottom of a shallow dish and pour in the hot dressing. Then let marinate for 10 to 15 minutes.

Finely chop the parsley and stir into the Jerusalem artichokes just before serving.

Baking and sweet things

Apple muffins
with rosemary

MAKES ABOUT 25 TO 30 MUFFINS

2 sticks softened butter
2 cups jaggery, plus extra for sprinkling
    onto the vanilla seeds
5 organic eggs
⅔ cup whole blanched almonds
1⅔ cups all-purpose flour
4 apples, such as Cox or Ingrid Marie
1 rosemary sprig, leaves picked and
    finely chopped
½ vanilla bean, split lengthwise and
    seeds scraped out

Beat the softened butter and sugar together thoroughly, then beat in the eggs, one at a time. Incorporate each egg well before you add the next to prevent the batter from splitting.

Chop the almonds finely in a food processor and stir them into the muffin batter along with the flour. Mix well until the batter is smooth and supple.

Cut the apples into quarters, remove the cores, and dice them into small cubes. Put the apples in a bowl and mix them with the finely chopped rosemary and the seeds from the vanilla bean—if you scrape the vanilla seeds out onto a cutting board and sprinkle a little sugar on them, you can separate the grains from each other by crushing the sugar and vanilla seeds with the flat side of a chef's knife. That way, the vanilla is easy to combine with the apple filling. Add the apple filling to the batter and pour the batter into the cups of a muffin pan lined with paper baking cups or, use a silicone muffin pan.

Bake the muffins in a preheated oven at 400°F for about 15 minutes until they are baked through and golden on top. Remove the muffins from the oven and transfer them to a wire rack to cool slightly.

This muffin recipe is something between a traditional very light and airy muffin and a more dense spongecake. I am aware that rosemary is a flavor that doesn't agree with everyone when it comes to using it in the sweet kitchen, so if you really don't connect with the slightly soapy pine-needle taste, you should not feel obliged to include it. But I promise you, rosemary and apples make an extraordinary combination.

Tip Using this batter as a foundation, you can add whatever filling the season prescribes—hazelnuts, pear, and ginger, for example, or plums, almonds, and cinnamon. Obviously, you can also just fill it with chocolate, orange zest, and dried fruit. In fact, you can pretty much tailor-make the filling with your own favorite additions.

Apple pie with hazelnuts and vanilla

SERVES 10

Filling
2¼ lb apples, such as Filippa, Gråsten
    (Gravenstein), or Cox
½ cup apple juice (preferably unfiltered)
⅓ cup hard dry cider
½ vanilla bean, split lengthwise and
    seeds scraped out
1 tablespoon honey

Batter
2¼ cups skinned hazelnuts (see method
    on page 171)
2 sticks softened butter, plus extra
    for greasing
2 cups sugar
2 organic eggs
2 organic egg whites
1 cup all-purpose flour

Peel and core the apples, then cut them into smaller pieces. Put them in a bowl and toss them in the apple juice, hard cider, the seeds from the vanilla bean, and the honey, then let them soak for 10 to 15 minutes.

Chop the hazelnuts finely and beat them with the butter and sugar until completely smooth and creamy. Add the whole eggs and egg whites, one at a time, so that each egg is incorporated well into the batter before adding the next. Then add the flour.

Pour the batter into a buttered 10½- to 11-inch springform pan. Drain the apples (save the juice for later) and arrange them on top of the batter, giving them a light press with the flat of your hand so that they sink in a little. Bake the apple pie in a preheated oven at 325°F for 1 hour to 1 hour 10 minutes. If the pie browns too fast, you can cover it with foil for the remaining baking time. Remove from the oven and let cool slightly.

Reduce the liquid from the apples to a thick syrup and pour it over the slightly cooled pie. It will benefit from having 3 to 4 hours to absorb the syrup—it is almost better the day after, when it has "set." Enjoy the pie with lightly whipped cream, Yogurt Ice Cream (see page 246), or crème fraîche.

Crispy puff pastry apple pie

5½ oz frozen puff pastry (2 sheets),
    defrosted
all-purpose flour, for dusting
4 to 5 apples, such as Cox or Ingrid Marie
1¼ cups confectioners' sugar
2 tablespoons butter, melted
¼ cup Calvados

Roll the puff pastry out thinly on a lightly floured surface, creating long rectangular sheets. Cut each sheet in half to make 4 pie crusts. Alternatively, cut out 4 circles 4½ to 5½ inches in diameter. Place the pie crusts on a cookie sheet lined with parchment paper and let rest in the refrigerator for 10 minutes.

Core the apples and cut them into very thin slices (or leave the cores in the apples—it looks beautiful). Place the apple slices in a thin layer on the puff pastry, each slightly overlapping the last, sprinkle with the confectioners' sugar, and drizzle with the melted butter. Bake the pies in a preheated oven at 425°F for 15 minutes until the pastry has puffed up and the apples are beautifully golden and lightly caramelized.

Remove the pies from the oven and sprinkle with the Calvados while they are still hot. Serve warm with crème fraîche, Greek yogurt, or vanilla ice cream.

Apple sauce and apple sorbet
with roasted hazelnuts, dried apples, and sugar beet syrup

SERVES 6

Apple sorbet
1 lb 2 oz apples, such as Ingrid Marie, Belle de Boskoop, or Cox
1¼ cups water
1 cup jaggery
2 tablespoons glucose syrup
⅔ cup apple juice
lemon juice
hard cider

Apple sauce
1 lb 2 oz apples, such as Ingrid Marie, Belle de Boskoop, or Cox
¼ to ⅓ cup sugar
½ vanilla bean, split lengthwise and seeds scraped out
1 handful of lemon verbena leaves (can be left out or replaced by lemon zest)

To serve
¼ cup hazelnuts
2 tablespoons sugar beet syrup (see tip)
Dried Apples (see right)

First, make the sorbet. Wash the apples and remove the cores, but leave the peel on. (Reserve the cores—they contain lots of pectin, which helps to stabilize the finished sorbet.) Cut the apples into small pieces, put them in a saucepan with the measured water, sugar, glucose, apple cores, and apple juice and boil for about 3 to 4 minutes until the apples are tender.

Remove the cores, put the apples and the syrup in a blender, and blend until creamy. Pass the pulp through a fine sieve so that the blended apple mixture is completely smooth. Add the lemon juice and hard cider to taste. Now follow the recipe for Rhubarb Sorbet on page 60 from the third step to finish making the sorbet, including alternative methods if you don't have an ice-cream maker.

While the sorbet is freezing, make the apple sauce. Wash the apples, remove the cores, and cut them into large cubes. Put the apples in a saucepan with the sugar and the split, scraped vanilla bean and vanilla seeds. Cover with a lid and slowly bring the apples to a boil so that they release some juice, then let them simmer for about 10 to 15 minutes to create a dense, chunky apple sauce. Pass the sauce through a coarse sieve for a beautifully smooth consistency and season, if necessary, with a little extra sugar along with the chopped verbena. Let the sauce cool in a bowl.

Meanwhile, skin the hazelnuts. Place the nuts in a small ovenproof dish and toast them in a preheated oven at 350°F for 7 to 10 minutes. Remove the nuts from the oven, pour them directly onto a clean tea towel, and rub off the skins inside the towel.

Put them in a dry skillet, add 1 tablespoon of the sugar beet syrup, and bring to a boil, then simmer the nuts in the syrup for about 30 seconds until they are glazed and sticky (be careful—they burn easily). Remove the nuts from the pan and let them cool.

Arrange the apple sauce in deep dessert plates with the Dried Apples, roasted hazelnuts, a scoop of apple sorbet, and the last of the sugar beet syrup drizzled on top, to serve.

True dessert fanatics would probably like to pour something like cream, crème Anglaise, ice cream, or another creamy substance on top, and I guarantee that to be a winner as well. But sometimes I really like the pure and fresh juiciness of a fruit dessert such as this, so serve it to suit your taste.

· ·

Tip Sugar beet syrup is concentrated, unrefined sugar beet juice, as opposed to Swedish dark syrup, which is a mixture of white refined sugar and molasses derived from sugar cane. Sugar beet syrup has considerably more character and nuance than plain dark syrup. You will find it in most Meyers Deli shops and from online suppliers, or you can, of course, replace it with a good dark syrup.

· ·

Dried apples

½ cup water
2 tablespoons sugar
2 apples, such as Ingrid Marie or Cox

Put the measured water and sugar in a saucepan and heat to dissolve the sugar, then let the syrup cool.

Wash the apples, then cut into paper-thin slices. This is unquestionably easiest if you have a mandoline. I usually leave the cores in the apples because it looks so beautiful in the dried apples. However, if you don't like the extra crunch, remove them with an apple corer.

Dip the apple slices in the cooled syrup and place them on a baking pan lined with parchment paper. Place the apples in a preheated oven at 140°F, preferably with the fan on, and with the oven door ajar. Dry the apple slices for about 2½ to 3 hours until they are absolutely crisp but have not browned.

Remove the apples from the oven and let them cool before storing them in a tightly sealed, sterilized glass jar for up to 3 days.

Stewed apples
with vanilla yogurt

**1 lb 10 oz apples, such as Ingrid Marie
    or Cox**
2 tablespoons water
**2 to 4 tablespoons jaggery (depending
    on sweetness of apples)**
**½ vanilla bean, split lengthwise and
    seeds scraped out**

Wash the apples but leave the skin on, since there is plenty of nice apple flavor and lots of vitamins in it. (If you use apples with very thick skin, pass the apple sauce through a coarse sieve after cooking.) Cut the apples into quarters, remove the cores, and dice.

Put the apples in a saucepan with the measured water, sugar, and the split and scraped vanilla bean and vanilla seeds. Simmer, with the lid on, over low heat for about 8 to 10 minutes until tender and a little mashed. If necessary, add a little extra sugar to taste, then let the apple sauce cool. Serve cold or at room temperature topped with Vanilla Yogurt (*see* below).

Vanilla yogurt

1¼ cups Greek yogurt, 2% fat
**½ vanilla bean, split lengthwise and
    seeds scraped out**
2 tablespoons confectioners' sugar
**10 lemon verbena leaves (*see* tip),
    very finely chopped**

Stir the yogurt with the seeds from the vanilla bean, the confectioners' sugar, and the very finely chopped lemon verbena in a bowl.

Let the creamy mixture stand for 15 minutes before serving so the taste of verbena and vanilla is fully infused into the yogurt.

....

Tip Lemon verbena is an overlooked herb with a very fine lemon flavor. Verbena is great in September, but if you can't find it, use lemon balm instead. The dessert will also still be delicious without any herbs.
....
....

> **The staple apple**
>
> In the parts of Denmark where apples grow well, that is East Jutland, Funen, Zealand, and the Danish South Sea Islands, apples have for centuries played an important role as a year-round food staple. That is especially true in Lolland-Falster, where both fresh and dried apples and pears are included in many of the local dishes. The oldest recipe for apple pie dates back to the 1600s. However, it was only when sugar beet made the Danish production of inexpensive white sugar possible in the last decades of the 1800s that sweet dishes, such as apple pie, became an everyday dish for the Danes.

Baked apples
with beer ice cream

SERVES 6

2 star anise
½ cup porter (dark brown beer)
2 tablespoons dark brown sugar
**finely grated zest and juice of
    1 organic lemon**
2 tablespoons cold-pressed canola oil
seeds from 1 vanilla bean
6 Cox apples

Crush the star anise a little using a mortar and pestle or with the flat side of a chef's knife. Combine with the porter, brown sugar, lemon zest and juice, oil, and split, scraped vanilla bean and vanilla seeds in a bowl to make a pickling brine.

Wash the apples, place them in an ovenproof dish, and pour the liquid on top. Bake in a preheated oven at 300°F for 50 minutes to 1 hour, stirring the apples around a few times during baking. Scoop up and pour the pickling liquid over them so that they are baked evenly, while becoming beautifully glazed and shiny. Serve the apples warm with Beer Ice Cream (*see* right) and a little syrup from the dish.

Beer ice cream

2 cups half-and-half cream
¾ cup sugar
½ cup porter (strong dark beer)
**½ vanilla bean, split lengthwise and
    seeds scraped out**
5 organic egg yolks

Combine the cream, sugar, porter, and split, scraped vanilla bean and vanilla seeds in a pan. Gently warm the mixture so that the sugar dissolves.

Put the egg yolks in a bowl large enough to accommodate all the ingredients. Pour the hot cream mixture into the egg yolks slowly and carefully while whisking vigorously. Pour it all back into the pan and cook over low heat to thicken the cream until it reaches a temperature of 84 to 85°C and, although still runny, easily sticks to a wooden spoon.

When the texture is right, pour the cream through a sieve into a bowl. Let the cream cool for a while before pouring it into an ice-cream maker and churning it until it has the consistency of soft ice cream. You can now choose to serve the ice cream immediately, or you can transfer it to a plastic box with a lid and store it in the freezer for 1 to 2 hours for a firmer texture.

In contrast to other ice creams, it is not necessary to let this one sit at room temperature before serving—it is soft and delicious from the moment you take it out of the freezer.

....

Tip Beer ice cream is not well suited to other freezing methods. But if you don't have access to an ice-cream maker, you can freeze it in a container, chop it into small pieces, and blend in a food processor into a kind of soft-serve ice cream.
....

Elderberries

Elderberries begin to mature in September, and the birds are always the first to discover them. They also know which trees have the best berries. You will find elder trees in woods, thickets, managed hedges, and abandoned gardens. They can grow up to 26 feet tall, but often form shorter shrubs, especially if regularly cut back. The young branches are filled with soft, white marrow, and the leaves are divided into five to seven elliptical, jagged leaflets. The plant itself has a characteristic slightly sickly smell.

Using elderberries

Pick the ripe berries off the trees in bunches and rinse them. If are using them for juice, cut off the coarser stems. If you want to make a preserve, you will need to pick the berries off the stems with your fingers or using a fork. Be careful not to get the juice on your clothes, as it is a very intense colorant and virtually impossible to remove.

Try making some *grevskabets* preserve to have with your *æbleskiver* (Doughnut Holes, see page 243) using equal parts elderberries and tart apples cooked with sugar and seasoned with lemon juice. You can pickle the ripe red berries with apple cider vinegar and sugar just like beets, while the unripe green berries can also be pickled.

Dried elderberries

You can also try drying elderberries. Carefully pick the berries off the stems, preferably using a fork so that they remain nice and whole, as you may accidentally squash the berries if you use your fingers. Spread the berries on a sheet of parchment paper, sprinkle with confectioners' sugar, and bake in a preheated convection oven at 140°F for about 1½ hours, preferably with the oven door ajar. They should shrivel up a little and slightly resemble raisins. Let the elderberries cool, then seal them in a sterilized glass jar or other airtight container and store them in a cool, dry place. Eat them with yogurt or use them in a salad, on a cake, or in ice cream or cream—delicious.

Cinnamon swirls

MAKES 16 SWIRLS

Dough
2 cups cold whole milk
2-oz cake (⅓ cup) fresh compressed yeast (baker's yeast)
1 large organic egg, plus 1 extra, beaten, to glaze
2¼ lb all-purpose flour, plus extra for dusting
¾ cup sugar
1 tablespoon fine sea salt
2 tablespoons ground cardamom
1½ sticks butter

Filling
1¼ sticks softened butter
⅔ cup sugar, plus extra for sprinkling over the swirls
2 tablespoons ground cinnamon

Pour the cold milk into a bowl and stir in the yeast. Add the egg, flour, sugar, salt, and cardamom, and knead the dough until it is supple and glossy and has stopped sticking to the bowl. This will take about 20 minutes, so use an electric stand mixer fitted with a dough hook and set it on medium speed.

Now cut the butter into small cubes and add them to the dough. Then let the machine continue kneading for a further 20 minutes until the dough is smooth and shiny. (The long kneading times are absolutely crucial for the final result.)

Cover the bowl with a clean dish towel and let the dough rest for 1½ hours.

Place the dough on a floured surface and roll it out into a rectangle 16 inches wide and 20 inches long. Spread the softened butter over the dough, then sprinkle the sugar and cinnamon evenly on top and rub them into the butter with your fingertips. Fold one-third of the dough toward the center and fold the other third over the first so that you have 3 layers of dough. Roll out the dough again until it is 12 inches wide and 20 to 24 inches long, and then cut it into 16 strips.

Hold each strip at either end and give it 4 to 5 twists, but don't twist it so hard that you squeeze out the filling. Take the end of a twisted strip in one hand and wrap it twice around the index and middle finger of your other hand. Place the remaining snippet of dough over the 2 rings, put it between your index and middle finger, and pull it down with your fingers to secure the snippet inside the bun.

Put the cinnamon swirls on a couple of cookie sheets lined with parchment paper, twists facing upward. Cover with a clean dish towel and let rise in a warm room until doubled in size (about 2 hours).

Brush the cinnamon swirls with the beaten egg, sprinkle them with a little sugar, and bake in a preheated oven at 400°F for about 12 to 14 minutes. Transfer them to a wire rack to cool.

• •

Tip These cinnamon swirls are of Norwegian origin. When I wrote my baking book *Meyers Bakery*, we went on a field trip to visit Bakeriet in Lom, where I had previously sampled these wonderful, twisted little pastries that surpassed anything I had experienced before in the way of cinnamon buns. You can, of course, just shape the dough into ordinary cinnamon buns and still have some tasty baked goods. However, you will not get quite as much caramelized cinnamon filling as when you form it into swirls.

• •

Pears poached in elderberry juice
served with skyr and elderberry syrup

4 pears, such as Conference or Doyenne du Comice
1¾ cups water
1 cup jaggery, plus extra if needed
1¼ cups unsweetened elderberry juice
2 tablespoons apple cider vinegar
1 cup skyr

Peel the pears beautifully from the stalk to the base, leaving the stalks on. Place the pears in a pan with the measured water, sugar, and elderberry juice. Bring the pears to a boil and then cook gently over low heat for 20 to 25 minutes until tender but still with some bite. Stir a few times during this time so that they are evenly cooked.

Lift the pears out and place them on a plate. Reduce the pear juice until two-thirds remain and it has reached a syrupy consistency. Add the vinegar and possibly a little extra sugar to taste so that the balance between sweet and sour is perfect.

Place the pears back in the syrup and let them cool in the refrigerator, where they will keep for 25 to 30 days, as long as they are covered by the syrup (and you can resist them for that long!).

Flavor the skyr with some of the elderberry syrup and eat it with the beautiful, elderberry-colored pears. I highly recommend munching an Almond Macaroon (*see* page 114) or a toasted crumpet with your free hand.

Pear sorbet
with fennel seeds and aquavit

1¼ cups water
1 cup jaggery
2 tablespoons glucose syrup (*see* tip)
½ tablespoon fennel seeds
1 lb 2 oz ripe pears
juice of 2 limes
2 tablespoons aquavit (pear brandy is
    also a great option)

Combine the measured water, sugar, glucose, and fennel seeds in a pan and bring to a boil.

Wash the pears, cut them into quarters, and remove the cores, then cut them into small pieces—just leave the peel on. Put the pear pieces and the hot syrup in a blender and blend for 1 minute until the pear pieces are blended completely.

Strain the fruit syrup through a fine sieve to make it perfectly smooth, and season with the lime juice and aquavit. Now follow the recipe for Rhubarb Sorbet on page 60 from the third step to finish making the sorbet, including alternative methods if you don't have an ice-cream maker.

Serve the pear sorbet as a refresher for your palate after a heavy dinner in the fall. I like to eat it as it is, with its crystal clear pear and aquavit taste, but you can serve it with a crunchy little cookie or scattered with Crispy Crumbles (*see* page 60).

. . . .

Tip Glucose syrup is extracted from corn and is less sweet than ordinary sugar or sugar beet syrup, but it gives elasticity and creaminess when you use it in caramels, dessert creams, or, as here, in ice cream and sorbet. Glucose syrup is available in well stocked supermarkets and from online retailers for confectionery making.

. . . .

Rye bread crisp,
apple sauce, and blackcurrant preserve with whipped cream

9 oz dark rye bread (choose one that
    doesn't have too many whole grains)
½ cup sugar, divided
2 tablespoons butter
4 to 6 large apples, such as Cox
    or Belle de Boskoop
3 tablespoons water
seeds from ½ vanilla bean (optional)
¼ cup blackcurrant preserve
1 cup heavy whipping cream,
    freshly whipped

Grate the bread on the coarse side of the grater and mix it with ¼ cup of the sugar.

Melt the butter in a saucepan and add the bread and sugar mixture. Toast the bread over medium heat for 2 to 3 minutes until it starts to smell caramelized, then remove it from the pan and let cool. When it cools, the sugar will harden and the rye bread mixture will become nice and crisp.

Peel the apples (or leave the peel on if you like), cut them into wedges, and remove the cores. Cook the apples to a sauce with the remaining ¼ cup sugar, measured water, and possibly the split, scraped vanilla bean and vanilla seeds. The combination of vanilla and apple is a great marriage, but once in a while it can also be nice to let the apple flavor shine on its own, especially if you are dealing with an interesting old apple variety or a variety with a very short season, which should be enjoyed to the full.

When the apple sauce is done, after 15 to 20 minutes (maybe more or less depending on the apple variety), take the pan off the heat and let cool completely.

Add the rye bread crisp, apple sauce, and blackcurrant preserve in layers to a bowl (the first and last layer should be the rye bread crisp). Decorate with the freshly whipped cream before serving.

Princess pudding
SERVES 6 TO 8

⅔ stick butter, plus extra for greasing
⅓ cup sugar
½ cup all-purpose flour
finely grated zest and juice of
    ½ organic lemon
¼ vanilla bean, split lengthwise and
    seeds scraped out
1 cup lowfat milk
8 organic egg yolks
4 organic egg whites

Melt the butter in a heavy saucepan, add the sugar, flour, lemon zest and juice, and vanilla seeds from the bean and cook, whisking continuously, until the mixture becomes smooth and comes away from the side of the pan.

Heat the milk in separate pan, and when it reaches a boil, add it to the roux. Stir the batter well with a large spoon and let it cook lightly so that it firms and almost lifts from the pan. Let the batter cool slightly, then stir in the egg yolks, one at a time.

Whisk the egg whites until stiff and then fold them into the batter. I always briskly stir in a spoonful of the egg whites first, making it easier to gently fold in the rest of the whites and keep their airy texture.

Pour the batter into 12 to 16 small buttered ramekins or ovenproof dishes. Make a bain-marie by standing the dishes in a shallow baking pan and pouring boiling water into the pan to come halfway up the sides of the dishes. Bake the princess puddings in a preheated oven at 350°F for around 30 to 35 minutes until the batter has souffléd.

Turn the puddings out onto a serving platter. Serve them, still warm, with Apple Sauce (*see* left) or fresh fruit.

Winter

Seasonal ingredients

Cultivated produce

apples
beans and lentils
beets
Belgian endive
Brussels sprouts
cabbage
carrots
celery root
Chinese artichokes
cod
grains
haddock
hare
horseradish
Jerusalem artichokes

kale
kohlrabi
leeks
lumpfish roe
nuts
onions
oysters
parsley
parsnips
partridge
pears
pumpkin
red cabbage
redfish
salsify

Savoy cabbage
sloes
whiting

In the wild

oyster mushrooms
mussels
chickweed
velvet shank mushrooms
water mint
watercress
venison
Scots pine bark
perch
ramsons
scurvy grass

lumpfish
mussels
nettles
daisies
ground elder
wood sorrel
birch sap
coltsfoot
violets
dandelion leaves

Soups and appetizers

Mushroom soup
with wheat berries and chicken meatballs

1 lb 2 oz field mushrooms
2 shallots
1 garlic clove
5 thyme sprigs
2 tablespoons olive oil
sea salt flakes and freshly ground pepper
½ cup dry sherry, plus extra if needed
4 cups chicken stock or water
7 oz cooked wheat grains
Chicken Meatballs (see below)

Clean the mushrooms using a brush or a small vegetable knife, then cut them into thin slices. Peel and chop the shallots and garlic.

Sauté the mushrooms, shallots, garlic, and thyme in the olive oil until they are tender and the shallot turns translucent, then season with salt and pepper. Add the sherry and reduce to half its original volume, then add the chicken stock or water. Simmer for 10 to 15 minutes so that the mushrooms are still al dente but have imparted their flavor to the broth.

Add the cooked wheat grains to the broth and season to taste with salt and pepper and, if necessary, a little extra sherry.

Finally, add the Chicken Meatballs to the soup and let them heat up. Serve the soup with good bread.

Chicken meatballs

1 boneless chicken breast
sea salt flakes
1 organic egg, lightly beaten
½ cup heavy whipping cream
freshly ground pepper
1 thyme sprig, chopped

Remove any skin or tendons from the chicken breast and cut it into large cubes. Season the chicken with salt, chop it in a food processor, and then mix it with the egg and cream. Season with pepper and

the chopped thyme. The mixture should be worked until soft and smooth, but not for too long otherwise it might split.

Take a small lump of the meatball mixture, then poach it and taste it to check the seasoning. When you're happy with the flavor, form the mixture into balls with a small spoon, aiming for ¼ inch in diameter.

Poach the meatballs in a pan of salted water for 2 to 3 minutes. These meatballs are suitable for both clear soups and asparagus or pea soups (*see* pages 19 and 66).

Fish soup
with root vegetables and mashed fava beans

Soup
1 large apple
1 leek
1 parsnip or parsley root
1 onion
3 garlic cloves
2¼ lb bones of flatfish, such as flounder, halibut, or turbot
a few parsley stems
12 whole black peppercorns
1½ cups white wine
3 tablespoons heavy whipping cream
3 tablespoons wheat beer
1 tablespoon apple cider vinegar
sugar, to taste
sea salt flakes and freshly ground pepper

Filling
1 carrot
3½ oz celery root
3 tablespoons water
sea salt flakes
½ cup cooked dried fava beans (or use canned beans)
2 tablespoons olive oil
grated zest and juice of ½ organic lemon
freshly ground pepper
¼ handful of parsley, chopped

First, make the soup. Wash the apple (keep the peel on) and vegetables, then cut them all into small pieces and put in a pan along with the fish bones, parsley stems, and peppercorns. Pour in the white wine and add enough water to cover the vegetables. Bring the soup to a boil and skim off any foam or impurities that rise to the surface, then lower the heat and let simmer for 25 minutes.

Turn the heat off and let the soup stand for 20 minutes, then strain through a sieve and return to the pan. Add the cream and then reduce to the desired intensity and consistency. Season with the wheat beer and vinegar, and sugar, salt and pepper to taste.

Now make the filling. Peel and cut the vegetables into large cubes and add them to a small pan with the measured water and some salt. Steam the vegetables, with the lid on, for about a minute until tender but still al dente.

Mash the beans coarsely, adding the oil, lemon zest and juice, and salt and pepper to taste.

Pour any excess water from the steamed vegetables into the soup, then add the mashed beans to the pan along with the vegetables and let it all warm through. Place a large spoonful of vegetables and mashed beans in wide shallow soup bowls. Whisk the soup quite vigorously so that it is lightly foaming, then pour the hot soup over the vegetables and scatter with chopped parsley to finish. Serve with good bread.

Potato soup
with lumpfish roe and dill

14 oz baking potatoes
1 leek
1 tablespoon butter
3 thyme sprigs, leaves picked
1 garlic clove, minced
sea salt flakes and freshly ground pepper
3 cups water
3 tablespoons heavy whipping cream
7 oz fresh lumpfish roe with all membranes removed (*see* right)
1 handful of dill

Peel and slice the potatoes thinly, place them in a bowl of cold water, and let them soak for 10 minutes. Cut off the root and top of the leek, then slice into thin rings and rinse them thoroughly in cold water to remove all the soil.

Drain the potato slices and leek thoroughly. Melt the butter in a pan and sauté the vegetables for 3 to 4 minutes until they have softened a little. Season with the thyme leaves, garlic, salt, and pepper, and sauté for about 1 minute.

Add the measured water and simmer the soup over low heat for 15 to 20 minutes until the potato slices are tender. Add the whipping cream and cook for another 5 minutes.

Pour the soup into a blender and blend until smooth, but not for long otherwise it will become sticky in consistency.

Pour the soup back into the pan, warm it through, and season to taste with salt and pepper. Serve in wide flat soup bowls with a good spoonful of lumpfish roe and the dill on top. Serve this with some nice wholegrain bread.

Cleaning lumpfish roe

Lumpfish roes are held together by big membranes, and for the best dining experience they should be removed completely. It is pretty easy to remove the membranes yourself and much less expensive than buying the precious roe in a purified form. Just do the following. Remove the coarse outer membrane by hand. Put the roe in a bowl with a little cold water and salt. Whisk for a while so that the rest of the membranes cling to the whisk instead of the roe. Remove the membranes from the whisk a few times while whisking and continue until the roe is totally free of membranes. At this point, I usually leave the roe in the bowl and let it stand under the cold running water for a few minutes. When remnants of membrane no longer rise to the surface and into the sink, that means your roe is clean. Pour the roe in a sieve and let it drain for a while. Season with salt and your lumpfish roe is ready to be served. The roe can be stored in the refrigerator for a few days, or you can even freeze it.

Split pea soup
with parsley and canola oil

¾ cup dried green split peas
1 onion
1 rosemary sprig
1 garlic clove, peeled and minced
2 tablespoons standard canola oil
sea salt flakes and freshly ground pepper
2 tablespoons apple cider vinegar
½ handful of flat-leaf parsley
a little cold-pressed canola oil

Pour the split peas into a colander, rinse them with cold fresh water, and let them drain thoroughly. Peel and chop the onion.

Sauté the onion, split peas, rosemary, and garlic in the standard canola oil in a saucepan for 1 to 2 minutes without coloring. Add enough water to cover the ingredients by a depth of about 2 inches and bring to a boil, then simmer gently, with the lid on, for 45 minutes or until the split peas are tender.

Take the pan off the heat, save a few tablespoons of the split peas for the garnish, and scoop the rest of the soup into a blender. Remember to discard the rosemary sprig. It should definitely not go into the blender, as it could ruin both your soup and your blender. Blend the soup until smooth, and season to taste with salt, pepper, and the vinegar. If necessary, dilute the soup with a little water so that it has the consistency of yogurt.

Wash the parsley thoroughly, let it drain well, and then chop it. Serve the soup scattered with the chopped parsley and the reserved cooked split peas, and finish off with a drizzle of cold-pressed canola oil.

This soup makes a really nice appetizer, especially with a good scattering of Crispy Croutons (*see* page 128).

Potato soup »

Gravad salmon
with sweet and spicy mustard sauce
SERVES 8 TO 10

1 handful of dill (*see* tip)
1 tablespoon fennel seeds
1 teaspoon allspice berries
2 tablespoons coriander seeds
2 tablespoons juniper berries
1 star anise
¾ cup jaggery
½ cup sea salt flakes
½ side of very fresh salmon, skin on,
    scaled and pin-boned, about
    4½ to 5½ lb

Day 1
Wash the dill very, very carefully and let it drain, then chop finely. Crush all the spices thoroughly using a mortar and pestle and mix with the sugar, salt, and chopped dill. Place the side of salmon in a dish, skin-side down, sprinkle the spice mixture over it, and cover the dish tightly with plastic wrap. Let the salmon marinate in the refrigerator for at least 24 hours and preferably 48 hours, turning it over a few times in the process.

Day 2 or 3
Take the salmon out of the dish, slice thinly, and serve with good wholewheat bread and the Spicy and Sweet Mustard Sauce (*see* right).

Gravad salmon is a classic on the breakfast table, but it is also nice as an appetizer for a big dinner. I like to pair it with a beet salad, such as the Beet Tartare with Horseradish (*see* page 199), the sweetness of which goes really well with the gravad fish. If you don't finish all the gravad salmon at once, it can be kept for about 8 days in a tightly sealed container in the refrigerator.

• •

TIP I have used fresh dill when making gravad salmon throughout my life and have had no problems, but the fact is that soil bacteria can sometimes lurk in fresh dill,

and therefore in the professional kitchen we are forced to use dried dill. At home, however, I still always use the fresh herb, washing it thoroughly, of course. Now that you know the reality, and should you prefer to use dried dill weed instead, you will need about 1¾ oz (about 1 cup) for this recipe.

• •

Spicy and sweet mustard sauce

½ cup prepared Dijon mustard
½ cup prepared sweet French mustard
⅔ cup brown sugar
3 tablespoons cider vinegar
3 tablespoons cold-pressed canola oil
1½ tablespoons fennel seeds
½ handful of dill, chopped
sea salt flakes and freshly ground pepper

Combine the 2 kinds of mustard in a bowl along with the brown sugar and vinegar, and stir until most of the sugar has dissolved. Then add the oil, a little at a time, whisking vigorously until the sauce thickens and becomes smooth.

Season the sauce with the fennel seeds, first giving them a quick crush using a mortar and pestle or with the flat side of a chef's knife, the chopped dill, and salt and pepper to taste. Now the sauce is ready to serve.

Oysters
with apple and horseradish vinaigrette

2 apples
2 tablespoons canola oil
3 tablespoons apple cider vinegar
sea salt flakes and freshly ground pepper
1 teaspoon honey
2 tablespoons freshly grated
    horseradish, or to taste
16 Limfjord (native European) oysters
    (Brittany oysters can also be used)

Peel the apples, cut them into quarters, and remove the cores.

Mix the oil, vinegar, salt, pepper, and honey together in a bowl. Cut the apples into small cubes and add them to the vinaigrette. Season to taste with the horseradish. Let the vinaigrette stand for 5 minutes so that the flavor really develops.

To shuck the oysters, hold an oyster cupped-side down firmly in one hand with a dish towel. Insert the tip of an oyster knife close to the hinge between the "lid" and bottom shell and then twist the knife to prise the shells open, keeping the oyster level to prevent the juices from spilling out. Check them for stray pieces of shell and make sure they are nice and fresh (an oyster should smell fresh from the sea and have lots of lovely juice in the shell; if there is any doubt about the freshness, the oyster must be discarded).

Pour a little vinaigrette over each oyster and serve immediately.

Lumpfish roe
with blinis, red onion, and sour cream

Blinis
1¾ cups lowfat milk, divided
½ oz (1½ tablespoons) fresh compressed
   yeast (baker's yeast)
½ organic egg
½ teaspoon fine salt
1½ cups buckwheat flour
1½ cups all-purpose flour
1 to 2 tablespoons butter, for frying

Accompaniments
10½ oz fresh lumpfish roe
   (uncleaned weight)
sea salt flakes and freshly ground pepper
1 red onion
1 organic lemon
1 cup sour cream, 18% fat

Warm the milk to around 98°F—there is no need for a thermometer, just bring it to the warmest point your little finger can bear—and pour some of it into a bowl, then dissolve the yeast in it. Add the egg, salt, and both kinds of flour, then mix in the remaining milk and whisk into a smooth batter. Let the batter rise in the kitchen for about 1 hour.

Fry the batter in a little butter in a special blini pan for 1 to 2 minutes on each side until golden, to make small, thick pancakes. If you don't own a blini pan, use an ordinary small skillet. Keep the cooked blinis warm in a dish covered with foil while you cook the rest.

Clean the lumpfish roe (see page 188) and season with a little salt and pepper. Peel the onion and chop finely, and cut the lemon into wedges. Serve the warm blinis immediately with the lumpfish roe, chopped red onion, sour cream, and lemon wedges.

Fried tartare of cod
with beets, smoked bacon, and horseradish cream

5½ oz beets (about 2)
3 tablespoons plum vinegar
1 tablespoon jaggery
1 tablespoon olive oil
7 oz very fresh skinless cod fillet
sea salt flakes and freshly ground pepper
8 thin slices of smoked bacon
a few beet leaves or other bitter salad
   leaves

Wash the beets, put them in a saucepan of water, and bring them to a boil. Let simmer for about 20 to 30 minutes until tender but still al dente. Drain the cooked beets, submerge in cold water to cool a little, and then slip the skins off to expose the silky interior (wear plastic gloves if you don't want your hands to be stained red).

Cut the beets into large cubes and place them in a saucepan with the vinegar, sugar, and oil. Boil until the beets have absorbed the vinegar and they are glazed, and the marinade has the consistency of syrup.

Check that there are no stray bones left in the cod fillet and that the fish is really nice and fresh, smelling of the sea, not of the harbor. Cut the fillet into very small cubes—use a sharp knife so that the flesh is cut cleanly and not mashed. Put the cod in a bowl, season with salt and pepper, and mix well. Form into 4 small patties and place them in the refrigerator for 10 minutes so that they firm up before frying.

Heat up a skillet and fry the thin slices of bacon until they are crispy and starting to curl a little. Take the bacon out of the pan and place on paper towels.

Pour off the excess fat from the skillet and then fry the tartare patties for about 30 seconds on one side only—that way, they get a beautiful crust while still remaining raw. Serve the patties with the warm, glazed beets, the crispy bacon, a small salad, and freshly grated Horseradish Cream (see below).

I love the classic Danish dish of boiled cod with the works—pickled beets, bacon, grated horseradish, fish, mustard, and butter sauce—and this appetizer is my modern take on that ever-good combination.

Horseradish cream

½ cup lowfat milk
sugar, to taste
sea salt flakes and freshly ground pepper
finely grated zest and juice of
   ½ organic lemon
freshly grated horseradish, to taste

Heat the milk up in a saucepan and season to taste with sugar, salt, pepper, and the lemon zest and juice.

Remove the pan from the heat and season with as much freshly grated horseradish as you would like. Personally, I like it so that it tingles a little up the nose.

Pour the horseradish milk into a bowl and place it in the freezer for a few hours until completely frozen. Scrape the ice with a spoon to form a fine horseradish powder and use immediately as a garnish.

Salted halibut
with squash purée and chervil dressing

7 oz very fresh skinless halibut fillet
1 tablespoon sea salt flakes
1 teaspoon sugar
freshly ground pepper

Squash purée
1 butternut squash
2 tablespoons butter
3 tablespoons apple cider vinegar, plus
   extra if needed
sea salt flakes and freshly ground pepper
1 tablespoon acacia honey

Chervil dressing
1 shallot
3 tablespoons apple cider vinegar
3 tablespoons cold-pressed canola oil
1 teaspoon acacia honey
sea salt flakes and freshly ground pepper
1 handful of chervil

Day 1
Check the halibut for any remaining bones and mucus. Put it in a dish and sprinkle with the salt, sugar, and some pepper. Cover the dish with plastic wrap and let marinate in the refrigerator for 12 hours before serving.

Day 2
For the squash purée, peel and halve the squash, then scrape out the seeds with a spoon. Cut it into large cubes, saving a small piece for the chervil dressing. Put the rest of the squash cubes in a pan, cover with water, and bring to a boil. Let simmer for about 20 minutes until tender. Drain and place in a blender along with the remaining ingredients for the purée, then blend until completely smooth.

For the chervil dressing, peel the shallot and chop it very finely. Dice the reserved piece of squash. Put both vegetables in a bowl and toss in the vinegar, oil, honey, salt, and pepper. Chop the chervil coarsely and add it to the dressing.

Pour the squash purée into a pan, heat it up, and, if necessary, season with a little extra vinegar, salt, and pepper.

Take the halibut out of the refrigerator, and cut it into very thin slices. Serve it with the warm squash purée, drizzled with the chervil dressing as a nice appetizer.

· ·

TIP Make some extra squash purée (about half the quantity or so), put it in the refrigerator, and save it for the Bruschetta with Squash Purée and Goat Cheese (*see* page 224).

· ·

Terrine of wild boar
with squash chutney
SERVES 6 TO 8

2¼ lb shoulder of wild boar, boned and skinned (you can also use pork shoulder)
1 tablespoon olive oil
2 carrots
2 onions
sea salt flakes and freshly ground pepper
2 garlic cloves, peeled
5 thyme sprigs
2½ cups dark Danish beer
½ cup apple cider vinegar, plus extra if needed
1½ quarts chicken stock

Cut the shoulder into small pieces and brown in the olive oil in a large cast-iron pan. Peel and cut the carrots and onions into chunks, add them to the pan, and season with salt and pepper. Sauté until they start to brown as well.

Add the garlic, thyme, beer, vinegar, and stock, and bring the stew to a boil, then simmer with a lid on either on the stove over low heat or in a preheated oven at 300°F for 1 to 1½ hours until the meat is very tender.

Lift the meat out of the pan and cook the broth with the vegetables on the stove to reduce to one-third of its volume. Put the meat back into the broth and mash the stew lightly using a whisk so that the broth, meat, and vegetables combine to a soft and rustic consistency. Season with salt, pepper, and if necessary, a little extra vinegar.

Transfer the stew to a terrine mold, and cover with a piece of parchment paper. Add a little weight on top, such as a milk carton with a heavy cutting board placed on top to weigh it down further. Place the terrine in the refrigerator for 4 to 6 hours to set before slicing it. Serve the terrine with Squash Chutney (*see* right), some bitter lettuce leaves, such as frisée (curly endive), Belgian endive, or radicchio and some bread.

Squash chutney
MAKES 2 MEDIUM JARS

3¼ lb winter squash, such as Hokkaido or butternut
1 lb 2 oz red onions
1 lb 2 oz apples
3¼ cups jaggery
2 cups apple cider vinegar
2 tablespoons coarse sea salt
2 tablespoons coriander seeds
2 tablespoons fennel seeds
5 cardamom pods
2 whole red chiles
½ cup peeled and sliced fresh ginger root
2 garlic cloves, peeled and minced
1⅓ cup raisins

Peel and halve the squash, then scrape out the seeds with a spoon. Peel the red onions. Wash and core the apples, leaving the peel on. Then cut the squash, onions, and apples into large cubes.

Put the vegetable and apple cubes in a saucepan with all the remaining ingredients, except the raisins. Simmer over low heat, with the lid on, for 30 to 40 minutes until you have a dense compote, but don't cook the vegetables to the point of collapse. Remember to stir the chutney a few times while it cooks so that it doesn't burn.

Finally, stir in the raisins and then pour the chutney into sterilized preserving jars.

In my family, we often serve the squash chutney with meatballs or cold meat from the day before, and we also frequently use it in sandwiches. The chutney will keep fresh in the refrigerator for 4 to 5 months unopened, and 3 to 4 weeks after you have opened it.

Christmas terrine
with pickled beets

SERVES 12 TO 14

1 lb 2 oz pork liver
7 oz duck liver
10½ oz duck meat, such as duck breast
14 oz fresh or frozen hard pork back fat
2 apples, cored and cut into wedges
10 pitted prunes
1 onion, peeled
3 teaspoons ground allspice
2 teaspoons ground cloves
2 tablespoons Christmas aquavit
4 organic eggs
1 cup lowfat milk
⅓ cup all-purpose flour
sea salt flakes and freshly ground pepper
butter, for greasing

Run the livers, duck meat, pork back fat, apples, prunes, and onion through a meat grinder into a bowl. (The sweetness of the fruits goes really well with the liver.)

Add the spices, aquavit, eggs, and milk to the ground mixture and mix to a soft consistency. Add the flour toward the end of mixing, and stir it in gently. Season with salt and pepper. I always taste the raw pâté mixture at this stage to check it for seasoning, but if that's a bit too challenging for your stomach, bake a small sample in the oven.

Divide the mixture between 12 to 14 small buttered ramekins or individual foil trays. Place the terrines in a bain-marie by standing the dishes in a shallow baking pan and pouring enough boiling water into the pan to come halfway up the sides of the dishes. Bake in a preheated oven at 315°F for 35 to 40 minutes until they have set and are golden on top.

Serve on good rye bread with pickled beets as an accompaniment (*see right*). The baked terrines will stay fresh for 4 to 5 days in the refrigerator.

Tip When making quite a large quantity of pâté, as in this recipe, you can freeze some of the uncooked mixture directly in the dishes and then bake fresh terrines for any occasion. Take the dishes out of the freezer a few hours before you need to bake them so that the mixture can defrost, then bake as described in the recipe.

Two kinds of pickled beets

Here are my recipes for two ways of pickling beets—the first one is slightly spicy, and the other fruity, fresh, and slightly less sweet. Whichever you choose, you will end up with some very lovely pickled beets, excellent as an accompaniment to liver pâtés, cold cooked and cured meats, and ham and sausages, among others.

Pickled beets with orange, chile, and cinnamon
MAKES 3 MEDIUM JARS

4½ lb beets
sea salt flakes

Pickling brine
4 cups water
4 cups apple cider vinegar
3¼ cups jaggery
1 red chile
pared strips of zest and juice
    of 1 organic orange
1 cinnamon stick
3 star anise
10 whole black peppercorns
15 fennel seeds
1 small handful of coarse sea salt

Wash the beets free of soil and place them in a saucepan of salted water. Bring to a boil and skim off any foam or impurities, then simmer for 20 to 30 minutes, depending on their size, until just tender when pierced with a small knife (be careful not to overcook them). It is therefore important that the beets are all are about the same size so that their cooking time is the same. If they are not evenly sized, you will need to

adjust their cooking time to ensure that even the smallest still have some bite to them.

Drain the cooked beets and rinse them under the cold running water, then slip their skins off (wear plastic gloves if you want to avoid staining your hands red). When the beets have cooled, put them in sterilized preserving jars.

Put all the ingredients for the pickling brine in a saucepan and bring to a boil. Take the brine off the heat and let it stand for 10 minutes in the kitchen. Then pour the still-hot pickling brine over the beets, seal the jars tightly, and let them to pickle in the refrigerator for a minimum of 3 days before you eat them. The beets can be kept, unopened, for 6 months in the refrigerator and almost get better with time. Use within 3 months of opening

Pickled beets with blackcurrant and anise
MAKES 2 MEDIUM JARS

4½ lb beets
sea salt flakes

Pickling brine
4 cups apple cider vinegar
2 cups water
1¼ tablespoons coarse sea salt
2 cups sugar
4 star anise
3 tablespoons blackcurrant concentrate
    or cordial
6 lightly crushed black peppercorns
2½-inch piece of fresh horseradish root,
    peeled and sliced

Follow the first 3 steps of the previous recipe to prepare, cook, and skin the beets, then put them in sterilized preserving jars.

Put all the ingredients for the pickling brine, except for the horseradish, in a saucepan and bring to a boil. Take the brine off the heat and then add the horseradish slices (if the horseradish is boiled, it becomes bitter and can give the brine an unpleasant aftertaste). Pour the still-hot pickling brine over the beets, seal, and store as above.

Meat

My mother-in-law's glazed ham
with stewed kale

SERVES 12 TO 14

6½ lb lightly salt-cured smoked boneless ham in netting (order from your butcher's)
¼ cup Homemade Christmas Mustard (see right, or buy some good-quality mustard)
¼ cup brown sugar
finely grated zest and juice of 1 organic orange
1 teaspoon crushed star anise

Wrap the ham tightly in foil nice (you may need a few layers so that the ham is completely covered). Place the ham on an oven or roasting rack with a roasting pan filled with water underneath. Roast the ham in a preheated oven at 315°F for 2 to 2½ hours until it is quite firm and cooked through while juicy on the inside. If you own a meat thermometer, you can check the core temperature of the meat, which should be about 150°F.

Take the ham out of the oven and let it rest for 30 minutes in the foil. Meanwhile, combine the mustard, sugar, orange zest and juice, and crushed star anise.

Unwrap the ham, remove the netting, and score a criss-cross pattern in the fat with a sharp knife. Spread the glaze onto the scored side of the ham—the pattern will help it stick to the meat. Then put the ham back in the oven at 375°F for 8 to 10 minutes until the glaze is completely crisp and golden on top.

Remove the ham from the oven and serve it immediately with Stewed Kale (see right) and boiled potatoes. Homemade Christmas Mustard should also be on the table (see right).

TIP You can cook the ham the day before you need it and then glaze it just before serving. There is a lot of meat in a ham and it may be too much for certain occasions. If that is the case, you can just use a *kassler* (lightly salt-cured smoked loin of pork) or a saddle of pork instead of a whole ham and follow the instructions left.

Homemade Christmas mustard
MAKES 1 SMALL JAR

3 tablespoons yellow mustard seeds
3 tablespoons black mustard seeds
⅓ cup water
⅓ cup apple cider vinegar
¼ to ⅓ cup brown sugar
1 teaspoon sea salt flakes

Roast the mustard seeds lightly in a dry pan until they begin to pop. Pour them into a mortar and grind them to a fine powder with a pestle. You can also use an electric coffee grinder for this, which you should only use for grinding spices so that they don't taste of coffee.

Pour the ground mustard into a bowl and add the measured water, little by little, while stirring constantly. Add the vinegar and season to taste with the brown sugar and salt.

Pour the mustard into a small sterilized glass jar, seal it, and let stand in the refrigerator for 1 to 2 days for the flavors to combine well before using it. The mustard will keep fresh for several months in the refrigerator and will only taste better with time. Use within 6 months of opening.

TIP You can vary the flavor of the mustard by adding Christmas spices like star anise, cinnamon, and cloves.

Stewed kale

9 oz curly kale, stalks removed
sea salt flakes
2 tablespoons butter
¼ cup all-purpose flour
3¼ cups lowfat milk
2 to 3 gratings of fresh nutmeg
1 teaspoon sugar
2 to 3 tablespoons apple cider vinegar

Check the kale for any tough stalks and discard them. Wash the kale thoroughly in cold water, and let drain in a colander.

Blanch the kale in a large pan of salted boiling water for 3 to 4 minutes and then immediately plunge it into a bowl of cold water. Now press all the liquid out of the kale and chop it coarsely.

Melt the butter in a saucepan, whisk in the flour, and cook to make a smooth roux. Add the milk, a little at a time, while stirring vigorously until you have added it all and the sauce is smooth and lump free. Simmer the sauce until all the flour taste is cooked out and the sauce is completely smooth and supple.

Add the chopped, blanched kale to the sauce and let it stew for a while. Season with 1 teaspoon salt, the nutmeg, sugar, and vinegar to taste, and serve immediately.

Glazed ham »

Pigs' cheeks

2¼ lb pigs' cheeks
2 tablespoons standard canola oil
1 carrot
1 onion
1 garlic clove
5 thyme sprigs
1 cup dark beer (ale or porter)
1¾ cups apple juice
½ cup apple cider vinegar, plus
    2 tablespoons, divided
sea salt flakes and freshly ground pepper
2 cups chicken or beef stock
1¾ lb potatoes
10½ oz Brussels sprouts
3½ tablespoons cold butter, cubed,
    divided
1 handful of flat-leaf parsley or chervil
2 tablespoons whole almonds
¼ preserved lemon from the "Burnt"
    Leeks and Lemon in Oil (*see* page 166)

Start by removing the tendons from the pigs' cheeks. Put the cheeks on your cutting board with the tendon facing down flat against the board. Take a long, sharp knife and cut a small incision in the jaw just where the tendon is. Grip the tendon and then let the knife slide down the tendon so that it comes off in one long, clean cut. It is not easy the first few times, but let it take the time it takes. The key is not to carve off too much meat while cutting off the tendon. You may want to ask your butcher to do the work for you (and the butcher may already have removed the tendons as a matter of course).

Brown the cheeks in the oil in a large cast-iron pan so that they are golden on all sides.

Peel the carrot, onion, and garlic clove, chop into large chunks, and add to the pan to brown with the meat. Lastly, add the thyme sprigs, beer, apple juice, the ½ cup vinegar, salt, and pepper. Bring to a boil and cook until reduced by half. Add the stock, bring to a boil, and skim off any foam and impurities. Cover and place in a preheated oven at 300°F to braise for 1½ to 2 hours.

While the cheeks are braising, peel the potatoes, cut them into large cubes, and bring them to a boil in a saucepan of lightly salted water. Rinse the Brussels sprouts and remove the outer leaves, reserving the nicest ones for the garnish. Cut the rest into quarters and add them to the pan with the potatoes after they have cooked for 10 minutes. Cook the sprouts and potatoes together for a further 5 minutes until both are tender. Drain and add 3 tablespoons of the cold butter along with salt and pepper until the compote is seasoned to perfection.

When the cheeks are done, remove the pan from the oven and strain the broth into another pan, discarding the vegetables and leaving the cheeks in the cast-iron pan. Reduce the broth by half to a slightly sticky consistency with a shiny surface. Season to taste with the remaining butter, salt, and the remaining 2 tablespoons vinegar. When the sauce is flavored as desired, add the cheeks and heat them up.

Finally, make a quick salad of the reserved sprout leaves and parsley or chervil. Roast the almonds in a dry skillet until they take on some color, then chop them coarsely and mix them into the sprout salad. Cut the preserved lemon into small pieces and add it to the delicious salad, then dress this fresh bowl of goodness with a little oil from the preserved lemon. Serve the compote accompanied by a few pieces of cheek with a little sauce on top. Finish off with a handful of the salad and serve immediately.

Beet tartare
with horseradish and cold veal rump

1 lb 2 oz beets, divided
2 tablespoons cherry vinegar
sea salt flakes and freshly ground pepper
1 red onion
1 apple
1½ tablespoons prepared coarsely
    ground mustard
1 tablespoon olive oil
2 tablespoons freshly grated
    horseradish
1 tablespoon honey
½ handful of chervil, chopped
7 oz cold Roasted Veal Rump
    (*see* page 138), thinly sliced

Peel 3½ oz of the beets and cut them into very small cubes. Put the beet cubes in a bowl and marinate them in the vinegar seasoned with salt and pepper.

Cook the rest of the beets in a pan of boiling water for 40 to 45 minutes until soft. Drain the cooked beets, submerge in cold water, and slip them out of their skins (you can wear plastic gloves if you don't want your hands to be stained red, but then you will miss the lovely feeling of the silky beets slipping between your fingers).

Peel the red onion and chop it very finely. Core the apple and cut it into tiny cubes. Then cut the cooked beets into very small cubes as well and toss them with red onion, apple, mustard, and olive oil in a bowl. Add the raw marinated beets to taste along with the freshly grated horseradish, salt, pepper, honey, and chopped chervil.

The beet tartare should be fresh, sweet, spicy, and also have a hot element thanks to the horseradish and mustard. Serve the thin slices of roasted veal rump with the beet tartare. The tartare also goes well with smoked or Gravad Salmon (*see* page 190) or with hot-smoked salmon, meatballs (*see* pages 26, 137, 186, and 200), or meat patties (*see* pages 76 and 142). It is one of the few salads I know that goes with almost anything.

• •

Tip Making this beet tartare is great for practicing your seasoning skills. If you season it just a little, it is almost like a salad, but if you season it quite a lot, the tartare almost tastes like a pickle—both of which can be really nice with the meat.

• •

Lamb rump
with celery root and apple compote, and "stamped" potatoes

2 lamb rump steaks, 12 to 14 oz each
sea salt flakes and freshly ground pepper
5 thyme sprigs
2 garlic cloves, crushed

Cut the largest sinews and most of the fat away from the lamb rump steaks. Score the remaining fat with a sharp knife.

Heat a dry skillet and fry the rump steaks on all sides until brown, starting with the fatty side so that enough of it renders to fry the other sides in. Transfer the rump steaks to an ovenproof dish and season with salt, pepper, the thyme, and crushed garlic. Cook in a preheated oven at 350°F for 10 to 12 minutes so that they are slightly pink in the middle.

Let the rumps rest uncovered for 3 to 4 minutes before cutting them into slices. Serve with the Celery Root and Apple Compote and "Stamped" Potatoes (see below) or cooked grains or rice.

Celery root and apple compote

1 celery root, peeled and cut into
**   ½-inch cubes**
sea salt flakes and freshly ground pepper
¼ cup apple cider vinegar, divided, plus
**   extra to taste**
¼ cup olive oil, divided
2 apples
2 onions
1 garlic clove
2 tablespoons curry powder
½-inch piece of fresh ginger root, peeled
**   and thinly sliced**
½ cup apple juice
½ cup heavy whipping cream
4 celery stalks

Put the celery root cubes into an ovenproof dish and season with salt, pepper, half of the vinegar, and half of the olive oil. Bake in

a preheated oven at 350°F for 5 to 7 minutes or until softened but al dente.

Peel and core the apples, and peel the onions and garlic, then coarsely chop them all and add to a pan with the remaining 2 tablespoons of olive oil. Sauté for a couple of minutes, then add the curry powder and ginger and sauté for a further 2 minutes. Add the apple juice and the remaining 2 tablespoons vinegar and bring to a boil, then add the cream. Let the delicious mixture simmer for 10 minutes over low heat.

Use a hand-held stick blender to blend the mixture into a chunky compote. Add the baked celery root cubes as well as salt, pepper, and vinegar to taste—it might need an extra touch of acidity.

Rinse and finely chop the celery, then add it to the compote shortly before serving with the lamb so that it stays crisp. This compote is also good with chicken or pork chops.

"Stamped" potatoes

2¼ lb small potatoes
sea salt flakes
1½ tablespoons butter
1 tablespoon prepared coarsely
**   ground mustard**
finely grated zest of ½ organic lemon
freshly ground pepper

Rinse the potatoes thoroughly, add them to a pan of salted water, and bring to a boil. Then simmer for 12 to 14 minutes. Turn off the heat and let the potatoes sit in the hot water for a further 5 to 7 minutes. Drain the potatoes and leave them in the pan for a minute or so for the steam to rise. Coarsely mash with a whisk and add the butter, mustard, lemon zest, and salt and pepper to taste.

Firmly press the mashed potatoes into 4 small bowls, then turn them out onto a baking pan lined with parchment paper. Place the pan in a preheated oven at 425°F for 10 to 15 minutes or until they are crisp and golden. Serve the "stamped" potatoes with the lamb, or whatever you like—they go well with almost anything.

Meatballs in celery root sauce
SERVES 6

2 slices of wheat bread, crusts removed
1¼ cups lowfat milk
1 lb 2 oz mixed ground veal and pork,
**   5 to 7% fat**
sea salt flakes and freshly ground pepper
2 organic eggs

Sauce
4 cups water or light stock
**   (chicken or veal)**
1 tablespoon sea salt flakes
3 bay leaves
1 celery root
1 tablespoon cornstarch mixed
**   with a little cold water**
3 tablespoons heavy whipping cream
freshly ground pepper
juice of ½ lemon
a little sugar, if needed
1 handful of flat-leaf parsley, chopped

Soak the bread in the milk for about 10 to 15 minutes.

Put the ground meat in a bowl with salt, pepper, the eggs, and soaked bread and stir together to make a smooth meat mixture. It is a good idea to mix it for quite a while, as that will make it extra juicy when cooked. Let the mixture stand in the refrigerator for 15 to 20 minutes before making the meatballs.

To make the sauce, bring the measured water or stock to a boil in a saucepan and add the salt and bay leaves. When the water reaches boiling point, start forming the meat mixture into meatballs using a spoon. Submerge the balls in the broth, a few at a time, and poach them over very low heat for 4 to 5 minutes until they become firm and start floating to the surface. Lift the cooked meatballs out and put them in a bowl. Continue until you have used up all the meat mixture.

Peel the celery root and cut it into ½-inch cubes, then cook in the broth for about 3 to

4 minutes until tender. Strain the broth into another saucepan and simmer for 5 minutes, then add the cornstarch paste and simmer for another few minutes. Add the cream and cook the sauce for a further 4 to 5 minutes. Season with salt, pepper, the lemon juice, and possibly a little sugar if needed, to taste.

Add the meatballs and celery root to the sauce and let everything cook together to thoroughly combine all the flavors. Finally, scatter with the chopped parsley and serve with rice, boiled potatoes, or grains.

Roast pork
with crispy skin and gravy

**1¾ lb bone-in pork loin, skin on
coarse sea salt
10 to 15 bay leaves
2½ to 3 cups water
2 tablespoons all-purpose flour
1 to 2 tablespoons Apple Gastrique
    (*see* page 10)
sea salt flakes and freshly ground pepper**

Check that the skin is scored all the way down into the meat—if not, you will just have to do it yourself by taking a sharp kitchen or utility knife and scoring the skin at ¼-inch intervals. Wet your hand and rub the skin side of the loin with plenty of coarse salt. This makes the salt stick better, and the salt starts "cooking" the skin before the meat even reaches the oven so that it ends up nice and crisp. Insert the bay leaves into the cuts. Place the loin, skin-side up, on an oven or roasting rack with a roasting pan containing the measured water underneath.

Roast the pork in a preheated oven at 350°F for 1 hour 5 minutes to 1 hour 10 minutes.

Halfway through the cooking time, pour the liquid from the roasting pan into a saucepan for making the gravy; if you wait until the very end, there will be too much steam in the oven and the skin will end up not being properly crisp. Let the liquid stand for a while and then skim most of the fat off of the surface. Bring it to a boil and reduce the liquid to about 1¾ to 2 cups.

Turn off the heat and, once again, let the liquid stand until the fat settles on top. Sprinkle with the flour and let the fat absorb it. Then whisk vigorously and bring the liquid back to a boil. This way the finished gravy will come together nicely and the fat will also give it a little extra body (be careful not to leave too much fat in the gravy).

Simmer the gravy for 6 to 7 minutes and then season to taste with Apple Gastrique, salt, and pepper. Strain the gravy if needed.

Check the core temperature of the roast with a meat thermometer, which should be around 150°F when it is time to take the roast out of the oven—this will give you a pale pink and juicy pork loin (if the core temperature is higher than 150°F, the meat may well be dry). Let the meat rest for at least 15 minutes before slicing. Serve with boiled potatoes, Warm Red Cabbage (*see* page 201), and the delicious gravy.

Tip Roast an extra 1¾ pounds of meat and save until the following day to make a delightful roast pork sandwich—*see* page 222 for the recipe for the sandwich we sell in Meyers Deli. Also make sure that you have some extra cabbage for the sandwich.

Warm red cabbage
SERVES 10 TO 12

**1 red cabbage
juice of 2 organic oranges
1 cinnamon stick
3 star anise
4 bay leaves
⅔ cup superfine sugar
1¼ cups concentrated cherry juice
1 cup cherry vinegar
1¾ cups red wine
1 tablespoon sea salt flakes**

Slice the red cabbage into quarters and cut out and discard the stalk. Slice the cabbage finely and place in a large saucepan with the remaining ingredients and stir over high heat. Bring to a boil, then reduce the heat and let the cabbage simmer, covered, for 1 to 1½ hours, stirring occasionally. The liquid should all be absorbed, to result in a blank and clear appearance.

Crispy pork skin

There have been several techniques through the years for getting your pork skin crispy. Some pour water into the roasting pan and then put the rind face-down in the water for the first 15 minutes so that it is cooked first, before turning the roast rind-side up for the rest of the cooking, so that it ends up nice and crisp. I have found that you need to drain the liquid from the roasting pan halfway through the cooking, otherwise too much steam is formed for the skin to become properly crisp. When I roast pork, I keep the meat on the bone because it gives extra flavor and intensity to both the meat and gravy.

I rub the pork skin with a damp hand and plenty of coarse sea salt, then pour a small amount of water into the roasting pan to collect the juices, which I later use as the base for the gravy. I then pour off the juices into a pan halfway through the roasting time so there is not too much moisture in the oven and the skin can get nice and crisp. I roast the pork for 1 hour 5 minutes to 1 hour 10 minutes in a preheated oven at 350°F, and this way my roast turns out perfectly each time. And don't try finishing it off at the end with the oven door open and using the broiler, because you will just end up burning the skin.

Pork braised in milk, garlic, and rosemary

SERVES 6

2¼ lb piece boneless pork neck
1 tablespoon olive oil
sea salt flakes and freshly ground pepper
1 whole garlic bulb
½ to 1 organic lemon, plus extra lemon juice to season
3 rosemary sprigs
5 bay leaves
10 whole black peppercorns
1½ quarts whole milk

Brown the pork neck well on all sides in the oil in a skillet, then season with salt and pepper and add the garlic bulb (leave intact with the skin on, but cut it in half), the lemon, cut into quarters, rosemary sprigs, bay leaves, and peppercorns. Let it all sauté lightly before adding the milk. Once the milk reaches a boil, lower the heat and simmer for 1½ to 2 hours with the lid halfway on so that the milk can evaporate and the sauce is lightly browned. Turn the meat over a few times during braising.

When the pork is done, lift it out of the sauce, cut it into slices, and serve with White Barley Risotto (see page 147) or mashed potatoes and the lovely sauce seasoned with a little extra lemon juice, salt, and pepper.

• •
TIP You can also milk-braise veal rump or neck—just make sure that the meat is marbled with fat so it doesn't get too dry.
• •

Pork ribs
with apple mostarda

1¾ lb lightly salt-cured pork ribs (see tip)
1½ quarts water
1 bouquet garni, consisting of thyme sprigs, bay leaves, and parsley stems
sea salt flakes and freshly ground pepper
Apple Mostarda (see right)

Put the pork ribs in a large pan along with the measured water, bouquet garni, and some salt. Bring to a boil, skim off any foam and impurities that float to the surface, and then let simmer for about 40 minutes.

Take the pan off the heat and let cool slightly before placing in the refrigerator and letting the meat cool completely in the broth. For practical reasons, I usually do this part of the preparation the day before.

Lift the cold pork ribs out and season the broth with salt and pepper. Let the ribs marinate in half the quantity of Apple Mostarda for 30 minutes in the kitchen.

Cook the ribs under the broiler of the oven preheated to 425°F for 15 to 20 minutes so they are beautifully caramelized and crispy.

Serve the broiled pork ribs straight from the broiler with the Crudité of Turnip (see right), the remaining fresh Apple Mostarda, and good bread.

Apple Mostarda

6 red apples
2 to 3 tablespoons water
3 to 4 tablespoons apple cider vinegar
2 tablespoons brown sugar
2 tablespoons prepared mustard
sea salt flakes

Wash the apples and cut them into quarters, then put them straight into a pan with the measured water, without removing the skin or cores. Steam them, with the lid, on for about 7 to 8 minutes until they start to form a compote but some whole pieces still remain.

Pour the tender apples into a blender or food processor and blend well, then pour them through a sieve to remove the cores and seeds. Season with the vinegar, brown sugar, and mustard so that there is a good balance between sour, sweet, and "hot." Then season very slightly with salt.

The first time I came by mustard-pickled fruit was many years ago in Italy, but since then I have found out that we also used to pickle with mustard in medieval Scandinavia. This apple mostarda is my version of a medieval apple sauce. In addition to using it for barbecues and for dishes with white meat, it is a lovely accompaniment to cheese and smoked meats, as well as in a sandwich or in place of butter on a slice of rye bread with cold cuts, such as Danish rolled sausage.

• •
TIP You can order lightly salt-cured pork ribs from the butcher, or you can do the salting yourself. If so, sprinkle the ribs with 2 tablespoons coarse sea salt in a dish, cover the dish with plastic wrap, and place in the refrigerator for 12 hours so that they are ready to be cooked the next day, but remember to brush any excess salt off first.
• •

Crudité of turnip

½ turnip
2 red apples
2 ramson leaves (or equivalent quantity of lovage), chopped
1 small garlic clove, peeled
1 tablespoon cold-pressed canola oil, plus extra to season
2 tablespoons apple cider vinegar, plus extra to season
sea salt flakes and freshly ground pepper

Peel the turnip and cut or grate it into matchstick-thin strips about 1½ inches in length. Rinse in cold water and then let drain in a colander.

Peel the apples, cut them into quarters, and remove the cores. Cut into small cubes and then mash them into a creamy dressing with the chopped ramsons, garlic, and oil using a mortar and pestle. Adjust the consistency and flavor with the vinegar, and season to taste with salt and pepper.

Toss the turnip in the dressing and season with some more vinegar, oil, salt, and pepper.

Hotpot
with veal, licorice root, and beer

SERVES 6

2¼ lb veal blade or brisket
sea salt flakes and freshly ground pepper
2 onions
2 carrots
2 garlic cloves
2 celery stalks
3 tablespoons all-purpose flour
1 tablespoon standard canola oil
¼ red chile, seeded
5 bay leaves
4 rosemary sprigs
1 licorice root
½ cup apple cider vinegar, plus extra to taste
⅔ cup prunes, pitted
¾ cup dried apricots
2 cups dark ale (I use Gl. Carlsberg Porter)
4 cups thin veal stock or water

Inspect the veal and cut away the sinews and fat, then cut it into 4 to 6 big pieces. Season with salt and pepper and let rest at room temperature for an hour. I don't always have enough time to let the meat rest that long, but it is absolutely fine just to leave it while preparing the vegetables.

Peel the onions, carrots, and garlic, and rinse the celery, then dice them all coarsely. Dust the meat with the flour. Heat the oil in a deep ovenproof pan or Dutch oven and fry the meat until browned on all sides. Then add the vegetables and sauté them with the meat for a couple of minutes. Add the chile, herbs, licorice root, and vinegar and let the flavors soak into the meat for a few minutes before adding the dried fruit. Now add the beer and stock or water, bring to a boil, and skim off any foam or impurities that rise to the surface.

Cover the pan with a lid. Put in a preheated oven at 300°F for 2 to 3 hours until it is so tender that it just about falls apart.

Take the pan out of the oven, strain the liquid into another pan, and reduce to a sauce consistency. Season with additional vinegar, salt, and pepper if needed. Pour the sauce back into the meat pan and mix well but carefully so that the tender meat and vegetables don't fall apart completely. Serve the hotpot with cooked grains, mashed potatoes, or some good bread and a green salad.

• •

TIP I often make this hotpot with boneless leg of goat or beef cheek—both are surprisingly delicious given this beer, licorice, and dried fruit treatment.

• •

Pan-fried veal liver
with compote of apples and onions

Compote
3 onions
1 tablespoon butter
3 thyme sprigs
sea salt flakes and freshly ground pepper
2 apples
a little apple cider vinegar

Liver
1 lb 5 oz veal liver
all-purpose flour, for dusting
sea salt flakes and freshly ground pepper
2 teaspoons butter, for frying
2 teaspoons standard canola oil

For the compote, peel and chop the onions finely, then put them in a cold pan with the butter and thyme sprigs. Sauté the onions lightly and season with salt and pepper as they begin to brown. Wash the apples, cut them into quarters and remove the cores, then cut them into large cubes. Add the apples to the pan, mix well, and sauté until they have softened slightly but are still al dente. Season the compote with vinegar, salt, and pepper until there is a good balance between acidity and sweetness.

Remove any outer membrane or tendons from the liver and cut into slices about ¾ inch in thickness. Dust the liver slices with flour, season with salt and pepper, and fry in the butter and oil in a large skillet for about 1 minute on each side. Don't fry the liver until just before serving so that it is piping hot and delicious (liver should not be reheated, because it will become very dry). Serve the liver on rye bread with the warm compote on top and a nice cold pilsner in your other hand.

WATERCRESS
These crisp, dark, peppery leaves can often be found in winter growing in warm streams and channels.

Veal chops and pearled spelt salad
with apples and parsley

**4 bone-in veal chops with fat,
    9 to 10½ oz each**
1 tablespoon standard canola oil
sea salt flakes and freshly ground pepper

Scrape the chops with a knife to remove any bone fragments, and score the fat a few times so that it doesn't contract too much when fried. Rub the chops with the canola oil and season with salt and pepper.

Brown the chops in a hot skillet for about 1 minute on each side so that they get a beautiful golden crust.

Transfer the chops to an oven or roasting rack with a roasting pan underneath to collect any fat and juices. Cook in a preheated oven at 350°F for 7 to 8 minutes. By then they will be done but still pink and juicy around the bone.

Take the chops out of the oven and serve them with the Pearled Spelt Salad with Apples and Parsley (see below) and, if you wish, some herb butter and a green salad.

Pearled spelt salad with apples and parsley

½ cup pearl barley or pearled spelt
sea salt flakes
2½ cups boiling water
**2 tablespoons apple cider vinegar, plus
    extra if needed**
2 tablespoons cold-pressed canola oil
freshly ground pepper
1 tablespoon honey
1 parsley root
1 red onion
2 apples
1 handful of flat-leaf parsley

Rinse the pearled barley or spelt in cold water. Put it into a pan with the lightly salted measured boiling water and boil, with the lid on, for 20 minutes—it should be soft but still have some bite.

Take the pan off the heat and let stand, still with the lid on, for 5 to 10 minutes. Drain off any excess water and season the grains with the vinegar, oil, salt and pepper to taste, and the honey while still warm, as they will absorb the flavors better.

Peel the parsley root and onion, and wash and core the apples. Cut the vegetables into very small cubes and mix them with the pearled spelt. Chop the parsley coarsely and mix it into the salad. Mix well and, if necessary, season with additional salt, pepper, and vinegar.

Eat the salad with the fried veal chops. It is also a great accompaniment to meatballs, good sausages, or other fried food that could use a little edge and acidity.

Roasted duck
with prunes, baked apples, and gravy

SERVES 6

**1 duck, about 6½ to 8 lb, including
    giblets, neck, and wing tips**
sea salt flakes
**2¼ lb apples, such as Cox or Belle de
    Boskoop**
1 lb 2 oz whole pitted prunes
4 thyme sprigs, chopped
freshly ground pepper
⅓ cup all-purpose flour
1½ quarts water
**a little apple cider vinegar or other
    light fruit vinegar**
**a little sugar or Apple Gastrique
    (see page 10)**

Wipe both the cavity and outside of the duck with paper towels and then rub both with salt. Wash the apples, cut them into quarters, and remove the cores, then cut them into large cubes. Mix with the prunes, chopped thyme, salt, and pepper. Stuff the duck with the fruit mixture—it is important that you stuff it as full as possible, since the filling helps to retain the juices and thereby prevents the meat from becoming dry. Tie the thighs tightly up against the breast with butcher's twine, which will help to keep the breast fillets nice and juicy as well.

Place the bird, breast-side up, on an oven or roasting rack with a roasting pan underneath containing the duck's neck, wing tips, and giblets. Brown in a preheated oven at 550°F for 15 minutes then remove the roasting pan from the oven. Add the flour to the pan, and turn all the duck pieces over a few times so that all the fat is absorbed by the flour. Pour the measured water into the roasting pan and place it back underneath the duck. Turn the oven down to 300°F and roast for another 2 to 2½ hours. The duck is ready when the skin is beautifully golden and crisp and the thigh meat is creeping up the bone, which, by the way, should be about to fall off by itself.

Take the duck out of the oven and let rest for 20 to 25 minutes before you start carving it. Meanwhile, strain the gravy from the roasting pan through a sieve into a saucepan—the flour you added earlier will have thickened the juices into a sauce. If there is excess fat on top, skim it off (you can save it and use it another time). Adjust the consistency of the sauce, if necessary, and season with a little vinegar and sugar or Apple Gastrique, along with some salt and pepper, until it is just as good as your mother's gravy.

Cut the bird into 8 pieces (4 breasts, 2 thighs, and 2 drumsticks) and serve it with the fruit stuffing, gravy, and boiled, browned, or butter-fried potatoes or whatever you usually eat with roast duck. Red cabbage is probably just about mandatory, and as far as I am concerned, the warm vinegary version on page 201 is a good accompaniment.

Gravad beef top round
with celery root pickles

1 tablespoon coriander seeds
1 tablespoon fennel seeds
1 tablespoon cumin seeds
1 tablespoon juniper berries
1 cup coarse sea salt
1 cup jaggery or 1⅓ cups brown sugar
1¾ lb beef top round

Roast the spices in a dry skillet until they begin to give off some aroma, and then mix them with the salt and sugar. Put the beef in a dish and spread the mixture out over it. Cover the dish with plastic wrap and place in the refrigerator overnight.

The following day the spices and salt will have transformed into a brine. Turn the meat over to coat it in the brine.

Repeat the turning and coating procedure every day for the next 5 days. The meat is then ready to be served. Scrape some of the spice mixture off of the beef and cut it into thin slices. Serve with Celery Root Pickles (see below) and a little bread.

Celery root pickles

1 small celery root
sea salt flakes and freshly ground pepper
2 tablespoons cold-pressed canola oil
2 tablespoons apple cider vinegar, plus
    extra to taste
4 celery stalks
½ cup Homemade Mayonnaise
    (see page 68)
1¼ cups Greek yogurt, 2% fat
2 tablespoons prepared mustard
¼ cup capers, chopped
grated zest and juice of ½ organic lemon

Peel the celery root and cut it into thin sticks. Place the celery root sticks in an ovenproof dish, toss them with some salt and pepper, the oil, and vinegar and bake them in a preheated oven at 350°F for 20 to 25 minutes. Toss them around a few times

during cooking so that they are evenly baked. Take the celery root out of the oven and let cool.

Wash the celery, cut it into very fine strips and then mix with the baked celery root. Combine the mayonnaise, yogurt, mustard, chopped capers, lemon zest and juice, salt, and pepper in a bowl to make a dressing. Pour the dressing over the celery and celery root and toss to coat thoroughly. Finish by adding more salt, pepper, and vinegar to taste.

Leg of wild boar
SERVES 6

1 leg of wild boar, 3¼ to 4½ lb
1 organic lemon
3 to 4 garlic cloves
3 rosemary sprigs
sea salt flakes and freshly ground pepper

Lightly score the top of the leg with a sharp knife. Place the leg on an oven or roasting rack with a roasting pan filled with water underneath to collect the fat and juices while the meat is roasting. Cut the lemon into small pieces, and peel and crush the garlic cloves with the flat blade of a knife. Distribute the pieces of lemon, rosemary sprigs, and garlic evenly across the leg, and season with salt and pepper.

Roast in a preheated oven at 315°F for 2 to 2½ hours. Baste the leg about every 30 minutes with the juices that have collected in the roasting pan, and add a little more water to the pan if the liquid is about to evaporate completely. Check the core temperature of the leg with a meat thermometer before you take it out of the oven. At 150 to 158°F the meat will be nice and juicy and slightly pink.

Let the meat rest for 15 to 20 minutes before carving it into thin slices. Serve with Baked Squash and Potato Mash and Warm Vinaigrette with Orange, Red Onion, and Rosemary (see right).

Baked squash and potato mash

3lb 5 oz baking potatoes
1 lb 2 oz squash, such as Hokkaido or
    butternut
1 lowfat milk
1 stick butter, plus extra for greasing
sea salt flakes and freshly ground pepper

Peel the potatoes and squash, then halve the squash and scrape out the seeds with a spoon. Cut the potatoes and squash into small pieces and place them in a saucepan with water to cover. Bring to a boil, then simmer for 25 to 30 minutes until the vegetables are tender. Drain and let cool in the pan for 2 to 3 minutes.

Heat the milk in a saucepan. Cut the butter into small cubes. Mash the potatoes and squash using a masher or a whisk, add the hot milk and butter, and mash until completely smooth and soft. Season to taste with salt and pepper.

Fill a large buttered ovenproof dish with the mashed mixture, place on a cookie sheet and bake in a preheated oven at 400°F for 15 to 20 minutes until golden and crisp on top. Take the dish out of the oven and serve immediately.

Warm vinaigrette with orange, red onion, and rosemary

2 oranges
1 red onion, peeled and finely chopped
1 rosemary sprig, leaves chopped
3 tablespoons olive oil
3 tablespoons apple cider vinegar
sea salt flakes and freshly ground pepper
1 teaspoon honey

Peel the oranges, removing all the white pith. Cut the oranges into small cubes and put in a pan with the onion, rosemary, oil, vinegar, some salt and pepper, and the honey, and gently bring to a boil. Stir with a spoon until the dressing is smooth. Take the pan off the heat and let stand for 10 minutes before serving it warm with the wild boar and Baked Squash and Potato Mash.

Fish

Pan-fried salmon
with warm salad of pearl barley, broccoli, pea shoots, and hazelnuts

1 head of broccoli
sea salt flakes and freshly ground pepper
freshly grated nutmeg, to taste
2 cups low-fat plain yogurt
1¾ lb salmon fillet, skin on
2 tablespoons cold-pressed canola oil, divided, plus extra to season
1⅓ cups cooked pearl barley
3½ oz fresh pea shoots
¼ cup hazelnuts, coarsely chopped
2 to 3 tablespoons apple cider vinegar
1 pack or tray growing garden cress, chopped

Break the broccoli into small florets and rinse them in cold water. Bring a pan of salted water to a boil and blanch the broccoli for 30 seconds, then immediately transfer to cold water so that they keep their crispness and color.

Stir grated nutmeg and salt and pepper to taste into the yogurt in a bowl and let stand for 20 to 25 minutes before serving.

Use a knife to scrape the scales off of the skin of the salmon. Divide the salmon into 4 equal-sized pieces.

Heat a skillet and fry the salmon pieces in 1 tablespoon of the canola oil on the skin side for about 2 to 3 minutes, then turn over and fry for a further 2 to 3 minutes, so the salmon has a beautiful crust on both sides.

Transfer the salmon fillets to an ovenproof dish and roast them in a preheated oven at 325°F for 4 to 6 minutes.

Meanwhile, drizzle the remaining canola oil into the skillet and fry the cooked barley over high heat for 1 to 2 minutes, tossing the grains a few times. Add the broccoli florets, pea shoots, and hazelnuts, and toss to mix all the ingredients evenly. Season the grain salad with the apple cider vinegar, extra canola oil, lots of chopped cress, salt, and pepper. Give the salad another stir and add some more salt and pepper if needed.

Serve the salmon pieces with the warm grain salad, the yogurt dressing, and some good bread.

. . . .

TIP The grain salad is also good served cold, so if you have left over from dinner, it will make a nice lunch the next day.

. . . .

Spicy fish cakes
with white cabbage salad

1 onion
1 garlic clove
½ oz fresh ginger root
1 lb 2 oz skinless cod fillet (or pollack or coalfish)
7 oz crabmeat
½ cup mashed potatoes
finely grated zest of 1 organic lime
1 organic egg, plus extra if you wish
½ handful of fresh cilantro, chopped
1 tablespoon prepared mustard
sea salt flakes
1 tablespoon peanut oil, for frying

Peel and grate the onion, garlic, and ginger into a bowl. Coarsely chop the fish and add to the bowl with the crabmeat, mashed potatoes, lime zest, egg, cilantro, mustard, and salt. Work the fish mixture until you have a good, firm texture, adding an extra egg or so if you want a softer consistency.

Using a spoon, form the mixture into little crabcake-sized patties. Fry the patties in hot oil in a skillet for 3 to 4 minutes on each side until golden and crisp.

Eat the fish cakes with some good-quality sweet and sour chili sauce or Homemade Apple Ketchup (see page 235) for dipping. Pack in your lunchbox or serve for lunch or dinner with the White Cabbage Salad (see below), rice and vegetables.

White cabbage salad

¼ white cabbage, 10½ oz
2 shallots
1 apple
2 tablespoons apple cider vinegar
1 teaspoon superfine sugar
2 tablespoons cold-pressed canola oil
sea salt flakes and freshly ground pepper

Using a sharp knife, cut the cabbage into fine strips and add to a bowl. Peel the shallots and cut the apple into quarters, discarding the core. Slice the shallots and apple thinly and add them to the bowl.

Toss the cabbage, shallots, and apple with the vinegar, sugar, canola oil, salt, and pepper, and let marinate for 2 to 3 minutes. The cabbage will absorb the marinade and become soft.

. . . .

TIP Cabbage is a spectacular vegetable and it very often ends up in the salad bowl at my house. I vary the recipe depending on what I have in the refrigerator. For example, this salad could be made with kale, red cabbage, or finely shredded Brussels sprouts. The latter, because of their size, might be a bit of a struggle to shred, but trust me, they make a delicious salad! A nice cabbage salad such as this makes a great accompaniment to almost any dish.

. . . .

Steamed razor clams
with jerusalem artichokes, onions and white beans

3¼ lb razor clams (or mussels or cockles)
1 onion
1 garlic clove
4 Jerusalem artichokes
2 tablespoons olive oil
½ cup cooked white beans, such as
   navy beans or cannellini
10 thyme sprigs
1¼ cup white wine
sea salt flakes and freshly ground pepper

Immerse the razor clams in some fresh cold water for 5 to 10 minutes or until they have rinsed themselves through and discharged as much sand as possible (unfortunately they usually store up quite a lot). If you are using mussels, check that they are fresh—they should smell of the sea. Clean the mussels by scrubbing them thoroughly under cold water and removing the beards. Discard any mussels that don't close after being tapped lightly on a hard surface, and those with damaged shells.

Peel the onion, garlic, and Jerusalem artichokes, and chop them finely. Heat the olive oil in a large pan and throw in the vegetables, beans, and thyme. Sauté for 1 minute, then add the razor clams or mussels and sauté for another minute. Add the white wine, cover the pan with a lid, and let everything steam for 2 to 4 minutes. All the razor clams or mussels should open during steaming, but if there are any that remain closed, discard immediately—they are bad and not safe to eat.

Serve the razor clams or mussels straight from the pan or in a large bowl. Season beforehand with a little salt and pepper. Eat with some good bread to soak up all the delicious broth.

Octopus salad
with beans, leeks, and tarragon

1 octopus, 3¼ to 4½ lb
1 onion
1 garlic clove
1 carrot
sea salt flakes
10 whole black peppercorns
⅔ cup dried fava beans (or ½ cup green
   split peas), soaked in water overnight
finely grated zest and juice of
   1 organic lemon
2 tablespoons olive oil
freshly ground pepper
2 winter leeks
5 tarragon sprigs, leaves picked

Wash the octopus in cold water and remove the beak and any ink (or ask your fish dealer do the work for you). Peel the onion, garlic, and carrot, then cut them into chunks.

Put the octopus in a pan along with the vegetables, some salt, the peppercorns, and enough water to cover. Bring to a boil, then simmer for about 45 minutes to 1 hour. Turn the heat off and let the octopus soak in the broth for about 30 to 40 minutes until done—it should be tender but still al dente.

Drain the soaked beans (or split peas), place in a pan of fresh cold water, and bring to a boil. Then simmer for about 25 to 30 minutes until tender and drain in a sieve.

Lift the octopus out of its broth and cut it into small pieces. Put it into a bowl and add the beans. Toss thoroughly with the lemon zest and juice, olive oil, salt, and pepper.

Cut off the roots and tops of the leeks, then cut into rings about ½ inch in thickness and rinse them thoroughly in cold water so that all the soil is washed away. Bring a pan of salted water to a boil and blanch the leeks for about 1 minute, then immediately plunge them into cold water so that they retain their color and crispness.

Toss the blanched leeks and tarragon leaves into the octopus and bean salad, and season with additional salt and pepper if necessary. Serve the salad as an appetizer or a small lunch dish.

•••••••••••••••••••••••••••••••••

TIP Soak and then cook an extra ½ cup dried beans, then put them in a tightly sealed container in the refrigerator and save them for the Fish Soup with Root Vegetables and Mashed Fava Beans (see page 186).

•••••••••••••••••••••••••••••••••

SCURVY GRASS
When the winter frosts retreat, scurvy grass can be found on the beach or in meadows.

Pan-fried herrings
with dill, mustard, and melted butter

8 double herring fillets
2 tablespoons prepared mustard
1 handful of dill, chopped, plus extra
   to garnish
sea salt flakes and freshly ground pepper
½ cup all-purpose flour
3 tablespoons butter, divided
2 tablespoons apple cider vinegar

Check that the herring fillets are fresh and smell of the sea, not of the harbor. Put them in a dish, skin-side down, then spread the mustard onto the flesh side, scatter with the chopped dill, and season with salt and pepper. Fold the fillets together and toss them in the flour to coat.

Fry the fillets in a little of the butter (about 2 teaspoons) in a medium-hot skillet for about 3 minutes on each side so that the skin is beautifully golden and crisp. It may be necessary to press down slightly on the folded fillets with a lifter when you first add them to the pan to ensure they don't unfold.

Lift the herrings out of the skillet and transfer them to a plate. Add the rest of the butter to the hot pan and let it bubble into a golden brown butter sauce. Season the sauce with the vinegar and salt and pepper to taste.

Serve the fried herrings with the butter sauce and boiled potatoes, scattered with some chopped dill.

Pan-fried cod
with leeks, dill, and carrot and egg sauce

1lb 5 oz skinless cod fillet (or use other
   codlike fish such as haddock, lingcod,
   cusk, coalfish, or hake)
sea salt flakes
4 winter leeks
1 shallot
1 tablespoon cold-pressed canola oil
1 tablespoon apple cider vinegar
freshly ground pepper
1 tablespoon capers
½ handful of dill, chopped
1 tablespoon standard canola oil

Check that the cod is fresh and smells of the sea, not of the harbor, and remove any remaining bones. Cut the cod into 4 equal-size pieces, place in a dish, and season with a little salt, then let stand to lightly cure in the refrigerator for 10 minutes.

Cut off the roots and tops of the leeks, then cut into slices about 2 inches long and rinse them thoroughly in cold water so that all the soil is washed away. Bring a pan of lightly salted water to a boil and boil the leeks for 3 to 4 minutes until tender but still al dente.

Drain the leeks in a colander and swiftly shake all the water out of them, then put them in a bowl. Peel the shallot and slice it finely. Fold it into the hot leeks and add the cold-pressed canola oil, vinegar, salt, pepper, capers, and chopped dill.

Heat a skillet and fry the cod pieces in the standard canola oil for about 1 to 2 minutes on each side so that they are beautifully golden and crisp on the surface. Season with salt and pepper. Serve the fried cod fillets with the marinated leeks, the Carrot and Egg Sauce (see right), and boiled potatoes or grains.

Tip Buy an additional 7 ounces of cod, put it in a dish, and coat it in 1 tablespoon sea salt flakes and 1 teaspoon sugar. Cover the dish with plastic wrap and place it in the refrigerator to cure for 12 hours. Serve the cured cod with Squash Purée and Chervil Dressing (see page 192) as an appetizer the following day.

Carrot and egg sauce

1 carrot
2 organic eggs
1 tablespoon prepared mustard
sea salt flakes and freshly ground
   pepper
3 tablespoons apple cider vinegar,
   plus extra if needed
½ cup cold-pressed canola oil

Peel the carrot and cut it into small pieces. Add to a pan of boiling water and boil for 12 to 15 minutes until completely tender.

Meanwhile, boil the eggs in another pan for 8 minutes. Drain and peel the shells off of the eggs, then take out the yolks (you won't be using the whites).

Put the egg yolks in the blender along with the carrot and some of its boiling cooking water, the mustard, salt, pepper, and the vinegar, and blend it all to a smooth cream. Then slowly add the oil in a thin stream while the blender is still running. The end result should be a thick, creamy sauce. Taste the sauce to see if it needs a bit more salt, pepper, or vinegar.

Pan-fried cod »

Fried flounder with braised Belgian endive »

Fried flounder
with braised Belgian endive

2 whole flounders (or 8 flounder fillets)
sea salt flakes
4 Belgian endive
3 tablespoons standard canola oil, divided
2 tablespoons jaggery
juice of 1 orange
3 tablespoons apple cider vinegar
2 apples
freshly ground pepper
½ handful of parsley

If using whole flounders, rinse and clean them, making sure that they are free of blood and mucus. Cut out the fillets and skin them (or ask your fish dealer to do the work for you). Save the bones for making stock, soup, or sauce.

Cut the fish fillets in half. Place in a dish and sprinkle with salt. Put them in the refrigerator while you make the braised endive.

Halve the endive lengthwise, rinse in cold water, and drain well. Heat 1 tablespoon of the canola oil in a sauteuse pan. Add the endive halves, cut-side down, and fry for a few minutes so that they have a beautiful golden crust. Flip them over, sprinkle with the sugar, and let caramelize slightly (watch that the sugar doesn't burn). Add the orange juice and vinegar and simmer for 4 to 5 minutes until the endive halves absorb about half of the liquid.

Wash and core the apples, then cut them into small cubes. Add them to the pan and simmer with the endive halves for 30 seconds. Toss to mix well, and season with salt and pepper. Finely chop the parsley and scatter it over the mixture, then round it all off by drizzling it with 1 tablespoon of the canola oil.

Fry the flounder fillets in the remaining tablespoon of oil in a hot skillet for 1 to 2 minutes on each side until they have a beautifully golden and crisp crust.

Arrange the endive halves on 4 plates—2 halves on each plate—and arrange the fried flounder on top. The endive halves can also be served by themselves as a small dish or as a side to fried poultry.

Pan-fried haddock
with fava bean stew

1⅓ cups dried fava beans, soaked in cold
   water for 12 hours
8 slices of bacon
2 shallots
2 tablespoons standard canola oil, divided
10 thyme sprigs
sea salt flakes and freshly ground pepper
1¾ to 2 cups water
2 tablespoons apple cider vinegar
1 lb 5 oz haddock fillet, skinned and
   pin-boned

Drain the beans, rinse them in fresh cold water, and let drain in a colander.

Cut the bacon slices into small pieces. Peel the shallots and cut one into small cubes and the other into thin rings (save the rings for the garnish).

Grease a sauteuse pan with 1 tablespoon of the oil, add the bacon and diced shallot, and sauté over low heat for 2 to 3 minutes. Add the drained beans, season with the thyme sprigs (save a few for the garnish), salt, and pepper and then pour in the measured water.

Bring the vegetables to a boil and then simmer for about 30 to 35 minutes until the beans are tender and have absorbed the water. Season with the vinegar and possibly some more salt and pepper to taste, then cover with a lid to keep the stew warm.

Make sure that the haddock is fresh and smells of the sea, not of the harbor. Check for any remaining bones and use a knife to scrape off any stray scales, then cut into 4 or 8 pieces.

Heat a skillet, add the remaining oil, and fry the haddock pieces over high heat for about

2 minutes on each side so that they develop a beautifully golden crust and remain juicy in the center.

Arrange the haddock on top of a couple of tablespoons of the bean stew and scatter with the raw shallot rings and reserved thyme sprigs. Serve with a bowl of Marinated Beets (see page 224) and some good bread, or make a nice crudité and some baked root vegetables.

RAMSONS
Along little streams, you'll find the first delicious green shoots of ramsons.

Home-smoked whiting
with beet tartare and horseradish cream

**whiting fillets, about 10½ to 14 oz
(or use cod)**
10 fennel seeds, crushed
2 tablespoons sea salt flakes
1 teaspoon sugar

You will also need
**a barbecue charcoal chimney starter
some straw (such as oats) or hay**

Day 1
Remove any skin and bones from the
whiting fillets (or ask the fish dealer to do
the work for you). Put them in a dish and
sprinkle both sides with the crushed fennel
seeds, salt, and sugar. Cover the dish with
plastic wrap and refrigerate for 12 hours.

Day 2
Take the whiting fillets out of the refrigerator
and gently pat dry with paper towels. Go
outside in the cold and stuff the bottom
of a barbecue charcoal chimney starter
full of straw or hay, ignite, and place it on
the ground. Lay the whiting fillets on a
barbecue grill and place it on top of the
starter so that the smoke goes right
through the fillets. Let sit in the smoke
for 45 seconds to 1 minute, then take
the fillets off of the grill and put in the
refrigerator to chill.

Cut the whiting fillets into thin slices and
serve with Beet Tartare and Horseradish
Cream (see right).

· ·

TIP If you don't have the courage or the
opportunity to smoke fish, you can preorder
it ready-smoked from your fish dealer. That
being said, the process is quite simple. All
you need is an ordinary charcoal starter and
some straw or hay. If you don't have a farm
nearby that can provide you with the straw
or hay, a pet supplies store will sell it.

· ·

Beet tartare

14 oz beets
**2 tablespoons cherry vinegar or other
fruit vinegar**
sea salt flakes and freshly ground pepper
1 cooking apple
1 red onion
1 tablespoon cold-pressed canola oil
1 handful of chervil, chopped
1 tablespoon honey
1 tablespoon prepared mustard

Peel 3½ ounces of the beets and cut into
minuscule cubes. Marinate the beet cubes
in the vinegar and some salt and pepper.

Wrap the rest of the beets in foil and bake in
a preheated oven at 400°F for 1 hour to
1 hour 10 minutes until tender.

Take the beets out of the oven and set aside
until cool enough to handle, then rub the
skins off.

Wash and core the apple, and peel the
red onion. Cut the baked beets, apple,
and onion into tiny cubes to match the raw
beet cubes and then mix them with the
raw beets. Add the oil, then season with
the chopped chervil, honey, mustard, salt,
and pepper. Toss it all around well and
season again—the tartare should be fresh,
sweet, and sharp, but at the same time well
rounded in flavor, to suit the smoked fish.

Horseradish cream

½ cup Greek yogurt, 2% fat
**finely grated zest and juice of
½ organic lemon**
**1 to 2 tablespoons freshly grated
horseradish, to taste**
1 teaspoon honey
sea salt flakes and freshly ground pepper

Mix all the ingredients together in a bowl.
Let the cream sit for 5 minutes in the
kitchen to allow the flavors to infuse and
then season, if necessary, with some extra
horseradish before serving.

Light dishes

Roast pork sandwich

SERVES 4

2 tablespoons Greek yogurt
2 tablespoons Homemade Mayonnaise
 (*see* page 68)
1 tablespoon prepared coarsely ground
 mustard
1 teaspoon apple cider vinegar
1 teaspoon acacia honey
sea salt flakes and freshly ground pepper
2 apples
4 pickled gherkins (preferably
 cornichons)
1 small portion of Warm Red Cabbage
 (*see* page 201)
1¾ lb leftover Roast Pork with Crispy
 Skin (*see* page 201)
4 good-quality buns

Mix the yogurt, mayonnaise, and mustard together in a bowl to make a dressing, and season with the vinegar, honey, salt, and pepper. Wash the apples, quarter them, and remove and discard the cores. Thinly slice the apple quarters and the gherkins.

Heat the red cabbage in a small saucepan. Reheat the pork in a preheated oven at 325°F for 10 to 15 minutes if you wish (reheat before slicing so that it doesn't become too dry).

Slice the buns and lightly toast them if you like. Spread the mustard dressing on both top and bottom halves. Cut the pork into 8 slices and place 2 slices in each bun. Sprinkle with a little salt and then garnish with the apple slices, warm red cabbage, and sliced gherkins. I usually drain the red cabbage in a sieve just before I add it to the buns to stop the juice from making them wet and soggy too quickly. Sandwich the buns together and serve. The pickled cabbage will eventually seep into the bread, so don't make the sandwiches in advance but enjoy them immediately.

The roast pork sandwich has become a classic in my Meyers Deli shops in Denmark, and we make it every fall and winter. At Christmas they sell really fast. The roast pork sandwich is lovely for lunch (not least on the day after a "wet" Christmas party), but would definitely make a nice dinner too.

Open-faced rye bread sandwich with smoked lumpfish and pickled onion
with celery root purée

1 red onion
1 tablespoon apple cider vinegar
sea salt flakes and freshly ground pepper
1 teaspoon acacia honey
1 smoked lumpfish or cod
1 apple
1 tablespoon cold-pressed canola oil
Celery root Purée (*see* below)
4 to 8 slices of rye bread
2 tablespoons skyr

Peel the red onion, cut it into thin wedges, and add to a bowl. Toss with the vinegar, salt, pepper, and honey, and let marinate for 30 minutes so that the onion softens a little but remains crisp.

Skin the smoked lumpfish and place the flesh in a bowl, discarding any bones. Wash the apple, cut it into quarters and remove the core, then cut it into very thin wedges. Add the apple to the marinated onion and toss with the oil and salt and pepper to taste.

Spread the Celery Root Purée over the bread slices, top with the lumpfish flesh, and finally add the marinated onion and apple. Garnish with a spoonful of skyr on top of the rye bread sandwich, and serve immediately.

Celery root purée

½ celery root
sea salt flakes
1½ tablespoons butter
finely grated zest and juice of
 ½ organic lemon
freshly ground pepper

Peel the celery root and coarsely cut it into pieces. Put them in a pan, cover with water, and add some salt. Bring to a boil and cook for about 20 minutes until it is tender.

Drain the celery root and blend in a blender or food processor with the butter and lemon zest and juice to a smooth purée. Season to taste with salt and pepper. The consistency of the purée should be smooth and slightly softer than mashed potatoes.

Let the purée cool slightly before using it. The purée is brilliant as a spread for rye bread or wheat buns, and will complement both cold meats and fish and seafood.

Salad with smoked cod roe

9 oz smoked cod roe
1 shallot
½ cup Greek yogurt, 2% fat
1 teaspoon honey
1 teaspoon prepared mustard
1 tablespoon apple cider vinegar,
 plus extra if needed
sea salt flakes and freshly ground pepper

Cut the smoked cod roe into small cubes and place them in a bowl. Peel and chop the shallot finely, then mix with the yogurt, honey, mustard, vinegar, salt, and pepper in another bowl to make a dressing.

Fold the cod roe into the dressing so that it is well incorporated but still keeps its shape and doesn't become mushy. Let the cod roe salad rest for 20 minutes in the refrigerator and then season with salt and pepper to taste and, if necessary, a little extra vinegar.

Serve the cod roe salad with crisp bitter lettuce leaves and some nice bread. This is an obvious choice for a lunchbox but it also works well for dinner, supplemented with cold or warm leftovers from the day before, such as a lentil stew. And if you top it off with a bun and a little cheese, you have a cozy snack meal—my kids love these fridge leftover evenings!

Smoked lumpfish salad
with marinated beets and apple sauce

SERVES 6

2 smoked lumpfish or cod
1 shallot
½ cup sour cream, 18% fat
1 teaspoon prepared mustard,
    plus extra if needed
1 tablespoon apple cider vinegar, plus
    extra if needed
sea salt flakes and freshly ground pepper
½ handful of chives

Skin the lumpfish, putting all the delicious smoked flesh in a bowl, discarding any bones. Peel and chop the shallot finely, then mix it with the lumpfish.

Add the sour cream, mustard, vinegar, salt, and pepper and mix together thoroughly, but make sure the fish still keeps its shape and doesn't become mushy.

Let the salad rest for 20 minutes in the refrigerator before you taste it and season with any additional salt, pepper, vinegar, and mustard if needed. At the very last moment, snip the chives and add them to give the salad a green finish. Serve the salad with Marinated Beets and Tangy Fresh Apple Sauce (see right), and possibly some fresh apple with a little of the marinade from the beets. Serve with good bread.

Marinated beets

3½ oz beets
3 tablespoons apple cider vinegar
3 tablespoons olive oil
1 tablespoon acacia honey
sea salt flakes and freshly ground pepper
1 to 2 teaspoons freshly grated
    horseradish

Peel the beets and cut into very thin slices using a mandoline or a sharp knife. Place the beet slices in a bowl and toss them with the rest of the ingredients. Let marinate for at least 2 hours or preferably 12 hours in the refrigerator before serving them, tossing the beet slices around a few times so that they are evenly marinated.

The marinated beets are also a good supplement to steamed or fried cod.

Tangy fresh apple sauce

3 tart apples, such as Belle de Boskoop
    or Bramley
2 tablespoons jaggery
finely grated zest and juice of
    ½ organic lemon
sea salt flakes and freshly ground pepper
1 tablespoon cold-pressed canola oil

Wash the apples, cut them into quarters and remove the cores, but leave the peel on. Save half an apple for garnish, then cut the rest into large cubes and place them in a small saucepan with the sugar and lemon zest and juice. Bring to a boil, then simmer with the lid on, for 4 to 5 minutes until the apples are tender and beginning to turn into a compote. Take the pan off the heat and let the apples stand, still with the lid on, for 5 minutes

Mash the apples through a coarse sieve, then season them to taste with salt, pepper, and the oil. Let cool slightly, then add the reserved raw apple, cut into cubes, and it is ready to be served.

Bruschetta
with squash purée and goat cheese

8 slices of day-old white bread
½ quantity of Squash Purée
    (see pages 192–3)
3½ oz log of goat cheese, thinly sliced
2 tablespoons olive oil
1 rosemary sprig, leaves picked
sea salt flakes and freshly ground pepper

Place the bread slices directly onto a shelf in the oven or on a grill rack, spread the Squash Purée over them, and top with the thin slices of goat cheese. Drizzle with the olive oil and season with the rosemary, salt, and pepper.

Bake the bruschetta in a preheated oven at 500°F for 3 to 4 minutes until the bread is crunchy and the cheese is crispy and golden. Serve the bruschetta immediately while they are warm, either as a snack or as an appetizer with a good salad.

SLOES
Remember to pick these blue-black fruits from the trees before the birds do!

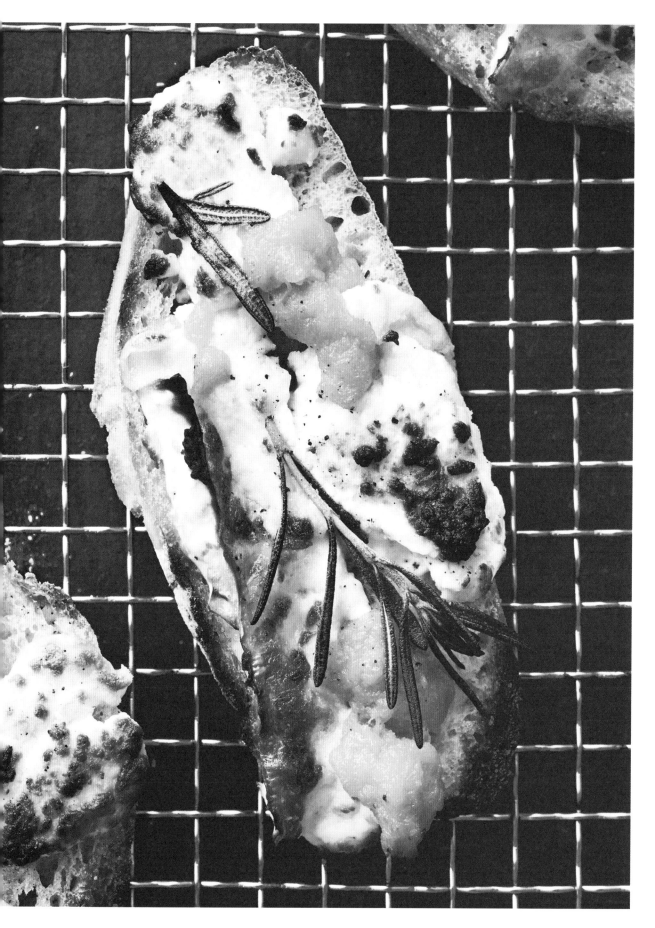

Dandelion leaves

A early as February, in mild winters, you may be able to pick the first leaves of dandelion from underneath a hedge, from your garden, or from a meadow. The small ribbons of barbed, bright green leaves are easy to spot against the bare soil. The plant is known for the milky sap that seeps out when you pluck a leaf. The taste is pleasantly bitter as long as the leaves are young; older leaves are stronger in flavor. Dandelions can be very different from plant to plant. In fact, there is not just one but up to 1,000 different species of dandelion, all with a roughly similar appearance.

Harvesting and using dandelion leaves

To harvest, cut off the plant with a sharp knife just below the surface of the soil so that all the leaves are still attached to the root. Wash them free of soil and pick off the smaller leaves. Always discard the old leaves from the previous year. The first dandelion leaves tossed with bread croutons, fried cubes of bacon, walnuts, and a nice vinaigrette give a wonderful feeling of spring.

If you "force" dandelion plants, your leaves will have a less bitter taste. This is an old tradition used, for example, in English kitchen gardens. Cut off the leaves of the growing dandelion and place a box, bucket, or flowerpot (remembering to cover the hole) over the plant. When the plant shoots, the leaves will be brighter in color and milder in taste.

You can blanch older leaves and make a stew with them just as you do with spinach. They are also good in a soup and, of course, on top of mashed potatoes.

Dandelion salad

Try this fantastic dandelion salad. It heralds spring and carries the promise of those piles of fresh lettuces and vegetables soon to come. You will need 7 ounces small, fresh dandelion shoots, 1 small red onion, 4 radishes, 2 tablespoons cold-pressed canola oil, 2 tablespoons apple cider vinegar, sea salt, and freshly ground pepper.

Wash the dandelion leaves thoroughly in cold water and put them in a colander to drain. Wash them again if necessary to make sure there are no traces of soil left, then let drain in the colander. Peel the red onion, nip the tops off the radishes, and shred both very finely. Mix the dandelion leaves, onion, and radishes together in a bowl, then toss in the oil and vinegar, and season to taste with salt and pepper. Dandelion salad is a lovely breath of fresh air to accompany steamed or braised meats, among other things.

Crispy onion pie

Dough
**¼ oz (1 tablespoon) fresh compressed
    yeast (baker's yeast)**
2½ cups lukewarm water
1½ lb all-purpose flour, divided
2½ cups wholemeal flour, divided
1 teaspoon fine salt

Topping
3 onions
⅓ cup olive oil
**3 rosemary sprigs, leaves picked
    and chopped**
coarse sea salt, for sprinkling
a little apple cider vinegar

This pie is not a pie in the traditional sense but more like a pizza without the cheese! Start by dissolving the yeast in the measured lukewarm water, then add half the flours and incorporate well. Add the salt and the rest of the flours (save a little flour for rolling the dough out), and knead thoroughly, either in an electric stand mixer fitted with a dough hook or by hand on a lightly floured surface, until smooth and supple.

Place the dough in a bowl, cover with a clean dish towel, and let stand in a warm place to rise for 1 to 2 hours until it has doubled in size.

Turn the dough out onto a floured surface and roll it out thinly into a circle. The thinner, the better, because then it is more likely to become crisp when baked.

Preheat the oven to 500°F with a baking pan inside the oven so that it is hot when the dough is placed on it. Place the rolled-out dough on a sheet of parchment paper for transferring to the hot baking pan. Peel the onions and cut them into very thin rings. Spread the onion rings evenly over the dough, drizzle with the olive oil, and sprinkle with the rosemary and some coarse salt.

Take the hot baking pan out of the oven and slip the parchment paper with the pie onto it. Return it to the oven and bake for 7 to 9 minutes until crisp and dark golden.

Remove the pie from the oven and drizzle a little apple cider vinegar on top, to balance out the sweetness of the onion. Cut the pie into pieces and serve immediately as a dish on its own with a good salad.

....

TIP I often make a large portion of the dough, roll it into several small bases, stacking them with parchment paper in between, and put them in the refrigerator. That way they are ready to be used the following day, and I have an easy dinner for the family.
....

Potato omelet
with smoked pork fat and purée of baked garlic

14 oz potatoes
1 tablespoon olive oil
**1¼ oz smoked pork fat (lard), cut into
    small cubes**
2 thyme sprigs
6 organic eggs
⅔ cup lowfat milk
sea salt flakes and freshly ground pepper

Peel the potatoes and cut them into small cubes. Fry the potato cubes in an ovenproof skillet with the olive oil and the smoked pork-fat cubes over medium heat for 4 to 5 minutes until the potatoes are tender and slightly golden while the pork-fat cubes have become crisp. Pick the leaves from the thyme sprigs and add to the potatoes.

Beat the eggs and milk together in a bowl and season with salt and pepper. Add the egg mixture to the skillet and stir lightly so that the potatoes and pork-fat cubes are evenly distributed. When the egg mixture has set, transfer the pan to a preheated oven at 500°F and bake for about 5 to 6 minutes. If necessary, turn on the broiler near the end of the cooking time so that the omelet is completely golden on top.

Remove the pan from the oven and slide the omelet gently onto a platter. Eat the omelet warm or cold with rye bread, the Purée of Baked Garlic (see below), and a good salad, such as a beet salad with a mustard dressing, which goes well with eggs, smoked pork fat, and potatoes.

Purée of baked garlic

2 whole garlic bulbs
2 tablespoons coarse sea salt
sea salt flakes and freshly ground pepper
1 tablespoon cold-pressed canola oil
1 teaspoon apple cider vinegar

Place the whole garlic bulbs (skin on) in a small ovenproof dish with the coarse salt. Bake in a preheated oven at 325°F for 35 to 40 minutes until the garlic is browned and crisp on the outside and tender inside.

Remove the garlic bulbs from the dish and let them cool slightly. Separate the cloves then crush them into a bowl, discarding the skins. Mash the garlic with a fork into a coarse purée and season to taste with salt, pepper, oil, and vinegar. The baked garlic has a unique, almost caramelized sweetness that turns the purée into pure candy. Serve the purée with the omelet; it is also great with roast meats and poultry.

....

The origins of potato omelet

Before we started feeding chickens, they didn't lay eggs in the winter, only in the summer. Omelets were therefore a rare but appreciated dish connected with summer, and in the oldest recipes dating back to the first half of the 1800s, they always appeared as a sweet dish. In the middle of the 19th century, a major expansion in poultry farming took place and this was reflected in the cookbooks of that time, which began to include eggs in savory dishes, first with bread and pork fat, then later with potatoes in place of the bread. Smoked pork fat and potato complement each other perfectly in an omelet.

Omelet
with cheese and leeks

1 leek
1 tablespoon standard canola oil
1 rosemary sprig, leaves picked and
    finely chopped
4 organic eggs
½ cup freshly grated hard cheese, such
    as Høost, Vesterhavsost, or Præstost,
    or ripe Gouda or Grana Padano
sea salt flakes and freshly ground pepper

Cut off the root and top of the leek, then cut into thin rings and rinse them thoroughly in cold water so that all the soil is washed away. Drain the leek rings thoroughly and then fry them in the oil with the finely chopped rosemary in a hot ovenproof skillet for 2 to 3 minutes so that they soften a little.

Beat the eggs and cheese together in a bowl and season with salt and pepper. Add the egg mixture to the skillet, then place in a preheated oven at 400°F and bake for about 6 to 8 minutes until it has set and is completely golden on top. Remove the pan from the oven, slide the omelet onto a plate, and serve while it is warm as part of a brunch.

Risotto
with oyster mushrooms and spinach

4 cups chicken stock or water, plus
    extra if needed
1 shallot
a little butter, for sautéing
1½ cups uncooked pearl barley
½ cup white wine
sea salt flakes
3½ oz fresh spinach
5½ oz mixed mushrooms
2 tablespoons butter, diced
½ cup freshly grated Parmesan cheese
freshly ground pepper
finely grated zest and juice of
    ½ to 1 organic lemon

Bring the stock or water to a boil in a saucepan. Peel and mince the shallot, then sauté it in a little butter until it is translucent and tender but without coloring.

Add the pearl barley and sauté for a few minutes, then add the white wine and allow the barley to absorb it. Add the boiling stock or water a little at a time so that the barley is constantly just covered, stirring as you go. Let the pearl barley cook for 15 to 18 minutes until it is soft but still has a little bite to it. It is important to season it with salt during cooking so that the pearly barley can absorb it, but do not add too much if your stock is already very salty.

Wash the spinach thoroughly, then place the leaves in a colander to drain. Shred the spinach using a sharp knife.

Clean the mushrooms with a brush or small vegetable knife, cut them into small pieces, and then fry them in a little butter in a pan for 3 to 4 minutes. Season the mushrooms with salt and pepper, then mix them into the pearl barley (saving some for the garnish).

Remove the pearl barley from the heat and stir in the diced butter and grated Parmesan to create a smooth and creamy consistency (you may want to add some extra stock or water to get the right consistency). Add the fresh spinach to the hot risotto so that it softens a little, then season to taste with salt, pepper, and the lemon zest and juice.

Serve the risotto with the reserved fried mushrooms on top and eat it immediately while it remains soft in texture but the pearl barley is still al dente.

Pearl barley risotto
with beets, goat cheese, and black pepper

½ cup uncooked pearl barley
3¼ cups chicken stock or water
1 to 2 beets, about 7 oz
⅓ cup freshly grated hard cheese, such
    as Høost, Vesterhavsost, or Præstost,
    or ripe Gouda or Grana Padano
2 tablespoons fresh goat cheese
2 teaspoons butter
1 to 2 tablespoons apple cider vinegar
sea salt flakes and freshly ground pepper
½ handful of parsley, chopped

Put the pearl barley and stock or water in a saucepan, bring it to a boil, and skim off the foam. Lower the heat and simmer the grains gently for about 30 to 35 minutes until they are tender and almost all the liquid has been absorbed.

Peel the beets and cut them into ¼-inch cubes. Add the beet cubes to the barley 10 minutes before the end of cooking time so that they also become tender.

Remove the pan from the heat and add the freshly grated hard cheese, goat cheese, and butter to give the barley a creamy consistency à la risotto. Season with the vinegar, salt, and pepper so that the balance is just right, and serve immediately scattered with the chopped parsley. This can be eaten as a dish on its own or as an accompaniment to meat or fish.

Vegetable accompaniments

Glazed beets
with plum vinegar, apples, and juniper

2¼ lb beets
sea salt flakes
1 tablespoon honey
½ cup plum vinegar or other
    dark fruit vinegar
1 tablespoon juniper berries
2 apples with good acidity, such as
    Belle de Boskoop or Cox
1 tablespoon standard canola oil
freshly ground pepper

Put the whole beets in an ovenproof dish with a little salt and bake in a preheated oven at 325°F for 45 minutes to 1 hour until tender, depending on size.

Take the beets out of the oven and set aside until cool enough to handle, then rub the skins off—a small kitchen knife can be helpful for this. Cut the peeled beets into chunky cubes.

Pour the honey and vinegar into a small saucepan, bring to a boil, and reduce for a few minutes until the mixture begins to thicken and become slightly syrupy.

Crush the juniper berries coarsely—just give them a heavy push with the flat side of your kitchen knife—and add them to the syrup. Then add the beet cubes to the pan and let them glaze in the syrup for a few minutes. Take the pan off of the heat and add the beets to a bowl.

Wash the apples, core them, and cut into cubes a little smaller than the beets, then add them to the bowl with the glazed beets. Mix well and season with canola oil, salt, and pepper. Serve these sweet, glazed beets alongside rich meats such as pork cheeks, hare, or game.

Celery root au gratin

1 celery root
sea salt flakes
1 cup full-fat crème fraîche
1 handful of flat-leaf parsley
1 tablespoon prepared coarsely
    ground mustard
⅓ cup freshly grated Parmesan cheese
freshly ground pepper
1 tablespoon olive oil

Peel the celery root and cut it into ¾-inch cubes. Bring a saucepan of salted water to a boil, add the celery root cubes, and cook for 2 to 3 minutes until they are tender but still have some bite. Strain, reserving the cooking water.

Put the celery root cubes into a small saucepan along with the crème fraîche and simmer for 4 to 5 minutes so that they are fully cooked and have integrated with the crème fraîche.

Wash the parsley and pick the leaves from the stems, then cook the leaves in the celery-root cooking water for 30 seconds to 1 minute. Lift the leaves out, squeeze out all the water, and chop coarsely. Add the parsley to the creamy celery root, take the pan off the heat, and season with the mustard, Parmesan, and salt and pepper to taste.

Grease a gratin dish with the oil and pour in the celery-root mixture. Bake the gratin in a preheated oven at 350°F for 15 to 20 minutes until it is slightly golden on top.

Remove the gratin from the oven and serve warm as a vegetarian dish or as a side to fish, roast meat, or poultry.

Salt-baked celery root and butter

1 celery root
plenty of coarse salt, about 4½ to 6½ lb

Wash the celery root thoroughly with a sponge, or peel it with a vegetable peeler if it is very dirty and coarse. Pat it dry with some paper towels, place it in an ovenproof dish, and cover it with the coarse salt.

Bake in a preheated oven at 325°F for 2 to 2½ hours until it is quite tender. You can check if it is soft enough by inserting a thin skewer or very thin knitting needle into the celery root.

Remove the dish from the oven and let the celery root rest for 20 minutes. Then crack the salt shell with the back of a knife and lift the root out. Brush off the excess salt and cut the celery root into chunks.

This way of cooking celery root will bring you a flavor that is delightfully sweet and mild yet intense, and nothing like the way you normally experience the vegetable. Serve the celery root while it is hot with a good dollop of cold butter. Enjoy it as a lunch or as an accompaniment to a main course with some caramelized onions and bacon, along with some good bread.

TIP Save the salt from baking and use it as cooking salt when boiling potatoes or making stock.

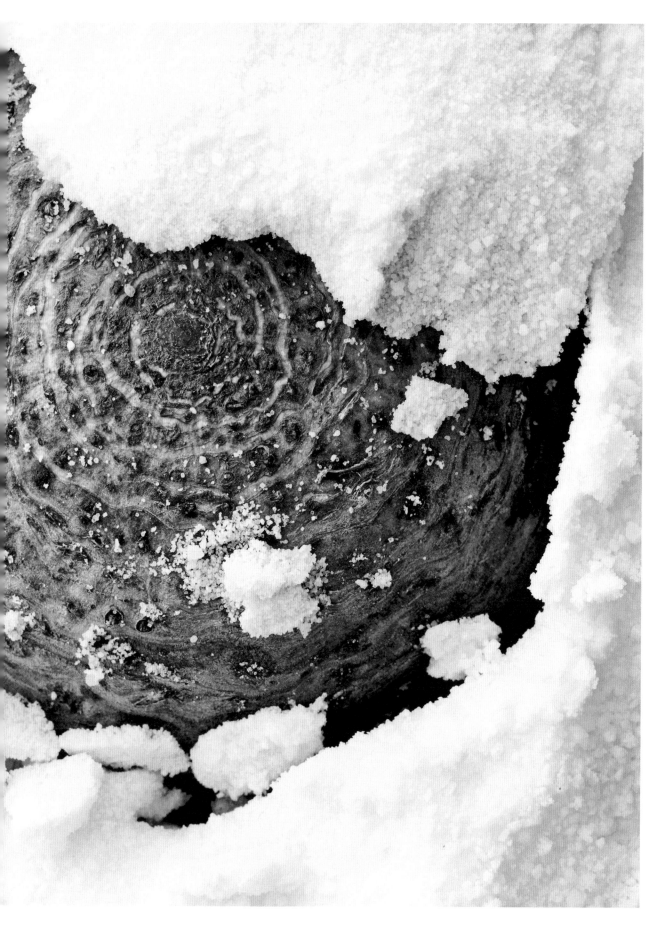

Potatoes fried in duck fat
with apple ketchup

1¾ lb baking potatoes
1 tablespoon duck fat
sea salt flakes
5 thyme sprigs, leaves picked
freshly ground pepper

Wash the potatoes thoroughly, leaving the skin on. Cut them into large cubes. Place the potato cubes in a bowl and let sit under cold running water for 2 to 3 minutes. This step removes the starch so the potatoes become more crisp when you roast them.

Drain the potatoes thoroughly and toss them in the duck fat. Season them with salt and the thyme leaves. Spread them out on a baking pan lined with parchment paper and bake in a preheated oven at 350°F for 35 to 40 minutes until they are perfectly crisp and golden.

Remove the potatoes from the oven and season with pepper and a little extra salt. Eat the potatoes with Apple Ketchup (see below) as part of a Sunday brunch.

Apple ketchup

1 onion
1 garlic clove
2 apples
1 tablespoon olive oil
3½ tablespoons jaggery, plus extra to season
2 star anise
10 coriander seeds
sea salt flakes and freshly ground pepper
2 x 14oz cans peeled plum tomatoes
3 tablespoons apple cider vinegar, plus extra to season

Peel and chop the onion and garlic—you don't have to worry about how finely, as the ketchup will be blended later on. Wash and core the apples, then cut them into pieces.

Sauté the onion, garlic, and apples in the olive oil in a pan for 3 to 4 minutes without letting them take on too much color. Add the sugar, star anise, coriander seeds, salt, and pepper and cook until the onions and apples caramelize in the sugar. Add the tomatoes and vinegar and cook over low heat for about 45 minutes until reduced to a dense compote.

Blend the compote in a blender or with a hand-held stick blender to a smooth purée, then pass it through a very fine sieve (use a spoon to press the purée through). Season to taste with sugar, salt, and vinegar, and then pour the ketchup into a bowl and let cool. If you are not using the ketchup immediately, pour it into a sterilized preserving jar, seal, and store it in the refrigerator, where it will keep for 50 to 60 days, or 10 to 15 days once opened.

Baked potatoes
with crisp bacon, mushrooms, and crème fraîche

4 large or 8 small baking potatoes, such as Russet
sea salt flakes
3½ oz oyster or button mushrooms
2¾ oz bacon
1 cup crème fraîche, 18% fat
1 tablespoon prepared mustard
finely grated zest and juice of ½ organic lemon
½ handful of parsley, chopped
freshly ground pepper

Wash the potatoes and pat them dry with paper towels. Place the potatoes in an ovenproof dish, sprinkle with salt, and bake in a preheated oven at 350°F for 1 hour until they are fully cooked.

Clean the mushrooms with a brush or a small vegetable knife and slice them into small pieces. Cut the bacon into small pieces and fry them in a dry skillet until they have rendered all their fat and are crisp. Pour the fat out of the pan, then add the mushrooms to the crisp bacon.

Mix the remaining ingredients together in a bowl and season with salt and pepper. Make an incision in each potato, squeeze them so that they open out, and fill with the bacon and mushrooms and the crème fraîche sauce. Serve while still warm as a dish in its own right or as an accompaniment to roast poultry or meat.

Kale salad
with carrots and apples

7 oz curly kale with stalks removed
2 carrots
2 shallots
8 dried figs
2 cooking apples, such as Belle de Boskoop or Bramley
2 tablespoons standard canola oil
2 tablespoons apple cider vinegar
1 tablespoon jaggery
sea salt flakes and freshly ground pepper

Remove any remaining stalks from the kale, wash it thoroughly in cold water, and let drain in a sieve. Then chop the kale finely and put it in a bowl.

Peel the carrots and shallots, then cut them both into thin slices. Cut the figs into thin slices. Wash the apples, quarter them, and remove the cores, then cut them into thin wedges.

Add all the prepared ingredients to the kale, and toss together with the oil, vinegar, sugar, and salt and pepper to taste.

Enjoy this salad the day you make it while it is still crunchy. Serve it with dried, salted fish, duck, ham, or sausages as an alternative to stewed kale on days when you fancy a fresh, green side.

Brussels sprouts

The vegetables of the cabbage family, of which Brussels sprouts are a member, are the rough diamonds of the Nordic kitchen garden. With their ability to withstand winter's snow and cold, and their delicate texture, crunchiness, and mildly bitter keynote flavor, they are unlike any other vegetables. They are also possibly the most nutritious vegetables of all that grow in the Nordics.

Brussels sprouts originally came from Belgium and only arrived in Denmark in the late 1800s. At the outset, it was only the uppermost crust of society who consumed the vegetable and, in contrast to its relative the cauliflower, the Brussels sprout had some difficulty making it into our kitchens because of its slightly sharper flavor. During the cold winters, however, frost helps to mellow that sharp flavor. The plant also survives outdoors all winter, to the great pleasure of the local wildlife, from hares to deer.

Cut off the stalks and bring them in as you need them, or find a Brussels sprouts producer and buy the stalks directly from the field—they will easily stay fresh on the stalk for two weeks in a cold cellar or in the refrigerator. If you dig them up by the roots during a mild period and plant them in your garden, you will have fresh supplies throughout the winter. But don't worry if you can't eat them all. The small fresh shoots that come up in the spring are among the most delicious vegetables you can have, and are just as delectable as green asparagus. Eat the shoots raw or blanch them, and then toss them in a good vinaigrette to coat.

The worst thing you can do to Brussels sprouts is to overcook them. If you give them more than 5 to 6 minutes, they develop a fusty, bitter taste and lose their beautiful green color. I prefer sprouts raw and marinated, either cut into thin slices or picked as whole, beautiful leaves. Try blanching sprouts for a few minutes in boiling water and then frying them in butter. Alternatively, glazing them in butter and apple cider vinegar tastes really quite amazing. Brussels sprouts also make a luscious purée.

Sliced Brussels sprouts

Wash the sprouts, then remove the outer leaves if they are damaged, and cut off the bottom-most part of the root. Slice the sprouts into very fine strips with a sharp knife or using a mandoline.

Brussels sprout leaves

Wash and prepare the sprouts as above. Using your fingers or an herb knife, carefully peel off as many leaves as you possibly can until you reach the very heart of the sprout. The leaves are great in salads with root vegetables, apples, or pears. Note that the leaves should soak in the marinade for a little longer than sliced sprouts—about 2 to 3 minutes in total—before serving.

Boiled Brussels sprouts

Wash and prepare the sprouts as before. You can cook them whole or halved; personally, I prefer to halve them because the cooking time is shorter and you can cook them until tender while retaining their beautiful green color and wonderful juiciness. Bring a pan of salted water to a boil, add the sprouts, and cook until tender. As a rule of thumb, cook halved sprouts for 2 to 3 minutes and whole sprouts for 4 to 5 minutes. Once done, if they are to be used cold, plunge them directly into iced water so that they keep their color and crunch. If you want to serve them hot, just take them directly from the pan to the table. Please don't let sprouts stand around for too long after they are cooked—it will ruin both their fragrance and their flavor.

Brussels sprout salad

You will need about 3½ ounces Brussels sprouts, 2 tablespoons apple cider vinegar, 2 tablespoons cold-pressed canola oil, sea salt flakes, freshly ground pepper, and, if necessary, a little sugar.

Wash the sprouts and drain them thoroughly. Prepare them as before and then slice very finely (see left). Dress with the oil and vinegar, then season to taste with salt and pepper. Depending on the type of apple cider vinegar you have used, you may want to balance it with a little sugar.

Kale purée
with nutmeg and almonds

sea salt flakes
9 oz curly kale with stems removed
5½ oz ricotta
⅓ cup freshly grated Parmesan cheese
⅓ cup whole blanched almonds
finely grated zest of ½ organic lemon
¼ cup cold-pressed canola oil
a little freshly grated nutmeg
freshly ground pepper

Bring a pan of lightly salted water to a boil. Check the kale for any pieces of stalk and discard, then wash the kale thoroughly in cold water. Add the kale to the boiling water and blanch for about 2 minutes, then immediately plunge it into a bowl of cold water. The kale should be tender but retain its beautiful green color and freshness.

Wring all the water out of the kale in a clean dish towel or between your hands, then place it in a food processor along with the ricotta, Parmesan, almonds, lemon zest, and oil. Process to a coarse purée and season to taste with nutmeg, salt, and pepper.

TIP This purée is perfect for spreading on toast, for tossing with pasta, or as a dip for fried poultry and fish.

Bitter salad greens
with deep-fried onions and mustard and honey vinaigrette

Deep-fried onions
1 onion
sea salt flakes
4 cups standard canola oil
a little all-purpose flour

Salad
1 head of radicchio
½ frisée lettuce (curly endive)
½ handful of flat-leaf parsley

Dressing
1 shallot
3 tablespoons apple balsamic vinegar
1 tablespoon prepared mustard
2 tablespoons honey
sea salt flakes and freshly ground pepper
3 tablespoons cold-pressed canola oil

First make the deep-fried onions. Peel the onion and cut it into very thin rings. Sprinkle the onion rings with salt and let stand in the kitchen for 10 to 15 minutes until softened.

Pour the oil into a pan and heat it up slowly to about 315 to 325°F. It is important that the temperature of the oil is just right—check it by dipping the wooden end of a match into the oil. If the oil bubbles a little around the match, the temperature is correct.

Dip the onion rings in a little flour and shake off the excess. Add the onion rings to the hot oil, a few at a time, and fry them for 1 to 2 minutes until golden and crisp. Remove with a slotted spoon and place them on paper towels to absorb the oil.

For the salad, tear the radicchio and frisée leaves coarsely, rinse them thoroughly in cold water, and dry them in a salad spinner or pat dry with a clean dish towel. Wash the parsley and pick the leaves from the stems.

Now make the dressing. Peel and chop the shallot, then put it in a blender with the vinegar, mustard, honey, salt, and pepper. Blend until the mixture is smooth, then slowly add the oil in a thin stream while the blender is still running to create a thick and smooth dressing.

Toss the salad with the parsley and dressing, and serve with the crispy onion rings on top. This salad is great with fried meat, where it provides a fresh and bitter contrast.

Crispy Brussels sprout salad
with orange, walnuts, and pearl barley

SERVES 6

½ cup uncooked pearl barley
3½ cups water
sea salt flakes and freshly ground pepper
10½ oz Brussels sprouts, rinsed
2 organic oranges
¼ cup walnuts
4 to 5 flat-leaf parsley sprigs
2 tablespoons apple cider vinegar
¼ cup cold-pressed canola oil
1 tablespoon honey

Rinse the pearl barley in cold water, place in a saucepan, and add the measurement water. Bring to a boil and cook the barley, with the lid on, for about 20 minutes until it is tender and has absorbed the water. Remove the pan from the heat and let stand, still with the lid on, for 5 to 10 minutes. Now season with salt and pepper and let the barley cool completely.

Remove the outer leaves of the Brussels sprouts and discard them, then cut off the bottom-most part of the root. Slice the sprouts finely with a sharp knife or using a mandoline and place in a bowl. Grate the zest of the oranges finely and add to the sprouts. Peel the oranges, cut the orange flesh into small cubes, and add them to the sprouts.

Break the walnuts into small pieces and mix them into the sprout salad, along with the cooked, cooled barley.

Pick the leaves from the parsley stems, wash them well, and chop coarsely, then toss into the salad. Now add the vinegar, oil, honey, salt, and pepper, and mix well. Taste the salad—it might benefit from a little extra vinegar, salt, or pepper. Serve the Brussels sprout salad as an accompaniment to Pigs' Cheeks (*see* page 199) or other main courses, or as a salad for lunch.

Crispy Brussels sprout salad »

Baking and sweet things

Raisin buns

MAKES 15 TO 20

2 cups lowfat milk
2½ oz (½ cup) fresh compresssed yeast
   (baker's yeast)
1 stick softened butter
⅓ cup sugar
1½ teaspoons fine salt
2¼ lb all-purpose flour
2 teaspoons ground cardamom
1 teaspoon vanilla sugar (*see* tip,
   page 246)
3 organic eggs
1 cup raisins
1 organic egg, lightly beaten

Warm the milk a little (95 to 104°F), pour it into a very large bowl, and stir in the yeast. When the yeast has dissolved, add the softened butter, sugar, and salt and stir well to combine. Then mix in the flour, cardamom, and vanilla sugar. Finally, add the eggs, one at a time, and knead the dough for 10 to 15 minutes. Don't add the raisins yet—I will come back to those.

Let the dough rise in the kitchen, covered with a clean dish towel, for about 1 hour. Meanwhile, soak the raisins in cold water, which will prevent them from scorching during baking.

Drain the raisins and knead them into the risen dough. Divide the dough into 15 to 20 pieces and shape into buns. Put the buns on a cookie sheet lined with parchment paper. Let rise until doubled in size.

Brush the buns with the beaten egg and bake in a preheated oven at 425°F for 6 to 7 minutes until they are completely golden.

Take the buns out of the oven and transfer them to a wire rack to cool slightly. Serve them with a little butter—nothing else. These buns are the best on the day of baking, but if you can't eat them all, they can be frozen and then defrosted and reheated as you need them.

Buns
with grated carrots and sunflower seeds

MAKES 20

3 cups lukewarm water
¾ oz (2 tablespoons) fresh compresssed
   yeast (baker's yeast)
1 tablespoon acacia honey
2 tablespoons standard canola oil
2 cups wholemeal flour, plus extra
   for dusting
⅓ cup sunflower seeds, chopped
3 teaspoons fine salt
5½ oz peeled carrots
1¾ lb all-purpose flour

Pour the measured lukewarm water into a very large bowl and stir in the yeast until dissolved. Add the honey, oil, wholemeal flour, chopped sunflower seeds, and, finally, the salt. Stir to combine. Grate the carrots and add them to the dough. Add the all-purpose flour, a little at a time, then knead the dough in the bowl for 10 to 15 minutes. Cover with plastic wrap and let the dough rise in the refrigerator for 8 hours.

Remove the dough from the refrigerator and place it on a floured work surface.

Divide the dough into 20 pieces and shape them into buns. Place the buns on a cookie sheet lined with parchment paper and let rise in the kitchen for about 20 minutes.

Bake the buns in a preheated oven at 400°F for 12 to 14 minutes. The buns are ready if they sound hollow when tapped on the base.

Take the buns out of the oven and let cool slightly on a wire rack. Eat them freshly baked, or use them as your lunch bread.

•••••••••••••••••••••••••••••••••••

Tip I often bake a large batch of these buns at the start of the week and freeze the few that my family haven't devoured freshly baked. It is easy to defrost a single bun or two for packed lunches or for a snack during the week.

•••••••••••••••••••••••••••••••••••

St. Lucia saffron buns

MAKES 10

⅛ teaspoon saffron threads
1¾ cups cold whole milk
1¾ oz (5¼ tablespoons) fresh
   compressed yeast (baker's yeast)
1 organic egg, lightly beaten,
   plus 1 extra beaten egg for brushing
1¾ lb all-purpose flour, plus extra for
   dusting
1 tablespoon sea salt flakes
½ cup sugar
1 stick butter, melted
raisins or currants, to decorate

Grind the saffron threads finely using a mortar and pestle. Pour the milk into a bowl and stir in the yeast. Add the egg, half the flour, the salt, sugar, ground saffron, and melted butter, and knead in the bowl.

Incorporate the rest of the flour, but hold back a little—the dough should not be too firm, so it is up to you to determine whether you need it all. Knead the dough for 5 to 6 minutes, either in an electric stand mixer fitted with a dough hook or by hand in the bowl, until you have a supple and smooth dough.

Let the dough rest, covered with a clean dish towel, in the kitchen for about 2 hours.

Turn the dough out on a floured surface, divide it into 10 pieces and form each piece into a curved shape: the Lucia classic is a tightly closed "S," but get creative with curved and braided crosses, snails, curly "U"-shapes, rams' horns, and so on. Place the shapes on a cookie sheet lined with parchment paper and let rise for 1 hour.

Brush the shapes with beaten egg, decorate with raisins or currants, and bake at 400°F for 10 to 12 minutes. Take the buns out of the oven and let cool slightly on a wire rack. Eat the sweet, yellow bread freshly baked and warm (they taste of a happy childhood just as they are, or quite sinful with butter).

Buttermilk pancakes

MAKES ABOUT 20 PANCAKES

2 organic eggs
2 tablespoons jaggery
finely grated zest of 1 organic lemon
½ vanilla bean, split lengthwise and seeds scraped out
½ teaspoon fine salt
1 teaspoon baking soda
1 teaspoon baking powder
2½ cups all-purpose flour
2½ tablespoons butter, melted, plus a little extra for frying, if needed
1¼ cups buttermilk
½ to ⅔ cup lowfat milk

Beat the eggs with the sugar, lemon zest, vanilla seeds, and salt in a bowl. Mix the baking soda and baking powder with the flour and then sift into the egg mixture. Stir the butter into the batter and then slowly stir in the buttermilk and milk. Let the batter rest in the refrigerator for 3 to 4 hours.

Fry the batter in a small skillet, a ladleful at a time, for 1 to 2 minutes on each side until golden. There is butter in the dough, but depending on the pan I use, I might also add a little butter to the pan while frying. My old blini pan is so "saturated," it doesn't require any grease, but with other pans, I sometimes notice that the batter sticks to the pan if I don't add a little butter after making each pancake. Keep the cooked pancakes warm in a dish covered with foil as you cook the rest. Enjoy the warm pancakes with syrup and fresh fruit. You can also bake the pancakes in advance and reheat them before serving.

Tip If you replace half the all-purpose flour with wholemeal flour and remove the sugar, you have a great pancake recipe for savory dishes—delicious as part of a brunch or in your packed lunch. Sometimes I add a handful of steamed spinach (drain off excess water) or freshly chopped herbs to the batter for a savory meal.

Danish doughnut holes
with orange and cardamom

3½ cups all-purpose flour
½ teaspoon fine salt
2 teaspoons sugar
1 teaspoon ground cardamom
1 teaspoon baking soda
½ teaspoon finely grated orange zest
3 organic eggs
1¾ cups buttermilk
3 tablespoons standard canola oil, plus extra for frying
juice of ½ organic orange
confectioners' sugar, for dusting

Mix the flour, salt, sugar, cardamom, baking soda, and orange zest together in a bowl. Separate the eggs into yolks and whites, then beat the yolks with the buttermilk and stir into the dry ingredients. Add the oil and the orange juice, then let the batter rest in the refrigerator for about 30 minutes.

Beat the egg whites until stiff and then fold into the batter—I always stir the first spoonful of the beaten egg whites in very thoroughly, then I can easily fold the rest gently into the batter without losing their airiness.

Warm a doughnut hole or *æbleskive* pan (*see* panel) and pour a little oil into each hole—this is only necessary for cooking the first round of batter, not for the rest because the oil is already added to the batter. Fill each hole three-quarters full of batter. When the doughnut holes begin to stiffen and rise at the edges, use a fork or a skewer to turn them upside down, and continue to turn them several times during cooking to make them perfectly round. Check whether the doughnut holes are done by poking them with the skewer—if any batter adheres to the skewer when you remove it, keep cooking a little longer.

You can keep the cooked doughnut holes warm in the oven while you finish cooking the remaining batches of batter, or place them in a dish covered with foil. Serve the doughnut holes with a light dusting of confectioners' sugar, and enjoy them with homemade jams and compotes.

Danish doughnut holes or *æbleskive*

Pastries are very regional. This also applies to the Danish æbleskive, literally meaning "apple slice." The currently familiar form—cakes baked in a special pan with semicircular indentations— is known only in Sweden, Norway, and Denmark, and most evidence indicates that it was originally Danish. The æbleskive, earlier also known as "monks," probably emerged as slices of apple dipped in a batter and baked in fat. However, the special æbleskive pan, which made it possible to bake the small round cakes with much less fat, has been around since the 1500s. The southern Danish islands of Lolland and Falster had their own version, known as svupsakker, created by poking a hole in the cake with your thumb and filling it with brandy.

Christmas cookies

MAKES 25 TO 30

½ cup whole unblanched almonds
2 cups all-purpose flour
½ teaspoon baking powder
1 cup confectioners' sugar
1 vanilla bean
2½ sticks softened butter
1 organic egg, beaten

Put the almonds into a heatproof bowl, pour boiling water over them, and let them soak for 30 seconds. Drain and then peel off the skins. Dry the almonds with paper towels or a clean dish towel and grind them finely in a food processor. Check for any remaining large pieces, because they could clog the pastry bag later.

Sift the flour, baking powder, and confectioners' sugar into a large bowl and mix in the ground almonds. Split the vanilla bean lengthwise, scrape out the seeds, and mix them thoroughly into the flour mixture—it is easier to do this if you first sprinkle a little flour on the cutting board and mix the vanilla seeds into the flour with the flat side of a chef's knife. Stir the softened butter into the dry ingredients until you have a smooth paste, then mix in the beaten egg to create a supple dough.

Fill a pastry bag, fitted with a small star tip, with the dough and pipe small rings onto a cookie sheet lined with parchment paper (you will probably need 3 cookie sheets in total). If you find piping all the rings too arduous, you can pipe the dough into long strips, cut these into 4-inch pieces with a knife, and then assemble the rings by hand.

Bake the vanilla cookies in a preheated oven at 325°F for about 8 minutes, or until they are light golden around the edges. Take the cookies out of the oven and transfer to a wire rack to cool completely before you pack them into airtight cake cans, where they will remain crisp for 1 to 2 weeks.

Chocolate cream mousse

SERVES 8

6 organic egg yolks
⅔ cup superfine sugar
1 cup lowfat milk
1½ cups heavy whipping cream
10½ oz good-quality dark chocolate, such as Valrhona Caraïbe 66%, chopped

Using an electric hand mixer or a balloon whisk, whisk the egg yolks and sugar together until white and foamy.

Pour the milk and cream into a saucepan and bring to a boil, then pour into the egg mixture and continue whisking. Pour the mixture back into the saucepan and cook over low heat until thickened slightly, whisking constantly. Don't let it reach boiling point.

Remove the custard from the heat and pour through a sieve into a bowl containing the chopped chocolate. Stir with a spatula from the center outward so that you create a supple core of melted chocolate that gets bigger and bigger as you work your way outward. Stir until all the chocolate is melted as it meets the warm cream. Pour into a bowl and place in the refrigerator for 3 to 4 hours until firm.

This chocolate cream is a mix between a light truffle and a mousse, and it can be scooped up beautifully with a spoon dipped in hot water. Serve with candied or baked fall fruit or fruit sauce.

Bread pudding
with apples and golden raisins

2 tablespoons butter
¾ cup jaggery, divided
½ loaf of day-old white bread
3 to 4 apples
⅔ cup golden raisins
4 organic eggs
1¼ cups heavy whipping cream
1¼ cups lowfat milk
1 vanilla bean
2 tablespoons confectioners' sugar, plus extra for sprinkling

My home is a high bread-baking and bread-consuming household, so we usually have some day-old bread in stock that is a little dry around the edges. I have developed a wide repertoire of use-the-bread-to-the-last-crumb recipes and this easy bread pudding is one of them.

Grease an ovenproof dish with the butter and sprinkle with 2 tablespoons of the jaggery. Cut the bread into thin slices. Wash and core the apples, then slice them into thin wedges. Arrange the bread and apple slices in alternate layers in the dish, sprinkling the golden raisins in between.

Beat the eggs, cream, milk, and the rest of the jaggery together in a bowl. Split the vanilla bean lengthwise, scrape the seeds out, and add both the seeds and the scraped bean to the egg mixture. Pour the mixture over the bread and apples in the dish, sprinkle with the confectioners' sugar, and bake in a preheated oven at 350°F for about 25 minutes until the pudding is golden and crisp on top.

Dust the pudding with a little extra confectioners' sugar before serving, and enjoy it warm with a little crème fraîche, ice cream, or lightly whipped cream.

Tip You can replace the apples with red berries to make a summer pudding. Raspberries, blackcurrants, redcurrants, and blackberries are all very well suited to this dish.

Yogurt ice cream
with pomegranate

3 cups plain yogurt, 10% fat
1 cup sugar, divided
1 to 2 teaspoons vanilla sugar (*see* tip)
2 pasteurized egg whites
1 pomegranate

Pour the yogurt into a bowl and add ¼ cup of the sugar along with the vanilla sugar—the better the quality of vanilla sugar, the richer and more delicious the vanilla taste. Mix well and place in the freezer for about 1 to 1½ hours, stirring it occasionally.

Pour the egg whites into a clean, dry bowl (this is very important, because any impurities or moisture will prevent the whites from becoming perfectly stiff) and whisk them until stiff using an electric hand mixer. Add the remaining sugar and whisk again until the whites are dense and shiny.

Take the yogurt out of the freezer, gently fold the egg whites into the ice cream, and put it back in the freezer. Freeze the ice cream for about 2 to 3 hours until it is solid but still has a creamy consistency. The ice cream can stay in the freezer for longer than 2 to 3 hours, but after several days it will become too hard.

Split the pomegranate and knock the seeds out with the back of a spoon. Serve the ice cream sprinkled with the beautiful fresh pomegranate seeds.

. . . .

Tip I use the good trick of saving empty vanilla beans in a preserving jar and filling it with light jaggery. Every time I have a scraped vanilla bean, I put it in the jar and then top it off with sugar whenever I use some of the contents—it makes a very nice flavored sugar.

. . . .

Crème brûlée
with stout and orange salad

1 cup stout
½ vanilla bean
1 cup heavy whipping cream
3 tablespoons lowfat milk
⅓ cup sugar
3 organic egg yolks
finely grated zest of 1 organic lemon
jaggery, for sprinkling

Pour the stout into a saucepan and reduce to half its original volume.

Scrape the seeds from the vanilla bean and add the seeds and the bean to a saucepan with the cream, milk, and sugar. Bring to a boil, then pour the warm mixture into a bowl with the egg yolks. Add the stout and lemon zest and mix to a smooth mixture. Let cool in the refrigerator for 2 to 4 hours.

Pour the cream into 6 to 8 ramekins, place them on a baking pan, and bake in a preheated oven at 195°F for about 1 hour. The mixture should be firm but won't rise like soufflés. When cooked, let cool in the refrigerator. Sprinkle a thin layer of the sugar on top of the cold cream and caramelize with a chef's torch until the surface is crisp. This can also be done under a broiler, but make sure the broiler is preheated to high beforehand so that you don't also heat the cream. Serve immediately with the Orange Salad (*see* below).

Orange salad

3 organic oranges
1½ tablespoons whole blanched almonds
2 mint sprigs

Peel the oranges, making sure you remove all the white pith, then cut the orange flesh into small cubes, discarding any seeds. Chop the almonds and mint coarsely and then mix with the orange.

White glogg
with fruit brandy and pear

2 cups good-quality cold-pressed or
    clear apple juice
1¼ cups water
1 cup elderflower concentrate or cordial
juice of ½ lemon, plus extra if needed
2 tablespoons jaggery
1 star anise
3 whole black peppercorns
1 cardamom pod
1 slice of fresh ginger root, ¼-inch thick,
    peeled, plus extra if needed
¼ to ½ cup pear or apple brandy
1 pear
3½ tablespoons golden raisins

Place all the ingredients, except the brandy, pear, and golden raisins, in a saucepan and bring to a boil. Take the pan off the heat and let the glogg stand for 30 minutes to 1 hour for all the spices to infuse.

Strain the glogg through a sieve and slowly heat it up again, taste it, and possibly add a little extra lemon juice or ginger—do not let it boil, because this changes the taste from distinctly gingery to intensely burning. When using fresh ginger root, the trick is to grate a little on the fine side of a grater and then squeeze the pulp between 2 spoons so that only the pure, strong ginger juice goes into the glogg.

Remove the glogg from the heat. Season to taste with the brandy, but again, do not let the drink boil after you add the brandy.

Wash the pear, cut it into quarters, and remove the core. Then cut the flesh into small cubes. Divide the pear cubes and golden raisins between 6 to 8 heat-resistant glasses and pour the hot glogg on top. Serve immediately as a refreshing and spicy winter drink that will get the heat back in your cheeks after a walk in the cold.

. . . .

Yogurt ice cream »

Index

A

æbleskive 242–3
almond
  & cabbage salsa 162
  & chocolate cake 108–9, 112
  macaroons 113, 114, 120
apples 174
  baked 174–5
  with braised pork knuckle 140
  in bread pudding 244
  Brussels sprout, chickpea & caper salad 164, 166
  & celery root compote 200
  crispy puff pastry pie 170–3
  dried 171
  & horseradish vinaigrette 190–1
  & Jerusalem artichoke 142, 157
  ketchup 235
  mostarda with pork ribs 202
  muffins 170
  & onion compote 205
  pearl barley salad 161
  in pearled spelt salad 206
  pie with hazelnuts & vanilla 170
  with roast duck 206
  sauce 180, 224
  sorbet with apple sauce 171
  stewed, with vanilla yogurt 174
  turnip & horseradish compote 160
  windfalls 132
artichoke, Jerusalem 142, 157, 160, 167, 213
asparagus
  & cauliflower with yogurt dressing 86
  & chervil mousseline 20
  & fennel crudités 33
  green 19, 20, 33, 36, 86, 92, 98–9, 100
  griddled vegetables 100
  with potato salad 36
  salad with shrimp 92
  with smoked curd cheese 19
  soup 19, 66
  summer vegetable tartlets 98–9
  white 19, 20, 66, 92, 98–9

B

bacon
  apple & artichoke compote 157
  with braised peas 72
  burning love 139
  with fried tartare of cod 192
  in meatloaf 135
barbecues 75, 86–7, 102–3

barley
  bread 52–3
  fried porridge 42
  pearl barley & asparagus soup 66
  pearl barley, onions & parsley 76
  pearl barley risotto 147, 230
  pearl barley salad 128, 161, 210, 238–9
  porridge 78
beans, white 213
beef
  gravad top round with celery root 209
  hanger steak with frisée lettuce 74, 75
  heart 82
  patties 76–7
  ribs with potato & squash purée 136–7
  sausages 81
beer ice cream 174–5
beets
  baked, with yogurt & dill 161
  with cottage cheese, pork fat & tarragon 105
  with fried tartare of cod 192
  in gastrique 24
  glazed 232
  horseradish & dill salad 82
  marinated 224
  with pan-roasted herrings 131
  pearl barley risotto 230
  pickled 195
  in rye salad 94
  sauce, with roasted veal 138
  tartare with cold veal 199
  tartare & smoked whiting 219
Belgian endive, braised 218
blackberries
  almond & chocolate cake 113
  parfait with aquavit 120
  red berry compote 116, 118
  in rye salad 94
  with sugar-roasted rye bread 121
  trifle 120
blackcurrants 116, 118, 180
blinis, with lumpfish roe 192
blueberries 95, 116, 118
bread 10
  barley 52–3
  brioche with smoked salmon 40
  bruschetta with squash purée & goat cheese 224–5
  buns 240–1
  cheese on toast 126
  crispy croutons 128

  dark rye 55
  focaccia 54–5
  pudding with apples & raisins 244–5
  quick & easy rye 108
  roast pork sandwich 222–3
  salted cod sandwich 155, 156
  smoked lumpfish sandwich 222
  smoked venison sandwich 160
  sourdough starter 52
  Swedish syrup bread 52
  toast, thin & crunchy 84–5
Brussels sprouts 236–7
  salad 164, 166, 210, 236, 238–9
buns 240–1
burning love 139
buttermilk
  dessert 121
  doughnut holes 242–3
  dressing 39
  ice cream 61
  pancakes 243
  in sour milk 116

C

cabbage
  & almond salsa with parsley roots 162
  with braised pork knuckle & apples 140
  crispy summer salad 105
  with crudité of turnip & pears 131
  with lamb fricassee 76
  & mushroom pie 155
  pea & dill salad 72
  pickled with pears 167
  red cabbage 135, 201, 210
  salad with fishcakes 210
  sauerkraut 135
  with skate wings 36
  spicy sugar-browned 139
  summer vegetable tartlets 98–9
cake
  almond & chocolate 108–9, 112
  cinnamon swirls 178–9
  rhubarb 58–9
carrots
  baked 161
  in buns 240
  carrot & egg sauce 214
  glazed 142–3
  griddled vegetables 100
  with marinated herring 131
  purée with dill seeds & vinegar 146
  root vegetable rösti 138

tartare sauce 152–3
cauliflower 86, 100–1, 152–3
celery root 27
   & apple compote 200
   au gratin 232
   pickles 209
   purée 222
   root vegetable rösti 138
   salt-baked 232–3
   sauce with meatballs 200–1
chanterelles 148–9
   & cheese with eggs 95
   onion & sausage stew 78
   shallot & chicken salad 95
   stew on toast 94, 96–7
cheese
   fynbo, with pear mostarda 157–9
   on toast 126
   see also type of cheese
chervil 18, 20, 68, 75, 98, 102, 192
chestnuts 162
chicken
   honey-glazed with black pepper 33
   livers, pan-fried 40–1
   meatballs, with mushroom soup 186
   with pea, cabbage & dill salad 72
   roast, with carrot pureé 146
   roast, with peas, onions, bacon & lettuce
      72–3
   salad with shallots & chanterelles 95
chickpeas, in salad 164, 166
chocolate
   dark 108–9, 244
   white 60
Christmas
   cookies 244
   mustard 196
   terrine 194–5
chutney 36, 57, 193
cinnamon swirls 178–9
cockles 213
cod
   fish cakes 152
   fish & chips 152
   orange & fennel-marinated 150–1
   pan-fried 214–15
   salted cod sandwich 155, 156
   smoked cod roe salad 222
   tartare patties with beets 192
compote,
   red berry 116, 118
   rødgrød 116, 118
cookies, Christmas 244

cottage cheese 46–7, 105
crab 39, 68–71
crayfish, with dill mayonnaise 68
cream
   chocolate cream mousse 244
   dessert with elderflower jelly 121
   licorice parfait 60
   rhubarb 57
cream cheese, with chervil & lemon 102
crème brulée 246, 248
crispbread, homemade 157–9
crispy crumbles 60
croutons, crispy 128
cucumber
   cold soup 66–7
   cream-stewed 34
   refrigerator-pickled 78
   sautéed, with pan-fried mullet 91
   in smoked curd cheese dressing 92
curd cheese, smoked 16
   with asparagus 19, 66
   cream 19
   dressing with cucumber & dill 92
   with potato pillows 16–17
   sandwich dressing 45
   with shrimp & crispy potatoes 44–5
   custard 113, 120

D
dandelion leaves 32, 226–7
Danish cooking 6, 8
dill 34, 36, 46, 68, 72, 75, 132, 154, 161
dips 22, 46, 102
doughnut holes 242–3
duck 33, 195, 206–7, 235

E
eggs
   & carrot sauce 214
   poached, with chervil soup 18
   in pots, with chanterelles & cheese 95
   see also omelet
elderberries 176–7, 178
elderflowers 114, 121, 246

F
fava beans 186, 213, 218
fennel
   & asparagus crudités 33
   asparagus & shrimp salad 92
   beet, horseradish & dill salad 82
   crudités, with mustard vinaigrette 88
   mayonnaise 68–9

& orange-marinated cod 150–1
   with roast pork 32
   with skate wings 36
   tartare sauce 152–3
   with veal stew 27
fish
   & chips 152
   fish cakes 152–3, 210–11
   fried with leeks, dill & carrot 214
   salted 155, 156, 192–3
   smoked 219
   soup with root vegetables 186–7
   see also types of fish
flavor, adjusting 10
flounder, fried with Belgian endive 216–18
focaccia 54–5
fruit bushes, leaves 61
fynbo, pear mostarda & crispbread 157–9

G
game 134
   see also venison; wild boar
garfish, pan-fried 36–7
garlic
   baked purée 228
garlic mustard 42
gastrique 10, 24, 201, 206
glogg, white 246, 249
goat cheese 104–5, 224–5, 230
gooseberries 86, 113
granita, elderflower 114
grevskabets preserve 176
ground elder 50

H
haddock 152, 218
halibut, salted with squash purée 192–3
ham, glazed, with stewed kale 196–7
hazelnuts 100, 137, 170, 210
healthy eating 8–9
herb butter 102
herring
   barbecued 86–7
   marinated with carrots & onions 130–1
   pan-fried 34, 87, 131, 154, 214
horseradish
   & apple vinaigrette 190
   in baked rhubarb 33
   beet & dill salad 82
   with beet tartare 199
   cream 192, 219
   pearled rye salad with blackberries &
      beets 94

with raw salmon 42
sweet & sour dip 46
turnip & apple compote 160
yellow split pea soup 126
hotdogs, homemade 81
hotpot, veal, licorice & beer 204–5

I

ice cream 61, 174-5, 246–7
see also parfait; sorbet
ingredients
seasonal 8, 10, 15, 65, 125, 185
sustainability 9

J

jams/preserves 110, 176
jelly (gelatin) 121

K

kale
creamy soup 126
purée 134, 238
salad 134, 210, 235
stewed 196–7
karbonader 142–3
ketchup 81, 235
kidneys, lamb 24
kohlrabi, in gastrique 24

L

lamb
chargrilled liver 82
chops, grilled 26
fillet with kale purée & salad 134
meatballs 26–7
pan-fried kidneys 24
roast leg 24
rump with celery root & apple compote 200
shoulder, oven-roasted 26
sweet & sour fricassee 76
langoustines, with tarragon & garlic 39
leeks
"burnt" and lemon in oil 165, 166
"burnt" summer 82
with cheese omelet 230
in octopus salad 213
with pan-fried cod 214
in potato soup 188
with steamed mussels 88–9
stewed 87
with vinaigrette 50–1
lemon mayonnaise 150

lemon verbena 174
lettuce 29, 72, 74, 75
licorice 60–1, 205
lingonberries 134, 135, 162–3
liver 40–1, 82–3, 195, 205
lobster, with lemon mayonnaise 150
lovage dip 102
lumpfish roe 39, 188–9, 192
lumpfish, smoked 222, 224

M

macaroons, almond 113, 114, 120
mackerel 45, 84–5, 86, 94
marmalade, mirabelle 110
mayonnaise 68
dill 68
fennel 68–9
lemon 150
quick tartare sauce 152–3
tomato 39
meatballs 26–7, 75, 186, 200–1
meatloaf 135
meringue, almond & chocolate cake 108–9
milk 114, 116, 121
mirabelles 110–11
mostarda 157, 202
mousse, chocolate cream 244
muffins 113, 170
mullet 66, 91
mushrooms
baked with hard cider & garlic 162
with baked potatoes & bacon 235
blue stalk 150
dried 149
oyster 154, 230–1, 235
St. George's 34
& Savoy cabbage pie 155
sheathed woodtuft 166
soup with meatballs 186
& spinach risotto 230–1
& squash with griddled pheasant 146
velouté 147
see also chanterelles
mussels 18, 20, 34, 88–9, 213
mustard 42, 88, 155, 190, 196

N

nettles 16–17, 40
Nordic Cuisine Manifesto 255

O

oats, toasted oat flakes 121
octopus salad 213

oil
dill 34
lemon 166
omelet
with cheese & leeks 230
with crispy Jerusalem artichokes 160
mackerel, potato & scallions 45
potato, with smoked pork fat & garlic purée 228
potato, spinach & smoked salmon 92–3
onion
& apple compote 205
baby 72, 78
baked with parsley & pearl barley 76
caramelized, with pork tenderloin 140
compote 42
crispy onion pie 228–9
crispy onion rings 46
griddled vegetables 100
with marinated herring 131
pickled 40, 222
soup, with cheese toasts 126–7
oysters 190–1

P

pancakes, buttermilk 243
parfait 60–1, 120
parsley roots, baked, with salsa 162
parsley sauce 78
pastry 98, 170, 173
patties 76–7, 142–3, 152–3
pears
with crudité of turnip & cabbage 131
mostarda with fynbo & crispbread 157–9
with pickled cabbage 167
poached in elderberry juice 178
sorbet 180
peas
cabbage & dill salad 72
cabbage & scallion salad 105
green potato salad 75
with onion, bacon & lettuce 72
with pan-fried mullet 91
pea & mint soup, cold 66
purée 100
split pea soup 126, 188
summer vegetable tartlets 98–9
pesto, wild garlic 22, 55
pheasant 132–3, 146, 160
pickles
beet 195
cabbage with pears 167
celery root 209

cucumber 78
elderberries 176
Jerusalem artichoke 167
lingonberries 134
onion 40
ramson buds 22
root vegetable 132
squash 132, 167
tomato 84
pie
    apple, with hazelnuts & vanilla 170
    crispy onion 228–9
    crispy puff pastry apple 170–3
    mushroom & Savoy cabbage 155
plaice, pan-fried 90–1
plums 110–11, 112, 113
pork
    belly in yellow split pea soup 126
    braised knuckle 138–9, 140–1
    burning love 139
    chops, marinated 82
    fat 105, 228
    in meatballs 200–1
    in meatloaf 135
    in milk, garlic & rosemary 202–3
    mock chicken 32
    pigs' cheeks 198–9
    ribs with apple mostarda 202
    roast belly 78
    roast loin 30–2, 201
    roast pork sandwich 222–3
    sausages 42, 78–9, 81
    smoked saddle, with spinach 28–9
    tenderloin, parsley-stuffed 29
    tenderloin medallions with caramelized
        onions 140
    & veal patties 142–3
    wild boar 193, 208–9
porridge
    barley, with chanterelles, onions &
        sausages 78
    fried 42
potato
    baked, with bacon & mushrooms 235
    baked, with salmon tartare & dill yogurt
        154
    barbecued new 102–3
    burning love 139
    chips, with fish 152
    compote 27
    crispy, with shrimp 44–5
    fried in duck fat 235
    mashed 139

omelet with hot-smoked salmon
    92–3
omelet with mackerel 45
omelet with smoked pork fat & garlic
    purée 228
& pea salad 75
pillows with curd cheese 16–17
with roast pork 26, 32
rösti 39, 138
with rye bread sandwich 45
salad 36, 50, 75
salt-baked 102
soup 18, 128, 188–9
& squash mash 209
& squash purée 137
"stamped" 200
stock 76
with veal stew 27
Princess pudding 180–1
prunes 52, 195, 206

Q
quail, warm salad 160

R
radishes, warm 29
raisins 240–1, 244
ramsons 18, 22–3, 26, 40, 55, 218
raspberries 113, 116–17
razor clams, steamed 212–13
recipes, using 10
red cabbage 135, 201, 210
redcurrants 116, 118, 119, 120
rhubarb 56–60
    baked 33, 57
    cake 58–9, 113
    in chutney 36, 57
    compote 58
    cordial 57
    gelatin with cream desert 121
    sorbet 60
    soup 57
    syrup 57
rillette, pheasant 132–3
risotto, pearl barley 147, 230–1
rødgrød 116, 118
root vegetables
    creamy soup 128
    in fish soup 186–7
    mash 26
    in meatloaf 135
    pickled 132

& potato rösti 138
with warm pheasant salad 160
rowan sprigs 24
rowanberries 98
rye
    crispy crumbles 60
    fried porridge 42
    pearled 66, 94
rye bread 55
    crisp with apple sauce & blackcurrant
        preserve 180
    quick & easy 108
    sandwiches 45, 160, 222
    sugar-roasted, with blackberries 121
    toasts, thin & crunchy 84–5

S
St. Lucia saffron buns 240
salad
    asparagus & shrimp 92
    beet, cottage cheese & pork 105
    beet, horseradish & dill 82–3
    bitter salad greens 238
    Brussels sprout 164, 166, 210, 236, 238–9
    cabbage with peas & scallion 105
    cauliflower & asparagus 86
    cauliflower, hazelnut & celery 100
    chicken, shallot & chanterelle 95
    dandelion 227
    green potato 75
    kale 210, 235
    pea, cabbage & dill, with chicken 72
    pearl barley 161, 210
    pearled rye, with blackberries, beets
        & horseradish 94
    pearled spelt, apples & parsley 206
    pheasant, scorzonera & carrots 160
    potato 36, 50, 75
    seafood 68
    smoked cod roe 222
    squash, lingonberry, bacon & chestnut
        162–3
salmon
    gravad with mustard sauce 190
    hot-smoked, in omelet 92–3
    pan-fried with warm salad 210
    raw, with lime, horseradish & garlic
        mustard 42–3
    tartare with baked potato 154
salmon, smoked 40, 128–9
salt, ramson 22
salt-baked vegetables 102, 232–3

samphire 84
sandwiches 45, 155, 156, 160, 222–3
sauce
  apple 171
  béchamel 98
  beet 138
  carrot & egg 214
  mushroom velouté 147
  parsley 78
  sweet & spicy mustard 190
  tartare 152–3
sauerkraut, with meatloaf 135
sausages 79, 81
  chanterelle & onion stew 78
  with fried porridge 42
  yellow split pea soup 126
scorzonera & carrots with pheasant 160
scurvy grass 213
sea trout 86, 92
seafood 68, 213
  see also type of seafood
seasonal food 8, 10, 15, 65, 125, 185
seasoning 10
shallots, glazed 142–3
shrimp 45
  with asparagus soup 19
  crispy fried 36
  crispy potatoes & curd cheese 44–5
  salad with asparagus 92
  with veal stew 27
skate wings, with cabbage in broth 36
skyr 66, 178
sloes 224
smelt, pan-fried 34–5
sorbet 60, 116–17, 171, 180
  see also ice cream
sorrel 50, 100
soup
  asparagus 19
  chervil, with poached eggs 18
  cucumber 66–7
  fish, with root vegetables & mashed fava
    beans 186–7
  kale 126
  mushroom, with meatballs 186
  mussel 18
  nettle 16–17
  onion, with cheese on toast 126–7
  pea & mint, cold 66
  potato 18, 128, 188–9
  rhubarb 57
  root vegetable 128
  shore crab 71

split pea 126, 188
sourdough starter 52
spelt grains 60, 66, 206
spinach 28–9, 46–7, 92–3, 230–1
split peas 126, 188, 213
squash
  chutney 193
  with griddled pheasant & mushrooms
    146

  lingonberry, bacon & chestnut salad
    162–3
  pickled 132, 167
  & potato mash 209
  & potato purée 137
  purée, bruschetta & goat cheese 224
  purée with salted halibut 192–3
stew
  chanterelle, on toast 94, 96–7
  chanterelle, onion & sausage 78
  fava bean 218
  game, with white barley risotto 147
  leeks 87
  shore crab 71
  veal 27, 204–5
stock 76, 160
strawberries 114
  almond & chocolate cake 108–9
  with elderflower granita 114
  red berry porridge 116, 118
  with sour milk & honey 116
  with tarragon sugar & milk 114–15
  wild 108
summer vegetables 98, 100
Swedish syrup bread 52
sweet cicely 20, 68, 98, 114
syrup 52, 57, 178

T
tarragon 39, 105, 114, 213
tart
  spinach 46–7
  summer vegetable tartlets 98–9
tartare sauce 152–3
terrine 193, 194–5
thyme, wild 88
tomato
  ketchup 81
  mayonnaise 39
  pickled 84
  stuffed with wheat berries & goat cheese
    104–5
trifle 113, 120

turbot, gravad 88
turnips 27, 50, 131, 160, 161, 202

V
veal
  braised in milk, garlic & rosemary 202
  chops, with leeks 82
  chops & pearled spelt salad 206
  cold rump with beet tartare 199
  hotpot with licorice & beer 204–5
  liver 82, 205
  in meatballs 200–1
  in meatloaf 135
  & pork patties 142–3
  roasted rump with potato & root
    vegetable rösti 138
  stew 27
venison
  barbecued 75
  braised shoulder with Jerusalem
    artichoke & apple purée 142, 144–5
  chargrilled liver 82
  fillet with kale purée & salad 134
  heart 82
  meatballs 75
  smoked haunch, open-faced sandwich
    160
  stew with white barley risotto 147
vinaigrette 29, 50–1, 86, 88, 190, 209

W
watercress 205
wheat grains 60, 104–5, 186
whiting, home-smoked 219
wild boar 193, 208–9
wild ingredients
  fall 125, 137, 149, 150, 154, 162,
    166, 176
  spring 15, 18, 22
  summer 65, 88, 95, 108, 110, 116
  winter 185, 205, 213, 218, 224, 227

Y
ymer 58
yogurt
  dill 154, 161
  ice cream 246–7
  mustard cream 155
  vanilla 173

Manifesto for the New Nordic Cuisine

As Nordic chefs we find that the time has now come for us to create a New
Nordic Kitchen which, in virtue of its good taste and special character,
compares favorably with the standard of the greatest kitchens of the world.
The aims of the New Nordic Kitchen are:

✳

To express the purity, freshness, simplicity, and ethics we wish to associate to our region.

✳

To reflect the changes of the seasons in the meals we make.

✳

To base our cooking on using ingredients and produce that are characteristically from our own climate, landscape, and waters.

✳

To combine the demand for good taste with modern knowledge of health and well-being.

✳

To promote Nordic products and the variety of Nordic producers, and to spread the word about their underlying cultures.

✳

To promote animal welfare and ethical production process in our seas, on our farmland, and in the wild.

✳

To develop potentially new applications of traditional Nordic food products.

✳

To combine the best in Nordic cooking and culinary traditions with influences from abroad.

✳

To combine local self-suffiency with regional sharing of high-quality products.

✳

To join forces with consumer representatives, other cooking craftsmen, agriculture, fishing, food, retail and wholesales industries, researchers, teachers, politicians, and authorities on this project for the benefit and advantage of everyone in the Nordic countries.

Erwin Lauterbach

René Redzepi

Hans Välimäki

Leif Sørensen

Rune Collin

Mathias Dahlgren

Gunndur Fossdal

Roger Malmin

Hákan Örvarsson

Ejvind Hellstrøm

Fredrik Sigurdsson

Michael Björklund

Signed at The Nordic Cuisine Symposium, 18th November, 2004

An Hachette UK Company
www.hachette.co.uk

First published in Great Britain in 2016
by Mitchell Beazley, a division of
Octopus Publishing Group Ltd
Carmelite House
50 Victoria Embankment
London EC4Y 0DZ
www.octopusbooks.co.uk
www.octopusbooksusa.com

Distributed in the US by
Hachette Book Group
1290 Avenue of the Americas
4th and 5th Floors
New York, NY 10020

Distributed in Canada by
Canadian Manda Group
664 Annette St.
Toronto, Ontario, Canada M6S 2C8

ISBN 978 1 78472 162 6

Printed and bound in China

10 9 8 7 6 5 4 3 2 1

Group Publishing Director Denise Bates
Managing Editor Sybella Stephens
Translation DHC Translations
Copyeditor Jo Richardson
Creative Director Jonathan Christie
Photographer Anders Schønnemann
Designer Jack Storey
Senior Production Manager
  Katherine Hockley